GROUP HEALTH
ASSOCIATION

A Portrait of a Health
Maintenance Organization

Health, Society, and Policy,
a series edited by Sheryl Ruzek and Irving Kenneth Zola

EDWARD D. BERKOWITZ

AND

WENDY WOLFF

GROUP HEALTH ASSOCIATION

A Portrait of a Health Maintenance Organization

TEMPLE UNIVERSITY PRESS
Philadelphia

Temple University Press, Philadelphia 19122
Copyright © 1988 by Group Health Association
All rights reserved
Published 1988
Printed in the United States of America

The paper used in this publication meets the minimum requirements of
American National Standard for Information Sciences—Permanence of Paper
for Printed Library Materials, ANSI Z39.48-1984

Library of Congress Cataloging-in-Publication Data

Berkowitz, Edward D.
Group Health Association.

(Health, society, and policy)
Bibliography: p.
Includes index.
1. Group Health Association (Washington, D.C.)—History. I. Wolff,
Wendy. II. Title. III. Series.
RA413.3.G69B47 1988   362.1′0425′09753   87-18178
ISBN 0-87722-552-4 (alk. paper)

In Memory of
WILBUR J. COHEN

CONTENTS

PREFACE

In the spring of 1986, some members of the Group Health Association (GHA) approached us about writing a history to celebrate the fiftieth anniversary of the organization in 1987. They told us that GHA was one of the first health maintenance organizations in America, that it had fought an important battle with the medical establishment, and that it had been the setting for one of the first doctors' strikes in America.

We decided to undertake the project, even though we knew little about GHA and were not experts on the history either of health care in general or of health maintenance organizations in particular. We were intrigued with the idea, in part because of our interest in Washington's liberal community and in part because we noticed that many of the individuals we had studied in other contexts, such as social security administrators, belonged to GHA.

For the next year, Wendy Wolff worked with the GHA records in space that GHA provided at its administrative headquarters. GHA paid her salary, in return for which she prepared a short history of the organization that was distributed in 1987 as a GHA publication. She also performed the research for this longer volume. Edward Berkowitz continued his duties as a professor of history at George Washington University, where he devoted the bulk of his research time to drafting the chapters of this book. GHA reimbursed George Washington for his summer 1986 salary.

The book is therefore essentially a history of one particular HMO, rather than a history of HMOs in general. As such, scholars have had a varied reaction to it. Some found the "inside"

story of an HMO to be interesting in and of itself; others would
have preferred a comparison between GHA and other pioneering
HMOs and wanted to hear more about GHA's performance in such
areas as reducing costs. For our part, we decided to stick with our
original plan and tell the story of one HMO. In future volumes, we
may try to draw broader comparative points about health policy;
for now, we present this book as a biography of a pioneering
HMO, based on primary sources that have not been available to
other researchers.

We want to thank some of the people who helped us to write the
book. At Temple University Press, we benefited greatly from the
work of Janet Francendese and Doris B. Braendel. Odin W. Anderson, Richard Scotch, Irving K. Zola, and Daniel M. Fox read parts
of the book in manuscript and made many helpful comments. The
staff and trustees of GHA were extremely cooperative, making
available all relevant documents without attempting to steer us
away from the less favorable aspects of the organization's past.
They have encouraged us to submit this volume to a scholarly press
and to follow the usual peer review procedures. Harold Wool,
Henry Lowenstern, Erica Johnson, Benetta Waller, and Clement
Abeygoonewardene served as our liaisons with GHA, providing
endless help, hospitality, and guidance. Other Group Health members who read and commented on portions of this manuscript or
the shorter history were Mark Colburn, Harold Goldstein,
Maurine Mulliner, Robert J. Myers, Arthur Rosenbaum, Stanley
and Gertrude Ruttenberg, and staff members Meredith Higgins
and Daniel J. Sullivan. In addition, numerous other current and
former trustees and staff members contributed their time and experience in interviews we conducted during the summer and fall of
1986. Robert P. Forbes performed admirably as a research assistant
and as a competent critic. All have our thanks and, even more than

with most books, all have a dispensation from responsibility for what follows.

We dedicate this book to Wilbur Cohen, who died in the spring of 1987. For one of us, in particular, he was a friend and personal hero. A loyal GHA member (number 1431) almost from the beginning, he made his last public appearance at GHA's fiftieth anniversary celebration. We like to think that he would have enjoyed this book.

GROUP HEALTH
ASSOCIATION

A Portrait of a Health
Maintenance Organization

CHAPTER ONE

Introduction

This book tells the story of a half-century in the life of the Group Health Association of Washington, D.C. (GHA), one of this country's first health maintenance organizations. Group Health Association combines health insurance and the delivery of health care. In return for a fixed annual or monthly fee, GHA, acting through a group of salaried doctors, provides its members with a wide range of medical services.

GHA needs to be understood as an attempt to solve universal problems in the financing and provision of health care. For more than thirty years after its founding in 1937, GHA managed to solve those problems and become the preeminent "prepaid group practice" in the District of Columbia metropolitan area. Then, in the 1970s, GHA's difficulties began to mount, as a result both of internal contradictions inherent in GHA's structure as a consumer cooperative and of changes in national health policy. By the early 1980s, Group Health faced serious cost pressures caused by competition from other health maintenance organizations (HMOs), labor relations strife, and the high expenses of serving an aging membership.

On its fiftieth anniversary, GHA's survival remained in doubt. The association had gone from economic insecurity to relative prosperity and back to economic insecurity. In the following chapters, we will chronicle this cycle in the life of an early and influential HMO.

At first, GHA was on the cutting edge of change in the delivery and financing of medical care. When Group Health started in 1937, prepayment of medical expenses represented an innovation in health care financing. Well into the 1940s, most people went to a doctor or a hospital and then paid the bill. Alternative arrangements were limited in number and affected relatively few people. Through prepayment, GHA's founders hoped to substitute a sure small loss for a possible large one by pooling the risk of ill health. Catastrophic individual expense would become manageable group expenditures. In this regard, GHA acted as a health insurer.

At the time of GHA's founding, a large market in health insurance had not yet developed, partly because this type of insurance was difficult to sell on an individual basis, unlike such traditional insurance lines as life or property. Those who purchased health insurance on a voluntary basis were either healthy but wary of taking a risk or, more likely, worried that they might be sick. The more sick people who purchased the insurance, the higher would be the cost. As costs rose, healthy people tended to drop out of the market, leaving only those who knew they were likely to get sick. In this manner, the cost of health insurance would tend to rise until it exceeded most people's reach.

The solution was to sell this insurance on a group basis, spreading the risk across many healthy and a few sick individuals, in order to improve the actuarial odds. For this reason, private life insurance companies eventually developed "group" health insurance coverages. The health insurance policies usually worked by reimbursing the individual or the employer for medical expenses already incurred.

Even with large groups, the insurance companies needed to guard against excessive use of medical services. For this purpose, they relied on the good sense of the doctors, even though the physicians' desire for more business often conflicted with the insurance company's need to hold down costs. They also instituted such devices as "copayments" and "deductibles," which required the insured to pay for part of each hospital stay or visit to the doctor, thus, it was hoped, discouraging excessive consumption of medical care.

The insurance companies and others associated with health care financing realized that ill health posed three separate but related risks for consumers. The first was the cost of paying for the doctor. The second was the income lost by a worker who became ill or by the family of a worker who died. To guard against this second risk, life and disability insurance developed (earlier than health insurance, because they addressed more immediate problems and presented fewer actuarial difficulties). The third risk was the cost of paying the hospital bill, an expense that became increasingly prominent in the twentieth century. As Paul Starr has noted, the percentage of the nation's health bill devoted to hospital care increased substantially between 1918 and 1934, and individual variations in these costs became a national problem. Although few people were hospitalized at any one time, each incidence of hospitalization was expensive.[1]

High costs for individuals also reflected high costs for the providers of health care. Hospitals required a substantial source of funds to stay in business. Particularly in the depression, hospitals experienced financial problems, and they began to see the wisdom of prepaid hospital insurance. In 1929, a group of 1,200 school teachers in Dallas, Texas, contracted with the Baylor University Hospital to provide them with up to twenty-one days of semiprivate hospitalization annually in return for a monthly premium of fifty cents; thus, according to the conventional wisdom, began Blue Cross. In time, most American communities had some form of a Blue Cross program that was used to reimburse hospitals. The Blue Cross organizations were locally run and usually controlled by local hospitals. True to the community nature and origins of general hospitals, they operated on a nonprofit basis. Blue Cross plans also differentiated themselves from insurance companies by emphasizing that they provided services rather than cash indemnities. The Blue Cross plan in Washington, D.C., known as Group Hospitalization, Inc., was instituted in March 1934.[2]

As with hospitals, so with the doctors: prepaid health care assured doctors of a steady source of income and cushioned the blow of declining demand. As might be expected, far fewer prepaid doctors' practices developed than hospital financing plans, because of the lesser costs involved, but some doctors defied the censure of their colleagues and opened prepaid practices, often group practices in which physicians in different specialties worked together. The most famous example occurred in Los Angeles, where in 1929 the employees of the Los Angeles Department of Water and Power made arrangements with two physicians to receive both hospital and medical care. Other employee groups joined the Ross-Loos plan. By 1935, it had 37,000 members.[3]

In 1937, GHA offered the employees of the federal government comprehensive medical and hospital care for themselves and their families in return for a modest monthly premium. Unlike most of the organizations that preceded it in the prepaid health care field, GHA began not as an attempt to make money, fill hospital beds, or drum up business for doctors but rather as an employer-sponsored health plan.

The tradition here was an old one, although GHA helped to move it into new settings. Industrial clinics, in isolated or dangerous occupations such as railroading, mining, or lumbering, typically were financed through deductions from a worker's wages. Using the money, the employer or, in a few cases, the employees contracted with a physician or surgeon to provide treatment. Although this form of care originated as early as the middle of the nineteenth century, it was limited in its application to the working class. As hospital costs rose, however, and the difficulties of paying for health care mounted, it became feasible to adapt this old tradition to modern urban circumstances.[4]

Unlike an isolated coal mining valley, the cities already had doctors and hospitals; the emphasis of the new organizations would be on providing access to health care for the middle class. The Ross-Loos clinic and the early Blue Cross plans responded to this need from the provider side; GHA marked a consumer's response to the need.

Although GHA was rationalized in pragmatic terms as a means of making federal workers more efficient, its founders soon developed a sense of social mission. GHA's care was so different from that prevailing in Washington, the medical establishment's opposition to the notion of a prepaid group practice so extreme, that GHA's founders began to believe that they were single-handedly bringing a new form of health care to America. This attitude led GHA to draw closer to other consumer-oriented health care plans. The best known of these began in 1929 when Dr. Michael Shadid, a reform-minded doctor, had started a medical care cooperative in Oklahoma. Other consumer health cooperatives had been organized as part of the New Deal's agricultural program and were administered in part by Washington bureaucrats, who joined GHA in substantial numbers.[5]

GHA's sense of social mission and its devotion to consumer control heightened the financing dilemmas common to all health insurers. GHA offered complete health care, including hospitalization, at a universal rate to the entire community of federal employees. Private health insurers, in contrast, charged more for groups who cost more than others to insure. GHA's founders also sought to lessen or eliminate the multiple payments that were a feature of private health insurance. Instead, a person or family paid monthly dues and had no further out-of-pocket expenses. For GHA, even more than for private health insurers, the need to spread the risk of ill health was therefore paramount.

Since those who needed costly medical care would find Group Health to be a better deal than regular health insurance, the founders of GHA recognized the importance of examining prospective members carefully. People with "pre-existing conditions" faced special restrictions or were denied membership. By excluding such individuals, however, GHA's administrators called the utility of the prepaid group health approach into question. Exclusions grated against the sensibilities of GHA members, as did special fees for medical services.

From the beginning, therefore, GHA's social mission to reduce the incidence and the costs of ill health for its members conflicted with its need to remain financially solvent. In seeking to resolve those tensions, GHA, like the insurance companies before it, turned toward group memberships. Recruiting large groups was also a way of ensuring GHA's continued growth. Since its existing membership grows older with time, a health organization must continually recruit new young members. If it fails to do so, costs will rise because, other things being equal, older people consume more health care than young ones. A health plan, therefore, needs to be constantly on the prowl for new members or costs will rise, the dilemmas of adverse selection will heighten, and the plan will find itself out of business.

In the early days, federal employees joined Group Health as individuals rather than in groups from particular bureaus or departments. Although GHA began admitting members in groups after World War II, the units recruited were relatively small, rarely exceeding several hundred subscribers, and membership grew very slowly. During the 1950s, as employers increasingly began contributing to their workers' health insurance, GHA began courting Washington employers and unions, hoping to enroll one or more large groups that would bring in thousands of new members. After a long search, GHA recruited the union representing the 10,000 employees of the D.C. Transit Company. Two years later, in 1960, GHA's participation in the new Federal Employees Health Benefits Program attracted an additional 12,000 new members.[6]

As we shall see, the entry of these large groups created another level of conflict of GHA. Although they brought in additional revenue and helped to control the problems of adverse selection, their very importance to Group Health gave them great negotiating power in the organization, thus undermining the concept of consumer control. Here, the term "consumer" acquired an ambiguity. In the case of both the transit workers and the federal employees, the individual consumer who received the care was represented by a powerful umbrella organization—the D.C. Transit Workers Health and Welfare Fund and the Civil Service Commission, respectively. With federal employees representing as much as two-thirds of GHA's enrollment and the transit workers some 15 percent, the administrators of each wielded far more power in determining rates and benefits than did the individual members, shattering what had been a neat bilateral relationship between health care providers and consumers.

GHA was founded, and has continued to function throughout its fifty years, as a consumer-owned cooperative. Since a government agency could not sponsor a health care organization, GHA was owned by its members, who elected the organization's trustees. There was nothing ceremonial about GHA's trustees; they worked hard to translate consumer desires into policy, rather than simply lending their names to the letterhead.

Although GHA's cooperative structure began as a necessity, it soon became central to the organization's identity. In the depression years, supporters saw cooperatives as a defense against the excesses of both big business and big government. In an influential book published in 1936, journalist Marquis Childs described coop-

9

eration as a "middle course" between the "absolute socialization of Russia and the end development of capitalism in America."[7] By removing the profit motive, consumer cooperatives ensured quality merchandise at fair prices. In this spirit, many of the young New Dealers regarded GHA as a consumer cooperative that dealt in medical care. By joining GHA, they took a stand against the profit motive and monopolistic practices in medicine.[8]

With strong political and sentimental ties to the cooperative movement, GHA never veered from its cooperative structure, even after bringing in large groups and attaining substantial size. It did, however, adapt its practices to meet the demands of large subscriber groups, creating a continuing tension during its second quarter-century.

Consumer control and a cooperative structure also complicated the relationship between the patients and the doctors. At GHA the physicians were salaried employees of the nonprofit organization. In many of the other "flagship" HMOs founded prior to the 1970s, the doctors belonged to a for-profit partnership. Kaiser and the Health Insurance Plan of Greater New York (HIP) illustrate how such arrangements functioned.

In 1942, Henry J. Kaiser, the west coast industrialist, expanding on his earlier efforts to bring medical care to workers in remote areas, established two Permanente foundations that administered prepaid health care to 200,000 people. When enrollment fell off after the war, Kaiser decided to open up membership beyond Kaiser employees. In the late forties, his doctors staged a coup against both him and Dr. Sidney R. Garfield, their medical supervisor, and established their own for-profit medical partnership, which contracted to provide medical care to members enrolled by the Kaiser foundations.[9]

Meanwhile, in 1946, Mayor Fiorello LaGuardia had initiated the Health Insurance Plan of Greater New York (HIP) to provide prepaid care for the city's municipal employees. This plan functioned as what later became known as an independent practice association, with twenty-six medical groups providing care to the HIP members through their privately owned, for-profit practices. These medical groups were paid through a capitation arrangement, a flat fee for each patient they received, rather than on a fee-for-service basis.[10]

GHA provided as pure an example of the "staff model" health care program as could be found in America. At Kaiser, the doctors belonged to a separate partnership; at HIP, the doctors worked in private practices. At GHA, doctors were employees who worked for their patients. Very few other health concerns operated in this fashion; those that did often bore the group health name, as in the Group Health Plan of St. Paul, Minnesota.[11]

From the beginning, the medical staff at GHA has been responsible for hiring and firing individual GHA physicians. New doctors must meet such objective criteria as graduation from an accredited medical school, completion of accredited postgraduate training, and eligibility for a specialty board certification examination. Beyond their clinical skills, however, GHA's doctors need to possess the personality and philosophy suited to group practice and preventive medicine. Personal interviews with clinical department chairpersons and other staff physicians therefore focus on the new recruit's "interest in delivering care in an ambulatory setting," liking for people, intellectual curiosity to remain current with the medical literature, and desire to contribute to the group and community.[12]

Once hired, the doctors, who received salaries in return for specified services, were sovereign in the clinical realm, yet they were employees of the organization. In effect, they traded professional dominance over their medical practices for financial security. The security stemmed from knowing that they did not have to drum up business or worry about the many details of maintaining a private practice. Offices and patients came with the job, but so did mandated hours and a specified number of patient contacts a day. The

GHA doctor had both less discretion and, in a paradoxical sense, more freedom than other physicians. This unsettling combination often made for troubled relationships between GHA's doctors and its consumers.

The tensions tended to boil over in times of financial crisis, which, because of the adverse selection problem and other cost pressures, were endemic to GHA. At issue was the prepaid, comprehensive nature of GHA's care. In the search for additional revenue, the choice often lay between raising premiums or instituting fees for particular services, such as a nominal charge for each office visit. The physicians often preferred the latter approach, since they were sensitive to the relationship between the "marginal" cost—the extra amount a GHA member would have to pay for an office visit or for a medical procedure—and the consumption of that particular service or visit. If the marginal cost were zero, as it would be under a plan in which everything was paid for in advance, doctors feared that too much of the service would be consumed, and the provision of medical care would become unmanageable. The members, however, often objected that special charges diminished the quality of care by deterring people from seeking preventive treatment.

Cost and administrative control posed even more difficult problems in determining doctors' pay and working conditions. The result was a history of labor strife. The doctors hardly fit the traditional image of trade unionists as, say, plumbers or steelworkers, yet GHA has suffered two physicians' strikes within the past decade. Ironically, the members and trustees were, by nature, more sympathetic to labor unions than were the doctors. The same GHA members who joined the cooperative movement also had tended to support the trade union movement as it emerged in the thirties and forties. No similar ties connected the physicians with the labor movement, yet they formed a union that twice went out on strike against the trustees and the members of GHA.[13]

When the relationship between doctor and patient deteriorated into a labor relations battle, the identities of the participants were confused by GHA's cooperative nature. At such times, the members, who were also patients and, in other settings, workers, assumed the role of management. The employees, who were also doctors and, outside of the negotiating room, medical authorities with control over the members, took the unfamiliar role of labor.

At GHA, such shifts in identity applied to a broad spectrum of the organization's activities. Considered as a medical clinic, GHA functioned as a provider of health care; considered as a consumer cooperative, GHA acted as a consumer of health care. For acute care that could be provided in its medical centers, GHA was a provider of care, but when hospitalization was required, GHA became a consumer of hospital services, since it never owned its own hospital and depended instead on hospitals in the Washington community.

The Washington community, in fact, exercised a crucial influence over Group Health's development, as Chapters Two and Three reveal. GHA's location contributed both to its accomplishments and to its historical importance. When the organization began, the community, on the one hand, was a parochial setting for the provision of medicine, with existing hospitals and an established fee-for-service medical practice. On the other hand, Washington, D.C., was the national seat of government and the home of many reformers who wanted to change the way in which medical care was financed and organized. In the battle over the creation of GHA, this segment of the community helped GHA's founders to establish a prepaid, group practice in Washington. Significantly, local hospitals, the centers of modern medicine, became the chief battlegrounds.

Many middle-class residents of the District of Columbia worked for the federal government and wanted to advance policy goals such as racial integration. Washington was also segregated, a southern city with separate medical facilities and separate doctors for whites and blacks. Because GHA drew much of its membership from those who supported integration, it helped to break down the city's racial barriers.

With the issues of its survival in the community settled, GHA successfully sought to expand its membership. The sudden arrival between 1958 and 1960 of 20,000 new participants ushered in the years of GHA's greatest growth and success. Despite the clash of cultures caused by the arrival of blue-collar transit workers into the ranks of GHA's membership and the tensions that the large groups created in GHA's consumer cooperative (detailed in Chapter Four), new memberships rejuvenated the organization.

In the 1970s, however, the climate changed. As competition entered the scene after passage of the HMO Act of 1973, GHA began to lose its distinctive sense of mission. At one time, it would have been as unthinkable to have two prepaid health plans in a metropolitan area as to have two educational television stations. In the 1970s, for reasons detailed in Chapters Six and Seven, that no longer was true.

The consequences for GHA were many. No longer could it claim to be the only local organization that combined the delivery and financing of health care; no longer could it draw distinctions between the range of its services with their emphasis on prevention and wellness and those offered by traditional health insurers. Instead, GHA's unique identifying characteristic became its organization as a consumer cooperative, which, in the health care market, had always posed liabilities. Not only were the newer HMOs unburdened by an aging membership, they were also freer to select the groups who joined. They could concentrate on relatively young, inexpensive groups. Less ambivalent about the need to make money, the newer HMOs faced fewer initial labor conflicts. Often associated with hospitals or large health insurance companies, the HMOs could afford to sustain initial losses and were able to obtain potentially greater hospital discounts.

Furthermore, the new organizations were freer to depart from GHA's staff model and experiment with newer forms of prepaid health care. In independent practice associations (IPAs), for example, the doctors often do not work exclusively for the association, nor does the association own the facilities in which the doctors work. Instead, the IPA contracts with groups of physicians who work in their own facilities, paying them according to a fee schedule to provide care to its prepaid subscribers. A preferred provider arrangement (PPO) is similar, except that it permits patients also to receive care from doctors outside of the arrangement. Lower deductibles and copayments encourage the patient to use one of the preferred providers. PPOs, as authority Jack Meyer has noted, became the fad of the 1980s in health care finance.[14]

Despite its origins as a pioneer in prepaid group health, GHA foundered in the new environment, as the control of health care costs became the paramount issue and as organizations entered and exited the health care market with surprising rapidity. Consumer control often shackled the efforts of executive directors who sought to develop new strategic approaches to the health care market. Doctors and other employees became restive, as they began to fear a substantial erosion of GHA's market share. Recognizing that loyalty to a doctor or hospital, more than any other factor, accounted for people's decisions to join a particular HMO, GHA clung to its 140,000 members.[15] Whether these members' loyalty would be sufficient to sustain the organization in the years ahead, without a substantial modification of GHA's structure, was a question often asked during Group Health's fiftieth anniversary year.

What follows is a case study in the development of an HMO: from the challenging period of its founding, through its glory years, to its troubled present circumstances. Through the course of its fifty-year history, GHA sought simultaneously to cope with the vagaries of the health care market and to keep its principles intact. As we will see, the task became progressively more difficult.

CHAPTER TWO

Launching Group Health

G HA became an important health care legacy of the New Deal. Although it bore only an indirect relationship to the New Deal's self-conscious efforts at a health policy, it figured prominently in one of the era's most celebrated confrontations between the federal government and organized medicine. The Roosevelt administration supported GHA in its efforts to offer a new type of medical care in the nation's capital. The American Medical Association (AMA), which could not afford to ignore the fledgling organization, joined the Medical Society of the District of Columbia in leading a boycott that forced GHA to struggle for its very existence, until the Justice Department, in a landmark case, successfully prosecuted the AMA and the medical society for harassing GHA and violating the antitrust laws. For all the drama, however, GHA did not begin as an ideological challenge to organized medicine but rather as a pragmatic effort to reduce the costs of health care for a small group of federal employees.

EDWARD FILENE AND THE CHANGING HEALTH REFORM SCENE

GHA originated with Edward A. Filene's interest in prepaid health care. Filene, a Boston department store magnate and contemporary of Theodore Roosevelt and social worker Jane Addams, owed his fortune to his innovative merchandising methods, such as his store's well-known bargain basement. He became a public figure by advocating an "intelligently selfish" approach to management, which included instituting cooperative ventures, such as credit unions, in which his employees could participate.[1]

In 1926, Filene grew interested in health care when he learned that Paul U. Kellogg, the editor of *Survey* magazine and a leader in many progressive causes, wanted to "ventilate" the subject of medical economics in an effort to secure the "better organization of medical service."[2] Filene was sympathetic, believing that the poor organization of medicine produced "a very great waste of life and a great waste of the wealth of the nation." Ill health could be largely prevented through a system of comprehensive health care financed on a prepayment basis, which Filene likened to preventive maintenance, "much as an engineer would give to his machine." By 1927, Filene had sketched a prepaid health plan in which "any incipient disease or dangerous disease could . . . be immediately reported and the matter handled by the senior doctor in charge."[3]

Because of Filene's interest in prepaid health care, he joined an inner circle of doctors, scientists, and public health experts who, just at the time of Kellogg's visit, were investigating the problems of health care. Supported in part by Filene's Twentieth Century Fund and by other major foundations, the Committee on the Costs of Medical Care gathered $1 million to undertake its studies. Staffed largely by social scientists who would lead the fight for national health insurance during the next generation, the Committee issued twenty-seven research reports between 1927 and 1932, culminating in its formal recommendations.[4]

A majority of the Committee members favored a health system characterized by what historian Daniel Fox has called "hierarchical regionalism," a plan based largely on the promotion of hospitals and of group practice. Each section of the country would have its major research or teaching hospital staffed by medical specialists, that would both inform medical practice and treat the most difficult cases.[5] Inside and outside the hospitals, physicians would function as a team, in effect taking a "group" approach to medicine. Believing that no one should be denied medical care, the Committee majority recommended that the "the costs of care should be placed on a group prepayment basis."[6]

A minority of Committee members dissented strongly. Medicine was a craft that should be practiced by individuals, they argued. Under the majority plan, elite doctors in teaching hospitals would dictate medical practice to local doctors. Such an approach, concentrated in large hospitals, would mean, according to the minority members, that medicine would begin to resemble the mass production techniques of large businesses. Instead, the minority favored preserving and even elevating the status of the general practitioner, who, unlike the specialist, could treat a wide variety of problems. By 1934, the American Medical Association had officially endorsed this position.[7]

Despite the AMA's position, doctors grew more interested in financing mechanisms that would bolster their chances of getting paid during the depression. Confronted by a catastrophic loss of income, people either failed to pay the physician or hospital for services rendered, or they neglected to see the doctor. Doctors therefore looked with increasing favor upon government welfare plans that permitted people to attend to their medical problems. The depression and the New Deal also changed the outlook of reformers who were sympathetic to the use of government power to advance hierarchical regionalism. Now, they increasingly looked toward Washington, D.C., rather than the state capitals, to become the focal point of public action.[8]

New Deal officials, such as relief administrator Harry Hopkins, recruited members of the Committee on the Costs of Medical Care to work for the federal government. Among those who came were Edgar Sydenstricker, a former member of the Committee, and Isidore Falk, a former Committee staff member, both of whom worked for the Milbank Memorial Fund. In 1934, they joined the staff of a new panel, the Committee on Economic Security, entrusted with writing what became known as the Social Security Act.[9]

Although both Sydenstricker and Falk were firmly committed to promoting prepayment and the group practice of medicine, they faced obstacles in using the Social Security Act of 1935 for this purpose. In particular, they discovered that reformers were more concerned about solving the most immediate problem of the depression—the lack of money caused by unemployment and involuntary retirement. Nor did President Roosevelt want to expend precious political capital on negotiations over a national health insurance program.[10]

The outcome suited Edward A. Filene, who had never overcome his progressive era belief that government's proper role lay in mobilizing the private sector, rather than in acting on its own. He therefore encouraged his Twentieth Century Fund to continue its work in medical economics during the thirties. Two months after the President signed the Social Security Act in August 1935, the Fund decided to intensify its efforts.[11]

Following an approach approved by Filene, R. V. Rickcord, a Fund consultant, tried to spark interest in prepaid group health plans among a "few, well-chosen agencies" and to avoid publicity that might antagonize the American Medical Association. This strategy, the Fund officials believed, would lead to the creation of a few effective plans that could serve as the basis for a national publicity campaign. At first, Rickcord looked to the American Federation of Labor (AFL) and the fledgling Congress of Industrial Organizations (CIO) and the Chamber of Commerce for help in his efforts. This hope proved unfounded. Local Chambers of Commerce, according to Fund officials, were "too much dominated by the medical profession," and the national offices of the labor unions were preoccupied with implementing the Wagner Act.[12]

Early in 1936, the Executive Committee of the Twentieth Century Fund considered establishing a national association that would promote "agencies through which the public can budget their health costs through small fixed periodic payments." The new Health Economics Association would undertake "promotional activities" that would stimulate interest in such plans and would provide groups with advice on how to organize and operate a plan. Edward Filene approved of the idea, citing with favor the work of the Ross-Loos clinic in Los Angeles, which employed forty physicians, owned a clinic building, and treated 60,000 people in 1935 at an average monthly cost of $2.68 a family. With Filene's financial backing, the Health Economics Association, under consultant Rickcord's charge, began its activities on December 1, 1936.[13] At the end of the Association's first fiscal year, Rickcord reported that twelve plans had been organized and nine other organizations were "definitely committed."[14]

The organizations leaning toward establishment of a prepaid group health plan included the Home Owners Loan Corporation (HOLC), a government agency centered in Washington, D.C., which was a constituent agency of the Federal Home Loan Bank Board (FHLBB). The HOLC employees formed a nonprofit corporation to furnish medical care to themselves and their families. They named the organization Group Health Association.[15]

GROUP HEALTH GOES TO WASHINGTON

A direct connection between Filene and the Federal Home Loan Bank Board explained the creation of GHA. John H. Fahey, who chaired the FHLBB, served on the executive board of the Twentieth Century Fund and was very close to Filene.[16] Learning through the Fund about prepaid group health, Fahey discussed starting a plan with Raymond R. Zimmerman, the personnel director of the

HOLC, sometime in 1936. He put Zimmerman in contact with Rickcord. Together, Rickcord and Zimmerman visited Baton Rouge, Louisiana, to observe the operations of a health program that had been instituted for Standard Oil employees. Impressed, the two men drafted a plan that would translate the essential principles of prepayment and group practice to the Washington setting.[17]

As Zimmerman later noted, the HOLC plan would have to be carried on by the employees themselves rather than by the agency. As an employer, the federal government had less freedom of action than did Standard Oil, since it spent public money and its administrative actions were matters of public record. The employees could, however, voluntarily organize such a program. That consideration, and the fact that no Washington doctors were offering their services in the manner of the Ross-Loos clinic in Los Angeles, lay behind the decision to make GHA a consumer-controlled cooperative. "We were not motivated by any desire to build a cooperative association because of any special interest in cooperatives," Zimmerman later said. "We were primarily interested in adapting the experience of industrial concerns in this field to the needs of government employees."[18]

The formation of GHA fit the character of an organization in which management took a paternalistic interest in the employees. At the Federal Home Loan Bank Board, a nurse visited those who were absent due to illness, a service that the management believed would cut down on absenteeism. In 1937, management sent a memorandum to all employees with instructions on what to do for the common cold. The advice included rest, eating "nothing solid for a day or two," and ensuring "proper elimination." If the employees wanted to prevent illness, they were advised to keep their feet dry, to dress properly, to practice "good nose and mouth hygiene," and to use Kleenex, which was "more sanitary, convenient, and less of a strain on the family laundress" than cloth handkerchiefs. That the management of such an agency should also organize a health plan for its workers is hardly a surprise.[19]

By the fall of 1936, the health care plan became a matter of public discussion at HOLC. On September 17, Zimmerman made a presentation to the officers of the Credit Union. On October 1, Zimmerman presented his idea to the FHLBB, which appointed a committee to bring the program to the attention of all the employees.[20] Meanwhile, Zimmerman asked the lawyers about the propriety of a government agency creating a health plan and was told that, although the FHLBB could not foot the bill for employee health care, it could spend money investigating whether or not to start a health plan.[21]

Early in 1937, a twenty-nine-page blueprint for a health care plan began to circulate in Washington. Marked "confidential," it carried the imposing title, "A Plan for Cooperative Medical Service on Periodic Payment Basis for Federal Employees and Their Families in Washington." The product of Rickcord's work with the Health Economics Association, it described a plan that would provide federal employees with complete, affordable medical care financed "on a regular, budgetable basis."[22]

The analysis borrowed heavily from the work of the Committee on the Costs of Medical Care and reasoned that, if federal employees were typical of people in their income group, then they were not receiving adequate medical care. Fifty years earlier, this lack had not been greatly felt because, for example, the treatment of cancer "was as inexpensive as it was ineffectual." In 1937, although such diseases had a better chance of being cured, medical treatment entailed heavy expenditures that might well drive a family deeply into debt. The culprit was an imbalance between rapid advances in medical technology and slow changes in economic organization. Simply put, medical care was organized poorly. Doctors and nurses sat around unoccupied, waiting for patients to come to their offices; the large number of small medical offices multiplied the overhead costs of doing business; and, most important, general practitioners and specialists did not work closely with one another.

Doctors made a great deal of the fact that a patient should have a free choice of physician. But, according to the pamphlet, the average person chose a doctor "on the basis of hearsay" and was not qualified to judge the competence of a general practitioner, much less a specialist.

The proposed plan sought to remedy these defects and bring the benefits of better medical organization to the 119,000 federal employees, of whom perhaps a third could be expected to join (raising the number treated to as many as 70,000 when dependents were included). The nearly two-thirds of the federal work force with incomes between $1,500 and $4,500 were special targets of the program.

The proposal emphasized preventing illness and freeing families from the economically debilitating effects of sickness. Benefits, including annual physicals and obstetrical care for women who had been enrolled for twelve months, would be provided in a medical center, located downtown, equipped with x-ray apparatus, a lab, and a pharmacy. To support this center would require recruiting a group of at least 10,000 and raising $35,000.

The plan was quite explicit on the steps to be taken. A small initial group of committed people should be formed, then gradually be broadened into a large sponsoring committee of perhaps sixty individuals of "prestige and standing." After the initial working capital had been raised, the plan would be publicly announced. Assuming a favorable response, the organizers would then raise additional money through the advance payment of dues or through the sale of special shares. Only then could the clinic open for business.

With such elaborate plans in hand, Zimmerman called a meeting of all employees at the end of January 1937 to discuss the idea. Nearly all the employees attended the meeting and apparently they reacted favorably. By February 1937, Group Health Association had been formally incorporated as a nonprofit organization that would provide medical, surgical, and hospital care and operate a clinic, a hospital, and a pharmacy. GHA would be controlled by its members, who, according to the articles of incorporation, could be employees of any branch of the U.S. government, except the army and navy. To begin with, however, membership was open only to HOLC employees. An elected Board of Trustees would manage the organization.[23]

By March 1937, Zimmerman claimed that eight hundred employees had already signed applications for membership, and he fully expected another hundred to join once the plan was officially launched. Zimmerman used the language of scientific management to persuade the FHLBB, the parent organization of the Home Owners Loan Corporation, of the efficacy of group health. Ill health, according to Zimmerman, represented a natural management concern because, by interrupting work, it raised the costs of doing business. Illness cost the Federal Home Loan Bank Board more than half a million dollars annually; the group health plan would stimulate the employees to take steps that would prevent sickness.[24]

A draft brochure, designed to lure members, featured a down-to-earth explanation of the new plan's many advantages. The patient would find that "it would be perfect to have a doctor, and a staff of specialists, and a place where they have everything." Doctors would discover "a perfect way to practice," treating patients with whom they were familiar, while the "daily contact with a group of physicians" enriched their medical knowledge. Group health, the principle that would bring patient and doctor together, combined "under one roof a number of physicians, the modern devices, and the technical assistants required for complete medical care." The typical patient would receive a thorough medical examination, followed by careful laboratory studies, such as a urinalysis, and additional laboratory tests, such as x-rays and special blood tests, should they be required. Other touted benefits included an eye service, complete maternity care, comprehensive pediatrics, and the removal of tonsils, adenoids, and gall bladders.[25]

Despite these bold claims, GHA had not yet opened its doors, and Zimmerman had no desire for publicity beyond his agency. When Edward Filene urged a national publicity campaign, he was told that "all of the resources of organized medicine will be thrown against" plans like GHA. It was better, then, to organize "on the quiet" rather than to sustain a "powerful barrage" from the local and national medical associations.[26]

In the absence of this barrage, GHA made substantial progress during the spring of 1937. In March, GHA negotiated a formal contract with the HOLC that was soon ratified by the members. This agreement, later to be the subject of considerable controversy, gave GHA $40,012 to equip its clinic and to hire staff. In return, GHA agreed to provide physical examinations to HOLC employees, to manage the HOLC nursing staff and emergency room, and to reserve two places on the Board of Trustees for people appointed by the HOLC directors.[27]

By the end of April 1937, the members had held their first meeting, adopted bylaws, and chosen an eleven-member Board of Trustees and a five-member executive committee that quickly turned its attention to hiring a medical director.[28] Dr. Henry Rolf Brown, recently retired as chief of the Veterans' Bureau tuberculosis hospitals, agreed to serve as the medical director at a salary of $7,200. When Brown began to hire the rest of the medical staff, he noticed that many of the people he contacted "seemed slow in responding favorably." Nonetheless, the Board optimistically set August 1, 1937, as the opening date for the GHA clinic.[29]

COUNTERATTACK: THE RESPONSE OF ORGANIZED MEDICINE

At this point, word of the new organization could no longer be contained. As Dr. Brown interviewed local physicians for GHA jobs, the doctors began to talk among themselves; soon news about Group Health reached AMA headquarters in Chicago. On March 27, 1937, a member of the AMA staff received a letter from a D.C. correspondent describing GHA as "nothing but an entering wedge to the establishment of state medicine" financed by the Twentieth Century Fund. "Treat this information as though it blew in your window," the letter concluded. "Some of the prominent doctors in Washington are going to be wised up." The AMA quickly asked GHA for a copy of its charter and bylaws.[30]

As these intrigues occurred behind the scenes, representatives of the District Medical Society held a series of meetings with Dr. Brown and members of the GHA Board that began calmly and grew increasingly acrimonious. The GHA officials reassured the doctors that the new organization would be, in Brown's words, "highly ethical in our practice in every sense." But that did not mollify the local doctors, who suggested that GHA would rake off the paying patients and leave the medically indigent to the local physicians. The doctors claimed that such things had happened elsewhere, such as in Havana, Cuba, where 50,000 people joined a prepaid group practice and left the private doctors with the "riffraff." If Group Health were to serve all federal employees and their dependents, the doctors noted, then it would include one-third of the District's population, with serious consequences for "the general medical care of the whole community." Drawing their practice only from the remaining two-thirds of the population, the local doctors would have to assume "total obligation for the indigent, the unemployed, the dispensary and staff work of the hospitals and leaving the very large colored population to the colored profession in whose hands the practice largely rests."[31]

The physicians also pointed out that GHA was a corporation and thus forbidden by law to practice medicine; that GHA might not actually protect its members from heavy medical bills, because many members faced with serious illness would seek the best possible doctors, even if it meant paying extra to go outside GHA; and that people who paid for their medicine in advance tended to consume more than was necessary. The doctors proposed that GHA remedy this matter by paying for three-quarters of a patient's care rather than all of it.

Dr. Thomas A. Groover, the dean of the local doctors, stressed his concern for the quality of care. He had graduated from medical school in 1898 at a time when Germany, France, and England were leaders in medical science. "We were backward," he recalled. Since that time, however, all those countries had adopted a socialized approach to medicine, and as a result, "leadership has passed from Europe where these various social schemes were tried out, to the good old USA." The implication was clear: Groover saw GHA as a scheme organized along socialized lines that would cause the quality of care in the District of Columbia to deteriorate.

Not everyone felt so strongly. In an effort to be helpful, one doctor suggested that GHA change its approach. Instead of offering members a limited selection of physicians who worked exclusively for GHA, the organization might act more like an insurance company and simply reimburse local doctors for services rendered. If that were to happen, he declared, "I feel pretty certain that the Medical Society and this organization could get together and be very helpful to each other."

The two sides, however, could not reach agreement. The doctors brushed aside GHA's contention that it was needed to serve the medically indigent. As Dr. Groover explained, "Anybody can come into my office tomorrow, it has been so and I am sure it is so with all of these doctors here; their credit rating is never looked up before we treat them. . . . The question of getting paid for it is the last thing that is considered." Doctors, he said, extended "unlimited credit" to the point where most lost money because of their "rotten" business habits.

The GHA representatives challenged this view, asking whether individuals with an income of $1,800 or less really had a genuinely free choice of doctors or the chance for adequate care. Most of these people, Raymond Zimmerman argued, had no financial reserves and postponed physical examinations and other preventive measures. Then, when they got sick and could no longer avoid a medical appointment, "they are going to select their doctors from the group for whose services they can pay," said Zimmerman.

The discussion confirmed each side's worst fears about the other and ended in an impasse. One doctor predicted that Group Health would lead to the "necessary exodus of a large part of the medical profession of the District of Columbia." GHA officials countered that they might eventually absorb local medical practice and that their type of medicine would be superior to present practice. GHA would not alter its operation to subsidize the local fee-for-service medical profession, nor would the local doctors agree to work for GHA.

As a result, in the summer and fall of 1937, the Medical Society of the District of Columbia took steps to forbid its members from working for GHA. The Society reminded its members that Chapter IX of its constitution forbade local doctors to work for an organization that had not been approved by the Society.[32]

GHA: OPEN FOR BUSINESS

GHA, determined to win its battle with the local medical society, continued to plan for the opening of its clinic. A committee scouted possible locations and reported that the best available site was at 1328 I Street, NW. This space was on the second floor of a two-story building and consisted of a hollow shell approximately seventy feet long and twenty-five feet wide, with no partitions and few electrical lights. The building had no elevator. As a lawyer investigating the situation for the AMA reported, GHA would start its operations in "modest and unassuming style."[33]

Securing rental space and buying equipment were easy tasks in the depressed 1937 economy; recruiting physicians in the face of Medical Society opposition proved to be much more difficult. Not until October was Dr. Brown able to assemble his staff. It included a surgeon, a full-time pediatrician, and two internists.[34]

Meanwhile, the local medical society and the AMA shadowed GHA's progress. When a Washington attorney working for the AMA learned the location of the GHA offices on I Street, he went there himself to look around, posing as a potential GHA member (although the GHA staff had not yet moved in). The attorney funnelled back his reports to Dr. William C. Woodward of the AMA's Bureau of Legal Medicine and Legislation, who prepared an article denouncing GHA even before it opened for business.[35] Published in the *Journal of the American Medical Association (JAMA)*, the article showed a complete familiarity with GHA's confidential planning documents and echoed the complaints of the local doctors. GHA was running an insurance company without a license, using funds of doubtful origin to capitalize the effort. The dues were set at such a low level that it would be impossible for GHA to make money, requiring a permanent government subsidy. These dues were collected through a payroll deduction, which *JAMA* argued was illegal for government employees. Furthermore, GHA served an enormous area that would require building many clinics, and if GHA opened its membership to all government employees, it would have to admit blacks. By not offering its members a free choice of physicians, GHA would be regarded by local doctors as "on the outer verge of ethical practice, if not beyond the pale."[36]

A few weeks later, the same journal printed a statement on "group hospitalization," stressing that AMA approval of such plans required physician control, coverage only of hospitalization and not medical services, and a restriction to the poor. GHA met none of these requirements.[37]

Despite the criticisms, GHA decided to open its clinic on November 1, 1937, preceded by a weekend of festivities.[38] On Saturday, visiting dignitaries got their first glimpse of the GHA clinic, and that night GHA staged a banquet at the Mayflower Hotel. R. V. Rickcord and Evans Clark, the executive director of the Twentieth Century Fund, came down from New York. I. S. Falk, the expert on health insurance from the Social Security Board, also attended, as did many officials from the Home Owners Loan Corporation. They listened to Dr. Richard C. Cabot, a prominent physician and Harvard professor from the distinguished Boston family, explain the virtues of the group practice of medicine. "Better service for less money," he succinctly said.[39]

The initial impression of the GHA facilities was favorable. The *Washington Star,* an evening newspaper and the first to get out a story on the GHA clinic, reported that the facilities included a "beautifully appointed waiting room decorated with palms, baskets of flowers and paintings from the WPA art project." The *Star* reporter also seemed impressed with the offices and treatment rooms, "well equipped with scientific instruments." The *Washington Post* published an encouraging editorial that stressed GHA's value to the community. It "met a social need" by providing "efficient and dependable service." GHA promptly reprinted and distributed the editorial to its members.[40]

When the clinic opened for business on November 1, 1937, the staff handled forty cases, performed several minor operations, and made two house calls. Dr. Brown pronounced himself "delighted" with the first day's operations. Rickcord described the set-up as the most advanced in the country, a tremendous bargain at $2.20 a month for individuals and $3.30 for families.[41]

THE OPPOSITION BUILDS

The opening of the clinic represented a substantial achievement, yet for all of the euphoria it engendered, GHA still faced substantial economic and political problems. Even the *Washington Post,* in its favorable editorial, mentioned the fact that GHA was launched with government money. The *New York Times* ran its story on Group Health under the headline, "Possible Extension of Medical Service to Other Agencies Worries Capital Doctors." When Dr. Thomas E. Neill, the president of the District Medical Society, received his invitation to the inaugural banquet, he instructed his secretary to send a curt two-and-one-half-line note of refusal, without even a cursory wish for success. Another local medical official, writing to a friend, characterized GHA as a New Deal scheme to control American medicine. "The setup, without the shadow of a doubt, seems to have the smiling approval of the various New Deal officials and the Secretary of Labor [Frances Perkins] on through," he wrote.[42]

Having failed to co-opt GHA, the local medical society and the AMA tried to put it out of business. The campaign to hinder GHA took many forms. The local society used its implicit licensing powers to discipline its members, threatening them with expulsion and withdrawal of privileges to practice in local hospitals if they chose to work for Group Health. The society and the AMA also attacked the legal basis of GHA, questioning its right to practice medicine as a corporation and asking Congress to consider the legality of the funds provided to GHA by the FHLBB.

In November 1937, AMA and D.C. Medical Society officials met in Chicago to plot strategy. The District representatives were Drs. R. Arthur Hooe, who chaired the society's Contract, Compensation, and Industrial Medicine Committee, and F. X. McGovern, who had chaired the delegation that met with GHA. They came prepared with a statement on GHA that had the local society's backing: the AMA had a duty to oppose GHA as "an entering and possibly illegal wedge to the socialization of medicine."[43]

Yet it was not clear either to the AMA or the local officials exactly how to defeat the new organization. The local doctors were handicapped by the fact that D.C. residents had no vote and that local government officials were appointed. Since most had been selected by the Roosevelt administration, they could be expected to "cater to the desires of those whom they turn to for their bread and butter." Congress and the courts, far less beholden to the administration, appeared to be better bets for stopping GHA.

Would it not be possible to "contact the private physician of every congressman and senator and carry on a campaign that way," asked Dr. McGovern. No, replied Dr. Olin West, the secretary of the AMA, because such "political attempts always bring reprisals." Nor could newspapers be relied upon to advance the AMA viewpoint. West thought it far wiser to attack GHA quietly through the courts. "Nothing can be accomplished by a great public upheaval," he said.

Dr. W. C. Woodward, the director of the AMA's Bureau of Legal Medicine and Legislation, suggested that the District Medical Society secure "competent legal counsel" and offered to furnish some citations to relevant cases. The other legal avenue that the AMA officials encouraged was determining whether GHA was subject to the local laws regulating the insurance industry. Everyone realized that, if GHA were declared to be in the insurance business, the organization would then be required to possess sufficient reserves to meet its liabilities, and GHA's reserves were nowhere near adequate.

Other than that, the AMA officials promised only to bring the matter up at a forthcoming conference of secretaries of state medical societies. These influential doctors would be encouraged to contact their members of Congress in protest against Group Health.

The AMA officials discouraged many of the specific initiatives planned by the local doctors, yet they remained sympathetic to the basic objective of forcing GHA out of business. Tell people in simple language, Olin West said, that GHA will "destroy the private practice of medicine and the people will pay the penalty."

Dr. West's attitude reflected both the characteristic caution of a national organization composed of constituent local groups and a personal frustration that he had not been able to prevent GHA from opening. "We have done all that we could to oppose the Group Health Association Inc. in Washington," he told a Maryland doctor, "but in spite of our best efforts the scheme has gone into operation." "It is an outrage," he continued, "that an agency of the federal government should finance a corporation that is to engage in the practice of medicine."[44]

Returning to Washington, the local medical society leaders ignored much of the advice they had received and adopted many of the tactics that the AMA officials had considered futile. They felt that the threat to their immediate interests demanded that they take prompt and possibly risky action.

Between November 1937 and March 1938, the District Medical Society enlisted the aid of local hospitals to ensure that GHA doctors would be denied privileges. Refusing GHA doctors the right to hospitalize patients struck at the very heart of a modern medical practice. Without the use of local hospitals, GHA simply could not function. Through their actions in the ensuing months, both GHA and the local medical society implicitly acknowledged that the hospital was a key battleground in the fight to establish prepaid group health plans.

On November 3, the Society directed its Hospital Committee to find the best way of getting hospitals to see the ethical issues raised by GHA. As a draft of one Medical Society report put it, this step was taken "in an effort to hinder the operation of [GHA]." The Hospital Committee soon recommended "as a matter of educational policy" that teaching hospitals should make sure that their staffs (including their courtesy staffs) contained only members of local medical societies. The directive left little doubt that GHA doctors, who were barred from membership, were to be denied privileges. In February 1938, the Medical Society asked for a review of the hospitals' response and threatened to take "the appropriate disciplinary action" against noncomplying hospitals. Anxious to avoid the economic damage that could result if large numbers of physicians chose to hospitalize their patients elsewhere, the hospital administrators fell into line. By March, only one Washington hospital still had a GHA physician on its list and that only because it did not revise its list annually.[45]

Just as the AMA officials feared, however, open opposition by the Medical Society brought reprisals. Members of the United Federal Workers of America condemned the efforts of the local doctors to frustrate GHA and objected in particular to the pressure the District Medical Society was applying on the hospitals. One union official wondered how federal workers, who were being denied access to local hospitals, could in good conscience contribute to the Community Chest, the local charity (similar to today's United Way) that supported those hospitals.[46] The "Citizens Committee for Medical Freedom," an *ad hoc* organization in support of GHA, asked contributors to attach a special sticker to their Community Chest pledge card, stipulating that the pledge would become effective only after the Community Chest agreed to restrict its payments to hospitals that did not discriminate against GHA.[47]

Other *ad hoc* committees of federal employees worked to gather support for GHA. The Committee for Co-operative Medical Care for Federal Employees, the largest and most prestigious of these committees, contained executives from fifteen different agencies that had a total of 40,000 employees. The founding group for this committee included a former governor of the Virgin Islands and the head of the Department of Labor's Women's Bureau.[48]

Despite this agitation from federal employees, the local medical society persisted in its campaign against GHA. As a result, the GHA doctors found themselves in an impossible situation. They could only get hospital privileges if they were members of the local medical society, yet they were expelled from that society or refused admission.[49]

GHA's president, William F. Penniman, sent letters to the local hospitals. In a typical reply, a vice president of the Episcopal Eye, Ear and Throat Hospital said GHA patients would be welcome there, but admission of GHA physicians to practice on Episcopal's staff constituted a different matter.[50] The GHA doctors would have to be placed on what one hospital administrator called the "courtesy list of physicians." Attempts to get the GHA physicians on the courtesy lists led only to a bureaucratic runaround. At Sibley Memorial, for example, the request of GHA's surgeon to treat patients for minor and major surgery was routinely referred to the hospital's Advisory Committee on Surgery. On the form letter used for such purposes, however, a special notation was added, indicating that the applicant was "one of the salaried physicians of the . . . Group Health Association." The application, which would have been handled perfunctorily in most instances, thus met with considerable scrutiny and ultimate rejection.[51]

Dr. Raymond Selders, the GHA surgeon, became a special target of harassment. As a member of a county medical society in Houston, Texas, Selders would ordinarily have experienced no difficulty in becoming a member of the D.C. Medical Society. Instead, the Washington society wrote a special letter of inquiry to the Harris County Medical Society. The Texas secretary, who agreed with his D.C. counterpart that GHA was "inspired by some who are in high authority in our national government," replied enthusiastically. "Please let me know," he said, so that "charges of unethical conduct may be lodged against Dr. Selders." Although Selders was a member of the Harris County Medical Society in good financial standing, with a clear record and good academic and professional qualifications, he would be "subject to disciplinary action" for joining GHA. In January 1938, the Harris County Medical Society determined that it was unethical for Selders or any doctor to work for Group Health.[52]

In Washington, Selders faced a similarly negative reception.

Meeting at the Cosmos Club in December 1937, the Washington Academy of Surgery discussed Selders and Group Health. For a surgeon to gain hospital privileges, it was decided, his ethics should be considered, in addition to his surgical training and experience. Since the Medical Society considered working for Group Health to be unethical, this decision tended to undercut the routine letters of recommendation that the hospitals received in response to their inquiries about Selders, such as one from J. C. Alexander, a Houston doctor, who stated, "[his] professional qualifications are well above the average and ethically and morally he has always been above reproach."[53] By the end of 1937, GHA President William Penniman began to receive letters from local hospital authorities telling him that Dr. Selders' professional qualifications were unacceptable and that he would be denied hospital privileges. That left GHA in considerable disarray: the GHA surgeon could not get into the operating room.[54]

Dr. Mario Scandiffio, a GHA pediatrician, who was already a member of the D.C. Medical Society, could not be dismissed so easily by local authorities. Scandiffio persisted through disciplinary proceedings conducted by the Medical Society. Faced with formal charges of violating the Society's constitution, Scandiffio at first resigned from the Society and then thought better of it. Instead, he submitted to a formal trial, complete with legal counsel, before the Society's executive committee.[55] In the middle of March 1938, the Society voted to expel Dr. Scandiffio for violating the ethics of his profession. Scandiffio vowed to remain on the GHA staff and, as one newspaper reported, the feud between GHA and the D.C. medical community progressed from "sniping tactics to open warfare."[56]

GHA AS NATIONAL CONCERN

In late 1937, as local authorities were investigating GHA, Congress conducted its own investigation, according to its own special rules.

Democratic Senator Patrick A. McCarran of Nevada asked the General Accounting Office to explore the legality of the $40,000 provided by the FHLBB. The acting comptroller general told Senator McCarran that this expenditure was "without authority of law." McCarran promptly called for legislation to prevent the expenditure of money for purposes not specifically authorized by Congress.[57]

The appropriations committees in both houses of Congress took particular exception to spending government money on GHA. In the House of Representatives, Republican Congressmen Everett Dirksen of Illinois and Richard B. Wigglesworth of Massachusetts and Democrat Clifton A. Woodrum of Virginia grilled Fahey and Zimmerman during hearings on their budget requests for 1939. Zimmerman justified the financial contribution as a "morale building factor, . . . an inexpensive way to become a better employer." A Federal Home Loan Bank Board lawyer compared spending $40,000 on GHA to building a cafeteria. Congress certainly did not legislate on every cafeteria, he protested. With a characteristic flair, Dirksen began to ask questions. Would it be proper for the Home Owners' Loan Corporation in the name of efficiency to set up a "grocery store, . . . meat market or a wholesale store?" The other congressmen joined in the ridicule. A gymnasium, beauty parlor, barber shop?[58]

In the face of such criticism, Zimmerman prepared a more rigorous justification for GHA that contained a new (and misleading) interpretation of GHA's origins. Zimmerman now emphasized that the impetus for GHA came from the rank-and-file employees of the Federal Home Loan Bank Board and the Home Owners Loan Corporation, rather than from Fahey, the chairman, or from Zimmerman, the director of personnel. Group Health, Zimmerman maintained, was an "employee enterprise . . . organized, not on the initiative of the Board, but voluntarily by those of the employee body who felt the need."[59]

Furthermore, each of the questionable practices at GHA could be explained. The check-off system for paying dues, regarded by many in Congress and on the bench as illegal, was not mandatory. Instead, it existed for the employees' "convenience," should they wish to avail themselves of it. The Home Owners Loan Corporation gave GHA $40,000 because start-up capital was required and "the thought naturally suggested itself that these funds might well be supplied by the organization itself." The money, it was emphasized, represented a one-time investment and not a "recurring expense." Most of it went into medical equipment.[60]

Raymond Zimmerman tried to convince the congressmen that GHA was an investment that paid for itself. After all, it provided a group project for employees and produced an *esprit de corps*. It also reduced employee turnover, allowing the agency to retain competent people because it kept "abreast of the times in matters affecting its personnel." (This line of reasoning was undoubtedly novel, coming at a time of double-digit unemployment, when people were hardly likely to give up secure jobs.) GHA therefore merited the investment of $40,000 in government funds. Air conditioning, another such investment, cost the agency $380,000 to install and $27,000 a year to operate.[61]

This rhetoric failed to impress the members of the appropriations committees. Congressman Woodrum called it "a perfect farce" for the HOLC to spend money as it saw fit. The Committee members made sure that the appropriations bill for 1939 contained an amendment, passed by the House, stating that the appropriated money should be spent only for congressionally authorized purposes.[62]

As the battle over congressional appropriations unfolded, GHA and the local medical community spent the spring of 1938 engaged in guerilla warfare over control of the local hospitals. The hospitals respected the wishes of the local medical society to a meticulous degree. When GHA member Sarah Abbott arrived at the Central Dispensary and Emergency Hospital by ambulance with a fractured leg, she was sent to the emergency room and then admitted to the hospital. Dr. Selders asked to take over the case but was told that he was not on the courtesy list and could only consult. GHA therefore decided to send Miss Abbott, broken leg and all, to Garfield Hospital, where Selders could still practice (under temporary courtesy privileges that were subsequently revoked).[63]

Most of the hospitals would not even accept checks from GHA. Sibley Memorial, for example, returned a check to GHA with a note that it "was evidently sent to us by mistake." Subsequent letters from GHA were met with a firm refusal to cash the organization's check.[64]

Physicians who practiced in these hospitals refused to treat GHA patients. One cardiologist, for example, declined to see a GHA patient with a serious heart condition that was beyond the competence of the GHA staff, unless the patient agreed to become the doctor's private patient.[65] As a result, GHA could only hospitalize its patients by turning them over to non-GHA doctors who had hospital privileges. The patients paid the doctors and hospitals and were reimbursed by GHA.

Such incidents generated congressional debate. Two California Democrats, Representative Jerry Voorhis, who later headed the Group Health Association of America, and Representative Byron Scott, praised GHA on the House floor. Voorhis spoke of a crisis in medical care distribution and equated GHA with social progress. Scott threatened to introduce a resolution to revoke the District Medical Society's charter. Scott also emphasized the larger issues involved in the Group Health case. "Women and children are suffering," he said, "because of their membership in an institution which the President of the United States has seen fit to characterize as representative of other similar undertakings."[66]

Representative Paul W. Shafer, a Michigan Republican who served on the District of Columbia Committee's hospital subcommittee, argued that the Washington doctors did everything they could to cooperate with GHA but had to uphold the ethics of their profession. "The medical society could hardly be expected to abandon its own principles in order to comply with the ultimatum of the GHA," Shafer said.[67]

As the heated rhetoric suggested, the issue involved more than the establishment of a local medical plan. Instead, it had become a battle between the New Deal and the AMA. Proponents of the New Deal believed that the government should facilitate prepaid group health plans; followers of the AMA saw the issue as one testing the rights of private self-regulation and the limits of government control over people's actions.

For a small, struggling organization like GHA to figure in this debate was extraordinary. It had not come close to changing the nature of medical practice in the District of Columbia, let alone the nation. Instead, it owed its national prominence to its emergence as a symbol in the fight to establish prepaid group practices in urban settings, just when this fight had reached a critical juncture. The date of GHA's establishment put it in the path of history, because it coincided with two major historical events: congressional reaction against New Deal legislation, and the beginnings of a major campaign to reorganize national health care. GHA became a test of the government's ability to reform health care; government officials approved of it and it had indirect ties to the Committee on the Costs of Medical Care (and hence to the New Deal).

The battle, which was fought in different institutions at different governmental levels, centered on two major issues. The first concerned the propriety of the government's $40,000 cash contribution to GHA; the second, ultimately the more important, involved the legal right of local physicians to exclude GHA doctors from the hospitals. The resolution of the first issue affected GHA's internal development; the second issue produced one of the most important lawsuits in the history of American medical care. On the local level, the hospitals mattered most, but, at the national level, the courts, centers of the New Deal debate over executive authority, ultimately became the major battleground.

EXPANSION TO OTHER AGENCIES

It became increasingly clear that the $40,000 contribution could not be defended, because it put the federal government in the position of advancing the cause of prepaid group health without legislative sanction. Government did not have the same freedom in its personnel policies as did progressive private employers. Edward A. Filene's department store could experiment with cooperative health care; the federal government could not. Congress, in its zeal to restrict executive authority, would not tolerate the Federal Home Loan Bank Board's dabbling in group health.

The resolution of this issue had a significant effect on the development of GHA. It recast the organization into a form that was consistent with the terms of the political debate over national health care. The lack of a federal subsidy created a need for additional revenues, which in turn caused GHA to seek new members from other federal agencies. Since GHA's articles of incorporation permitted it to serve employees of all federal agencies, there was no legal impediment to such expansion. The arrival of the new members changed the very nature of the organization because, unlike the original subscribers who joined GHA as faithful employees of the FHLBB, the new members chose GHA because it was organized as a cooperative. What had been an incidental feature of GHA now became central to its identity.

Originally, if Zimmerman or Rickcord of the Twentieth Century Fund could have found a local doctors' group offering prepaid practice, they might well have asked the HOLC employees to join. Since none was available, they helped the employees themselves to organize Group Health as an independent, cooperatively controlled, nongovernmental agency. In fact, however, GHA took money from the government, and executives of the FHLBB dominated its affairs. The first Board of Trustees, for example, consisted entirely of high-salaried officials who, according to a report prepared by one early member, placed "considerable pressure" on FHLBB employees to join. In effect, the bosses ran the workers' medical plan in a paternalistic manner, as might be expected from a program that shared the intellectual heritage of welfare capitalism.[68]

Seeking new members, GHA turned to federal employees who believed in the group health cause. The efforts to meet congressional criticism, as reported in the press, had changed the public's perception of this cause. Forgotten were the roots of GHA as a management tool of welfare capitalism. Now, joining Group Health meant striking a blow against the medical establishment and for the people's right to medical care. As one early member of GHA put it, "I joined Group Health because I believed in it. If there had been socialized group health, I would have joined that."[69]

The first overtures to new groups came at the very end of 1937. In an effort to expand GHA's rolls to 2,500 members, Raymond Zimmerman investigated interest at the Rural Electrification Administration (REA), the Farm Credit Administration, the Social Security Board, and the Federal Reserve Board.[70] In January 1938, the outreach efforts began to pay off. More than two hundred employees from the Social Security Board and sixty-two from the Rural Electrification Administration joined GHA. By March of 1938 the target of 2,500 members was met.[71]

The new members soon became influential in the organization. By the summer of 1938, for example, the Department of Agriculture had more GHA members than did the HOLC, and the Social Security Board, Farm Credit Administration, and REA each contributed more than one hundred members.

The rise of new agencies at GHA meant the decline of the HOLC and the FHLBB. Membership among HOLC employees fell from 800 to 270 in little more than a year, dropping precipitously when the payroll deduction of dues, which Congress had so thoroughly condemned, was discontinued in July 1938.[72] Many of the initial 900 GHA members may have signed up more from a desire to please their superiors than from a genuine enthusiasm for the idea. Such members simply took advantage of reduced pressure from their supervisors and quietly dropped out. Nearly 30 percent of those dropping GHA membership had received no GHA services at all while they were enrolled, and nearly half had received services amounting to less than the value of their dues. In other words, they may have left because they thought it would be cheaper simply to pay the doctor on the rare occasions when they needed medical treatment.[73]

The enrollees from the new agencies, particularly the REA and the Department of Agriculture, believed deeply in the ideals of cooperation. They wanted to distribute economic power. As Agriculture employees, they worked to give food producers parity with food processors. As members of GHA, they hoped to create a balance between health consumers and health providers.[74]

This view of GHA as a democratic organization led the new members to expect a voice in its policies. As a result, some of the newer members turned to the device of an Advisory Council. The Board agreed and arranged for an Advisory Council election in April 1938. Made up of GHA members elected to represent their federal agencies, the Council took its role seriously and promptly began providing the Board with advice. To keep GHA members informed of Board actions and other important developments, the Advisory Council in June 1938 started a monthly publication, the *GHA News*.[75]

For its part, the Board of Trustees was also changing to reflect the importance of the newly recruited agencies. In February 1938, Perry R. Taylor of the Rural Electrification Administration was appointed to fill a vacancy. Other non-HOLC Board members followed, so that a year later, fewer than half the eleven Board members worked for the HOLC.[76]

In March 1939, both the Board of Trustees and the Advisory Council adopted a resolution that reflected the new priorities of GHA. It called the organization a "cooperative enterprise," with many qualified members who were willing voluntarily to donate time to its program. The resolution also assigned important responsibilities to the Council and created an elaborate system for choosing the members. A bridge between the trustees and the membership, the Council would meet with the Board at least four times a year, and its members would serve on GHA's standing committees. Each federal bureau with GHA members would be represented, at an approximate rate of one Advisory Council member for every twenty-five GHA members. The Advisory Council, then, functioned as a representative democracy within the emerging cooperative structure.[77]

FINANCIAL AND OPERATIONAL PROBLEMS

The consumer cooperative faced its first major internal crisis in the spring of 1938, when Dr. Brown, the medical director, resigned. Dr. Selders, the surgeon, took the post, but problems soon developed within the staff, and by the end of the year, the Board openly discussed replacing him. Selders, it was noted, suffered from "a lack of personality and diplomacy," and many people did not consider him a competent surgeon.[78] The Board pondered the difficulty: even if Selders was incompetent, the Board could not dismiss him without giving the impression of dictating to the medical staff. In January 1939, after two months of discussion, the lay Board of Trustees decided to ask Dr. Selders to resign. In a formal resolution, the trustees noted that they had received many complaints from members about Dr. Selders' work as medical director. Dr. Selders resigned the next afternoon.[79] On March 1, 1939, Dr.

Mario Scandiffio, the martyr of the D.C. Medical Society and a pediatrician known for his pleasant temperament, became the new medical director.[80]

Meanwhile, during the summer of 1938, the Board had taken steps to improve the administration of GHA and place it on a sound financial footing. It hired a full-time administrator, planned a fund-raising campaign, and contemplated opening up a hospital for GHA patients. After consultation with the Advisory Council, the Board decided on a goal of $100,000 for this campaign.[81] Although GHA's structure was becoming more democratic through the influence of the Advisory Council, elements of elitism remained. For example, the Board planned to have people "high up in each agency" take the lead roles in the fund-raising drive, anticipating a better response if the campaign had "the official sanction of the agency or department."[82]

Such sanction mattered because of the severity of GHA's economic problems. In an illustration of the organization's relative poverty, a special committee appointed in 1939 recommended such reductions in monthly expenditures as fifty dollars on laundry and twenty-five dollars each on gas, electricity, and the telephone. An organization for which such savings mattered was clearly close to the margin. Its status as a pariah in the medical community exacerbated the problem. In March 1939, for example, the Hartford Accident and Indemnity Insurance Company threatened to cancel GHA's malpractice insurance, forcing the organization to transact its business with Lloyds of London and raising its costs. The 1940 rate was $40,000.[83]

Similarly, Group Health decided to build a hospital—which clearly was beyond the means of the young organization—because the existing hospitals refused to accept GHA doctors and their patients. The first hospital drive in the summer of 1938 illustrated GHA's problems. Initially, GHA hoped to build a hospital in Chevy Chase, Maryland, but the Montgomery County Board of Commissioners, mindful of AMA opposition, denied the application in a unanimous vote. Then GHA went south and made a deposit on an Arlington, Virginia, estate. Valued at $60,000, the eleven-acre property overlooking the Potomac had a house large enough for a fifteen-bed hospital. In a few months, however, GHA, short of funds, allowed its option to lapse, and the Board considered asking Congress for special legislation to build a new D.C. hospital for GHA patients. By early 1939, however, the Justice Department had begun to prosecute the Medical Society and the AMA for harassing GHA, causing the D.C. hospitals, led by Garfield, to relent. Slowly, they began admitting GHA's patients and granting privileges to its physicians. Five Group Health doctors could practice at Garfield in January 1939. As a result, GHA decided to wait for more members before building its own hospital.[84]

Still under siege by the Medical Society and short of funds, GHA had constantly to cut costs, even if that meant undermining the prepaid concept. Chronic ailments posed particularly poignant dilemmas. A 1939 analysis of clinic records revealed that 10 percent of the patients were receiving 40 percent of the services. The entrance physical, with its five-dollar fee, screened some of these people from the membership rolls, but others, whose problems went undetected, slipped through and raised GHA's costs. The only solution was to back away from pure prepayment and to devise a way of recovering some of the expense of chronic care. The Board considered, and the membership approved, a plan under which chronically ill patients would have to pay the costs of care that exceeded half of their dues, if the illness came within three years of joining.[85]

Thus, even as the democratic views of its new members pushed GHA closer to the model of a prepaid group practice run in a cooperative manner, economic pressures forced it to modify the model. Although this basic tension between ideals and financial realities was to continue throughout GHA's history, the intervention of outside political authorities on GHA's behalf provided some temporary relief in the late 1930s.

THE COURT CONTEST

Congressional interest and the interest of the AMA had assured national attention for GHA almost from its inception. In the summer of 1938, this interest reached a climax, as the New Deal approached GHA from two directions. The social welfare bureaucracy was pressing the fight for national health insurance, and lawyers in the Department of Justice began investigating the practices of the American Medical Association.

National health insurance, although put aside in 1935 when the Social Security Act was passed, remained a concern of such officials as Josephine Roche, an assistant secretary of the Treasury in charge of the Public Health Service, Harry Hopkins, FDR's relief administrator, and Arthur Altmeyer, the chairman (after 1937) of the Social Security Board. Their views were represented in the work of a health subcommittee of the Interdepartmental Committee to Coordinate Health and Welfare Activities that submitted a confidential report to President Roosevelt in February 1938. The report, a product of many of the people whose interest in health insurance stretched back to the Committee on the Costs of Medical Care, stressed such themes as the need for preventive health services, particularly to improve the nation's performance in infant mortality, the need for more hospitals, and the need to find a means by which more people could afford health care.[86]

To highlight the drive to reform medical care, the administration arranged a National Health Conference in July 1938. As expected, more than two hundred participants agreed in principle on the need for a national health program. Mary Switzer, who had done the staff work for the conference and later became a major figure in federal health and welfare policy, wrote of the emotional impact of hearing "speaker after speaker tell from the experience of its own group the desperate need for medical benefits."[87]

Matters of emphasis separated the New Dealers from the members of GHA, but the two groups were basically in agreement. The New Dealers emphasized reorganizing medicine so as to allow the poor to gain access. GHA had a slightly different emphasis: it was in no way a charity organization. In June 1938, for example, New Dealer Josephine Roche spoke before the AMA and challenged the doctors to do a better job serving the poor. Although GHA used the same data as did Roche to demonstrate the need for medical care among the near-poor, it was more interested in cooperation and self-help than in reforming the entire health care industry. But these goals were hardly contradictory, as demonstrated by the fact that many of the people who devised the New Deal health program, such as Arthur Altmeyer, belonged to GHA. Altmeyer and his New Deal colleagues realized that both entities fought for prepaid, group practice and wanted to change medical care to bring it within the economic reach of the common citizen.[88]

At the same time that New Dealers cautiously began to advocate health insurance programs in the various states, the direction of the New Deal, if such a disparate and incoherent group of programs could be said to have a direction, was changing. During his first New Deal (1933), Roosevelt sought to remedy the nation's problems by cooperating with organized interests such as large industries or farmers and by sponsoring a temporary, emergency program of relief. Although this initial effort left behind a permanent bureaucratic residue, the initiatives of 1935 took a different tack. Confrontation with big business replaced cooperation, and permanent social welfare programs, designed to achieve security or set minimum standards of industrial conduct, replaced earlier, temporary efforts. At the same time, other New Deal programs worked toward a complex goal that might be called "empowerment," restoring labor, for example, to a position of parity with management. When the courts became more receptive to New Deal goals after the abortive court-packing plan of 1937, it became possible and appropriate for New Deal lawyers to confront big business in court over "unfair management practices," as in the 1935 Wagner Act, or fostering monopoly. The court, rather than the Congress, became the center of the effort to preserve and extend the New Deal. In this convoluted manner, the New Deal discovered antitrust prosecutions, an old item on the reform agenda. That, in turn, brought the New Deal lawyers into contact with Group Health.

More than any other individual, Thurman Arnold, a Wyoming lawyer with an Ivy League education, led the New Deal's antitrust efforts. When Arnold died in 1969, the *New York Times* described him as "a somewhat paunchy man whose suits looked as though he had slept in them" who was, at the same time, "one of the canniest and most successful lawyers in Washington." In March of 1938, Arnold, who had been teaching at Yale Law School, arrived in Washington to head the Justice Department's Antitrust Division. Arnold began a vigorous program that would lead to the filing of 230 lawsuits and the hiring of over two hundred attorneys and investigators before he resigned in 1943. Explaining the uses to which he put antitrust legislation, Arnold said he did not want to destroy big corporations but rather to hold them in bounds and keep the field open for "newcomers with fresh ideas."[89]

At Yale Law School some creative thought had already been given to the group health situation. One student, who later moved to Washington and joined Group Health Association, wrote a short note on "Group Practice and the American Medical Association." The article suggested remedies for a doctor, like Mario Scandiffio, who had been expelled from the local medical society. One suggestion was to attack the bylaws of the District Medical Society as "in restraint of trade and therefore contrary to public policy." The doc-

49

tor would argue, in effect, that "his expulsion was part of a scheme by which the Society hoped to destroy [GHA]" and preserve traditional fee-for-service medicine.[90]

What the student did not mention but what Arnold must have understood was that the government could also present this argument if it wished to use the Sherman Antitrust Act to initiate a suit against the American Medical Association. Such an extraordinary application of that statute would require arguing that medicine was a "trade" in the legal sense of the term, rather than an art or profession. The very audacity of the strategy may have appealed to Arnold.

The various strands of the New Deal health offensive came together in July 1938. First, the National Health Conference focused attention on health policy, and then Judge Jennings Bailey ruled that GHA was not "illegally or otherwise engaged in the practice of medicine or engaged in an insurance business." Four days later, Arnold, who had reportedly been investigating the situation since June, formally charged the American Medical Association and the Medical Society of the District of Columbia with violating the antitrust laws of the United States.[91]

Arnold proposed to present evidence to a grand jury and seek an indictment. The charges, he declared, were based on the threatened expulsion of GHA doctors from the local medical society and from the local hospitals. In Arnold's view, the law prohibited "combinations which prevent others from competing for services as well as goods." Arnold announced the charges in advance of the grand jury proceedings, he said, in order to warn the Medical Society and the AMA and give them a chance to change their policies.[92]

Starting in late May 1938, and continuing through the summer and fall, GHA worked closely with the Antitrust Division, passing along a steady stream of documents that government attorneys could present as evidence to the grand jury. The materials included affidavits by Group Health members whose physicians had been refused permission to treat them in certain hospitals, transcripts of meetings between Medical Society representatives and GHA trustees, correspondence in which the *Journal of the American Medical Association* rejected a GHA advertisement for additional staff doctors, and letters from hospitals refusing GHA checks. The Department of Justice and GHA worked in concert, and their actions were carefully timed to coincide with the administration's campaign for national health insurance.[93]

The AMA and the District Medical Society seemed to welcome a confrontation with Arnold. Lawyers for the doctors told the Department of Justice that the Medical Society was not "amenable" to the antitrust laws. Nothing "constructive" could be "accomplished by further discussions," the lawyers said. In September, the AMA's House of Delegates met in emergency session and urged the AMA to "oppose with its utmost power, even in the courts of last resort," any attempt to portray AMA as a monopoly. The two sides agreed to meet in court.[94]

Here was a perfect example of how the focus of public policy had shifted from the legislature to the courts in an important area of domestic affairs. As health insurance bills in Congress got nowhere, GHA, a small organization with severe problems that threatened its very existence, became the center of the battle over national health insurance in the United States.

In the fall of 1938, a grand jury was impanelled to hear evidence against the D.C. Medical Society and the AMA. On December 20, the grand jury indicted the AMA, the District of Columbia Medical Society, the Washington Academy of Surgery, twenty-one individual physicians, and the Harris County Medical Society in Texas for violating the Sherman Antitrust Act. Included in the indictment were such medical luminaries as Dr. Thomas E. Neill, president of the local society, and Dr. Morris Fishbein, editor of the *Journal of the American Medical Association* and author of a popular syndicated newspaper column. The indictment rehashed the incidents that had kept GHA doctors from joining the local medical society and practicing in local hospitals. In a *JAMA* editorial, Morris Fishbein responded to the indictment by vowing that the AMA would defend its position "to the utmost."[95]

Group Health now found itself on page one of the nation's newspapers, and the editorial columns featured extensive commentary on the case. Many of the editorials reflected the vituperative attitude of the newspaper editors toward the programs of the late New Deal. In Huntington, West Virginia, the local paper said that the antitrust prosecution was an idea "only the New Deal could have been expected to conceive." Sensing the relevant comparison, the newspaper said the action was "on a brazenness par with the attempt to pack the Supreme Court." The *St. Louis Daily Globe-Democrat* criticized Arnold for "making his own laws." The *New York Daily Mirror* made a bold comparison between Thurman Arnold and Adolf Hitler. "How much more of our freedom of action, of our liberties . . . must we sacrifice to the obsessions of legalistic department dictators in Washington?" the paper asked. The *Charleston Evening Post* explained that the issue was quite simple: a fight between organized medicine and "a movement toward socialized medicine."[96]

The case plodded through the courts. On July 26, 1939, District Court Judge James M. Proctor dismissed the grand jury's indictment on the grounds that medicine was not a trade and therefore not subject to prosecution under the Sherman Antitrust Act. The government tried to appeal this decision directly to the Supreme Court, but the Supreme Court refused to consider the issue. On March 4, 1940, the United States Circuit Court of Appeals reversed the lower court, paving the way for a trial.[97]

The principals returned to Judge Proctor's court on June 14, 1940. The defendants formed a semicircle in front of the judge and pleaded not guilty. They were released without bail.[98]

On February 5, 1941, the trial began, and a group of Washingtonians, including a housewife, a mailman, and a woman described only as "colored" were selected for the jury. The jurors were treated to a virtuoso display of courtroom technique. Prosecutor John Henry Lewin took more than a hour to deliver his opening statement and still did not have enough time to finish. He promised to put more than thirty witnesses on the stand to demonstrate the "harsh, outrageous, and unreasonable treatment" of GHA members at the doctors' hands. AMA attorney William E. Leahy addressed the jury the following day and spoke without notes for almost three hours. He characterized GHA as an organization of "haughty and arrogant men" that was dedicated to the "destruction of the hallowed tradition of the medical profession."[99]

The trial lasted almost three months, with extensive testimony on the Medical Society's campaign against GHA. The defense capped its case at the end of March by putting Dr. Henry Rolf Brown, the former medical director of GHA, on the stand. By this time, Brown had thoroughly recanted. "I resigned [from GHA]," he had written in an article for the AMA, "because lay control invaded the field of medical direction." The founders of GHA, he believed, confused cooperative medicine and socialized medicine. They communicated constantly with the Social Security Board, the White House, and Josephine Roche and spent government money in an improper manner. When they needed to use the long distance telephone, for example, they did not hesitate to use the government lines. It was the government, not local medical officials, who deserved prosecution.[100]

The defense attorneys for the AMA and the local doctors thus tried to make socialized medicine and professional control over medicine the issues in the trial. Because Brown had worked for GHA and become disillusioned, he made a perfect witness. With Brown's testimony, the defense rested.

The jury deliberated for nearly eleven hours. It had heard 118 witnesses and watched the presentation of 747 documents. When the jurors returned to the courtroom at 11:31 P.M. on the evening of April 4, 1941, they delivered a split verdict. They found the AMA and the D.C. Medical Society guilty, but they acquitted the individual doctors.[101]

When the Appeals Court affirmed the verdict, the AMA carried its fight to the Supreme Court, where Thurman Arnold argued the government's case. On January 18, 1943, a unanimous Supreme Court upheld the lower courts' decision. The AMA paid a $2,500 fine, and the local medical society paid $1,500. The case was finally over.[102]

By then the case had already been rendered irrelevant by changing circumstances. The Medical Society had relented in its fight against Group Health, perhaps aware of the fact that GHA was unlikely to take over a significant share of the health care market. The administration had long since given up fighting for national health insurance, which had faded from the public's mind as the economy heated up under wartime conditions and unemployment disappeared.

When the case was settled, the nation was preoccupied by war. Doctors, in particular, were in short supply, their depression insecurities gone. More people were working longer hours and earning enough money to pay for medical care on a fee-for-service basis. Nonetheless, the decision set an important legal precedent that encouraged the formation of prepaid group health plans elsewhere in the country.[103]

GHA AT THE VERGE OF THE SECOND WORLD WAR

From GHA's perspective, the Supreme Court case assumed great importance. The verdict left little doubt that both physicians and hospitals would have to make room for Group Health in the local market. At last, GHA was firmly launched.

In the intervening years, however, GHA itself had altered in response to changing circumstances. Begun as an experiment in progressive management, it had become a cooperative run by government employees. At Group Health, unlike other health care plans, the members themselves entered into a collaboration with the medical staff to manage the organization and provide care. Yet, as the leaders of GHA had already learned, organizing and financing such an operation were difficult tasks. GHA had both to solve the riddles of medical economics and to secure a niche in the Washington community. Despite all the notoriety that attended the organization's launching, these tasks still lay ahead. The delay created by the Supreme Court case meant only that GHA would attempt these tasks in a wartime economy rather than in a depressed one.

CHAPTER THREE

Interlude: GHA
as Small Cooperative

After the trial, GHA receded from public view and tended to its own affairs. To stay in business required increasing enrollment and holding services within limits. The war helped. It brought more people to Washington, D.C., forced members to conserve their use of medical care, and made doctors work longer hours. The problems of the postwar world, such as combatting inflation, integrating blacks into GHA, recruiting groups, coping with the exodus to the suburbs, and introducing new services into the prepaid group format, proved more difficult to solve. The result was that, as late as 1958, GHA remained a struggling, small medical cooperative.

WARTIME

The war produced a sudden and stark change in the nation's economy. New pressures to defer consumption and divert all available funds to the war replaced depression desires to spend and invest. Labor, which had been in extraordinary surplus, now came at a premium. Because the war altered people's routines and changed the normal flow of capital, it inevitably demanded sacrifice, creating internal political problems for Group Health Association.

GHA's location affected the type of sacrifice required. At first, GHA believed that the principal impact of the war would be an exodus of its members from Washington, as government decentralization efforts moved federal agencies to other parts of the country. It soon, however, became apparent that the problem would not be lack of members. As the war finally brought fiscal health to both the country and the government, it fueled a major expansion of public sector activities. As the center of a growing federal bureaucracy, Washington, and GHA as well, reaped the rewards. Toward the end of 1942, for example, GHA found its chief problem was not the loss of members to military service but rather the great influx of civilians into the city as part of the wartime bureaucracy. At the close of 1942, GHA had 161 members from the Office of Price Administration, 226 from the War Production Board, 186 civilian employees from the War Department, and 168 from the Navy Department. Between January 1942 and January 1944, GHA's total enrollment actually increased by more than 1,400.[1]

After Pearl Harbor, GHA, which served 7,800 people with a staff of thirteen full-time doctors, sought to play a patriotic role in a transformed community.[2] The lines between public and private activities, always blurred in the nation's capital, became nearly indistinguishable: all organizations were expected to contribute to the war effort. As part of the local civilian defense program, for example, GHA constructed a shelter in the basement of its clinic building as a location for emergency care. The *GHA News* published a list of first aid supplies to have on hand in event of an air raid. Responding to the mood, GHA also transferred its savings from bank accounts to war bonds and decided not to hold the annual membership meeting because of wartime transportation restrictions.[3]

During the war, patriotism took more mundane forms as well,

such as deferring medical procedures and working longer hours. In response to wartime emergency, for example, GHA made plans to shift essential operations, such as the delivery of babies, from hospitals to homes.[4] Following the lead of the federal government, GHA went on a forty-eight-hour work week and changed clinic hours to 9:30 A.M. to 6:30 P.M. to accommodate late-working federal employees.[5]

Inevitably, the goal of prevention gave way to the necessity of treatment. The organization could not even staff its clinic. Late in 1941, for example, medical director Dr. Mario Scandiffio made a recruiting tour of the prestigious east coast medical schools and returned enthusiastic about the warm reception he received. Then the war came, and Scandiffio's recruiting drive collapsed.[6] Instead of getting new doctors, GHA lost some of its old ones to military service. The remaining physicians became overburdened, and they were forced to spend their time attending to the most pressing cases. Such GHA procedures as entrance physicals, designed to spot emerging health problems, were dropped for the duration.[7] In December 1942, with only eight full-time and three part-time doctors left to serve its 8,000 participants, GHA asked members to postpone checkups and not to request house calls. The number of house calls declined from 2,100 in the first six months of 1942 to 1,300 during the same period in 1943; the number dropped even lower in 1944.[8]

At GHA, as elsewhere, the war tended to break down sexual and professional divisions of labor. Nurses successfully relieved doctors of routine duties, such as filling out forms and taking temperatures. Doctors performed work outside of their medical specialties. Internists worked as gynecologists, as allergists, and even as surgeons. Pediatricians saw patients of all ages and did orthopedic work.[9] Dr. Ruth Benedict, an internist, carried on the adult medicine practice almost by herself. "We could not have had a more conscientious person," said Dr. Henry Lichtenberg, a GHA pediatrician during the war and later its medical director. Dr. Natalie Deyrup, a pediatrician, he recounted, not only gave anaesthesia for tonsil and adenoid operations but also sutured wounds and strapped ankles.[10]

By the end of the war, as the number of full-time doctors dropped to five, the strain began to show. Trustees grew concerned over the "increasing number of complaints" and the "problems of low morale." The organization did what it could within the legal limits imposed by the war. It doubled salary scales and paid higher and higher fees for more and more outside services. Finally, in 1944, GHA reached the point where it became necessary to stop accepting new subscribers. By then, with victory in sight, the organization began to contemplate the postwar world.[11]

POSTWAR ASPIRATIONS

As it planned for future expansion, Group Health set the ambitious goal of attaining 25,000 participants in the immediate postwar era, although at war's end it had only 9,000. GHA hoped to reach the new level by admitting future members in groups, rather than just as individuals or families, as had been the practice. An article in *Fortune* magazine explained the need for the change, noting that when subscribers joined as individuals or families, "it would be a wonder if Group Health were not to pick up members sure to overutilize its services." The article described such adverse selection as GHA's "congenital weakness" and recommended that people be admitted in blocks to assure a more balanced membership.[12]

In order to meet the problems outlined by the *Fortune* article and expand its membership, GHA considered not only admitting new subscribers in groups but also opening enrollment beyond federal employees to include all workers in the Washington area. By early 1946, the Board had formally approved, and the members ratified, the principle of group admissions and broadening membership.[13]

The subject of group admissions forced GHA to confront the question of admitting black members. The trustees realized that, if groups were admitted, blacks could no longer be excluded. As the

GHA president wrote to the chairman of the Advisory Council, "If there are Negroes in an employee group wishing to join GHA, we cannot on any reasonable or objective basis discriminate against them."[14]

The war had both facilitated and hindered racial integration. At GHA, as in many other institutions that transacted business at the northern edge of the American South, the war divided an era of total racial segregation from a time of limited integration. Prior to World War II, Washington, D.C., was a racially segregated city. Medical care was as thoroughly segregated as other aspects of life, with black Washington residents cared for by black physicians and treated in black hospitals like Freedmen's. GHA, faced with serious opposition from the medical community, saw little point in further antagonizing local forces and accepted only whites.

This policy chafed at the sensibilities of a substantial portion of GHA's members who, after all, worked for the government and imagined themselves as bettering the lot of the downtrodden and disadvantaged. Many felt a dissonance, an inconsistency, between their egalitarian philosophies and the refusal of their member-owned organization to offer health care to black government workers. Throughout the war years, the question of whether GHA should admit blacks seethed below the surface and occasionally erupted. The issue was called to the attention of the Board of Trustees by those who perceived a gap between the organization's theory and practice.

At the annual membership meeting in January 1941, the members discussed, perhaps for the first time in GHA's history, admitting blacks. The trustees eventually decided to tell any Negro applicants that "GHA is still in the process of organization" and could not yet deal with the "controversial subject . . . of admitting Negroes."[15]

The pressure for action came from GHA members and outside organizations, not from blacks themselves. Twice in the spring of

1941, for example, a member of the CIO Ladies Auxiliary requested a meeting with the Board to discuss admitting Negroes. Two years later, in May 1943, representatives of the War Labor Board, the CIO, the Office of Price Administration, the Bureau of Labor Statistics, and the Department of Labor met with the GHA Board and contended that GHA should allow black members. They pointed to the growing number of black federal employees and observed that GHA's own bylaws stated that membership was open to all federal workers.[16]

Civil rights posed a serious dilemma for the trustees, who believed that the issue of the survival of a prepaid group health plan outweighed the need to improve civil rights in the nation's capital. Not without anguish, the Board in June 1943 voted, five to two, "that it is in the best interests of Group Health Association we maintain our present policy of excluding Negroes from membership."[17]

The matter was not so easily laid to rest. It arose repeatedly in meetings the Board held with the Advisory Council. The Advisory Council wanted to integrate GHA; the Board feared the effects of dissension in an organization already strained by the war. The Board members worried, in particular, that staff doctors might leave.[18]

After informing the members in November 1943 that it was not "practicable or feasible" to admit blacks, the Board received forty responses in less than two weeks. "As for myself, when the Negro comes in I shall go out," wrote one member. "I believe we should not discriminate on the basis of race," asserted another. The overwhelming majority of writers supported the Advisory Council and charged that the Board was disingenuous in, as one member said, hiding "behind the veil of 'wartime conditions.'"[19]

Early in 1944, the trustees approved a new statement of policy in which they noted that local hospitals did not admit blacks. Since GHA would have to hospitalize its black members in different hospitals from white patients, GHA would itself be providing discriminatory service. "Pressing this issue at this time would endanger the existence of Group Health," the statement concluded.[20]

The issue lay dormant for another two years until GHA began to explore the admission of nongovernment groups. By November 1945, the Board had formally approved the principle of group admissions and agreed to poll the members on the question. A letter accompanying the referendum on employee groups stated unequivocally that "adoption of the group admissions procedure . . . will mean that the Association cannot discriminate on grounds of race or otherwise in accepting new members." The membership took the matter in stride and overwhelmingly approved admitting groups without racial discrimination.[21]

Between 1944 and 1946, the Board changed its mind on admitting black members. Confidence bred of wartime and postwar prosperity played a role. The war had made Washington a larger and more cosmopolitan place. The strong political views of some members and the relationship between revenues and group admissions also motivated the change. By early 1946, GHA hoped to expand both its services and its enrollment. A mood of optimism replaced earlier fears and enabled the organization to accept all who qualified.[22]

As Group Health opened its membership to all races and began an active recruitment campaign, the trustees recognized the need to streamline GHA's operations. The trustees decided that the Association should have an executive director to supervise the business and clinic staffs, to be responsible for the day-to-day running of the organization, and to relieve the Board and the committees of administrative detail. The new executive would be coequal with the medical director, who supervised the physicians.[23]

To undertake the new responsibility, the trustees chose Melvin Dollar. A graduate of the University of Chicago, Dollar had spent three years on the staff of the School of Public Health Administration at the University of Michigan and five years as executive secretary of the Committee on Economics of the American Dental Association. He started in May 1946.[24]

In addition to hiring an executive director, the trustees wanted to expand the central clinic beyond its cramped quarters on I Street. The long-range goal was to build a GHA medical center, but office space was at a premium; the postwar housing squeeze was on. GHA had to settle first for renting space in a downtown office building and then purchasing the building it had been renting. Between 1948 and 1950, the administrative offices and a number of other GHA operations moved to rented space in the Arlington Building at 1025 Vermont Avenue, NW. In 1950, GHA decided to purchase the Arlington Building, financing the deal with a bank loan and a special assessment on all members. The goal was to unite its scattered clinic operations under one roof.[25]

In November 1952, the original I Street clinic closed, and all services were concentrated in the Arlington Building. The increased space improved the working conditions and made a political statement about GHA's permanence. As executive director Melvin Dollar put it, the move meant that "GHA has graduated out of attics and back rooms. We can now invite the public to see our facilities and show them with pride."[26]

Oriented toward Washington, GHA had located its medical center downtown, but the trustees were already eyeing suburbia as a location for satellite clinics. Starting at the end of the war, the movement of young families to newer, more outlying suburbs had become a national phenomenon. In the era of the baby boom, suburban clinics might prove attractive to mothers with young children. GHA members also knew from their own experience that Washington was becoming increasingly black, and those in the midst of white flight might find it convenient to receive medical care where they shopped and where their children went to school.

Expansion to the suburbs brought legal and political problems, since Washington's suburbs are located in Maryland and Virginia. In these states, GHA faced laws and regulations that, if not actively hostile, were not conducive to member-owned prepaid group medical plans.

In the mid-1950s, with all GHA's facilities safely ensconced in the Arlington Building, the Board discussed the idea of a branch clinic. A 1956 staff study favored locating a center in Montgomery County, Maryland (which nearly doubled its population during the forties).[27] Responding to the study, GHA lawyers checked on the feasibility of operating in Maryland, and concluded that it was safe to enter the state, as long as GHA served only its current members and did not try to sell new memberships there. With the legal situation clarified, the Maryland project moved rapidly. In November 1956, GHA's first branch center opened in the newly built Silver Spring Medical Building on Georgia Avenue. Although limited to pediatrics, general adult medicine, routine laboratory tests, and injections, the new clinic offered the suburban conveniences of location, easy access, and plentiful parking.[28]

With the Maryland clinic operating, the Board turned its attention to Virginia and discovered more difficult problems. Starting a Virginia clinic required changing the state law that permitted only medical plans run by physicians. This undertaking turned out to be complex, lengthy, and ultimately frustrating. In 1965, having failed in the legislative approach, GHA and its attorneys decided the best solution would be to comply with the law. In July 1965, the new GHA clinic opened in Annandale, Virginia, operated by a partnership of three GHA physicians.[29]

Facilities, whether urban or suburban, integrated or segregated, meant little in the absence of services. In the postwar era, Group Health worked to expand the range of its services and to finance as many of them as possible on a prepaid basis. GHA began programs

64

in dentistry and optical services, originally dismissed as too difficult for a prepaid group health plan to provide, and in such specialized areas as child behavior counselling.

The introduction of services followed a general pattern. GHA usually began a new program on a fee-for-service basis. That guarded against adverse selection by making the service less attractive to those who needed it the most. Someone with crumbling teeth would, for example, not be allowed to overcome years of neglect at GHA expense. As GHA gathered more data about costs and gained experience in providing the service, it offered the program on a prepaid basis in a separate plan or as part of its comprehensive plan.

The history of the dental program illustrates the pattern. Early in GHA's existence, members had considered offering a dental plan to supplement the medical services. At the annual meeting in April 1941, for example, members expressed an interest in participating in such a plan. That same year, a GHA committee prepared a detailed blueprint for a dental program. The committee estimated initial equipment costs at $9,000 and annual operating costs at $16,500.[30]

Although the 1941 proposal urged moving ahead with the program, it soon became apparent that wartime shortages and disruptions made it impossible. Not until the war ended did the organization take further action, and not until December 1947 did GHA members vote to equip a dental clinic.[31] The cost of the equipment came to $24,000, a considerable increase over the prewar estimate of $9,000.[32]

On January 1, 1949, the *New York Times* reported the opening of "the first planned dental program in the United States in which individuals have agreed to obtain complete, continuing dental care."[33] Because the members' teeth were so bad, seven years passed before GHA could put the dental plan on a prepaid basis. Finally, in April 1956, GHA announced the availability of prepaid dental care. Members agreed to pay for the initial restorative care on a fee-for-service basis. After that, they received cleaning, x-rays, emergency treatment, fillings, and minor oral surgery at a charge of three dollars per person per month.[34]

Hospital care was another service that was initially offered on a limited basis and then expanded. Always considered an essential adjunct to prepaid medical care, it nonetheless was provided only within limits to guard against excessive costs. During the 1940s and 1950s, GHA steadily expanded the number of days of hospitalization for which it would pay, from 21 days a year to 40 days in 1943, to 60 days in 1945, to 90 days in 1951, and 180 days in 1957. The limitation was removed entirely in 1960.[35]

In addition to adding services after the war, GHA also improved the quality of its medical care. After the 1943 Supreme Court ruling, the Association built closer relationships with area hospitals and medical schools, especially the George Washington University Medical Center. Many GHA physicians served on the GW clinical teaching staff, and the University also sent medical students to be trained in the offices of GHA doctors.[36]

More professional medicine also meant less personal medicine, as the case of house calls revealed. House calls were an essential part of the way most doctors at GHA and elsewhere practiced medicine in the 1930s and 1940s. During the fifties and sixties, however, home visits slowly fell into disuse, as physicians depended less on a comforting bedside manner and a prescription for penicillin and more on sophisticated laboratory tests, which could only be conducted in a clinic. Gradually, both GHA members and society as a whole came to recognize that a doctor's time was best spent in the office, seeing as many patients as possible, rather than in driving long distances to visit only a fraction of the number. During 1952, GHA doctors made a total of 8,400 house calls. From then on, even as the Association's membership was climbing, the number of house calls dropped steadily, with physicians making 4,000 home visits in 1960, 1,000 in 1968, and only 600 in 1973.[37]

POSTWAR REALITIES

Each of the postwar improvements, each of the attempts to make GHA more professional, cost money, and raising money always created difficulties for a cooperative like GHA. Some members felt, for example, that threadbare facilities were appropriate to GHA's noncommercial form of medical care; others feared entanglements with banks and other financial institutions (hence the attraction of self-help schemes such as selling bonds to members). Whatever the difficulties of raising money, perceived postwar realities left GHA with little choice. "To have more members we will need more doctors; to have more doctors we will need more clinic space; and to have more space we will need more capital," wrote the GHA News.[38]

GHA's primary way of raising money continued to be the dues and membership fees it charged its members. In these years before employer-sponsored health insurance, individual subscribers paid their monthly dues out of their own pockets. Each time dues increased, some members reached their financial limit and dropped out. Desperate to maintain its cash flow, GHA required prompt payment on the first day of each month. GHA never sent a bill. Instead, members could pay either at the business office or through voluntary "collectors" at work.[39]

During the war, although dues remained stable, GHA generated a surplus. Members paid monthly dues of two dollars for each adult and a dollar for each of the first three children, in addition to a five-dollar application charge and an initial membership fee of ten dollars, which represented their part in the ownership of GHA. Special charges, used to ration services and to make certain classes of members pay for services that they alone consumed, included one dollar for the first house call in an illness (two dollars for those who lived eight to fifteen miles from the center of Washington), and the first twenty-five dollars of hospital costs in maternity cases (raised to fifty dollars in 1941). Because of low staff costs—the doctors were off at war—and low per capita use of services—hypochondria was unpatriotic—these charges proved sufficient.[40]

In the immediate postwar era, rampant inflation put the GHA budget into deficit through 1947.[41] GHA's experience represented that of other of the nation's "firms" in microcosm. The staff, which had sacrificed throughout the war, wanted higher wages, and the members, who had also sacrificed, wanted more services. The result was increased costs, which somehow had to be matched with additional revenues. Translated into GHA's institutional terms, the situation called for raising the dues.[42]

The Board increased dues four times in five years, and new charges appeared as well. Before they stabilized in 1951, dues and membership fees had both doubled, dues reaching four dollars a month for adults and membership fees rising to twenty dollars. New charges included two dollars each for x-rays and electrocardiograms, one dollar for a physical therapy session, and a maternity deductible of one hundred dollars.[43]

Democratic decision making in the GHA cooperative posed two sorts of conflicts. One concerned the basic need to gain the members' approval for raising the rates, and the other, more philosophical in nature, involved the apportioning of expenses between people who used particular services (pregnant women, for example) and all members. Raising rates was never easy. The members, whose preferences were clear, required convincing that the increase was actually needed and not simply an effort to pad the administrative or medical budget and add waste or frills. The result was a form of fiscal discipline that differed from that of most health care providers. GHA, in one trustee's words, had to "operate on an actuarial basis as far as possible and on a cooperative basis at the same time." In the second type of conflict, democracy in the economic sense of the free market, in which individuals paid only for what they consumed, conflicted with democracy as understood in health care politics, in which a community rate covering many services made treatment accessible to all. Resolution of both sorts of conflicts tested GHA's leadership, as the events of 1948 and 1951 illustrated.[44]

Although GHA president William Warne told the members in 1948 that GHA was "the biggest medical bargain in the United States," they were not happy at the prospect of a third dues increase in as many years. At the annual meeting in February 1948, they asked the Board to reconsider and submit an alternative proposal. Some expressed a preference for less service rather than higher payments. In response to the members' concerns, the Board offered a choice between its proposal to raise dues and a package that included one-dollar charges on all clinic visits to a doctor. Much to Warne's relief, the members voted to raise the dues.[45]

In April 1951, the Board again proposed to increase dues and service fees, and once again the members raised objections. Attending a special meeting at the Federal Security Auditorium on May 3, three hundred GHA members complained of "inefficiency, waste and sloppy administration" and voted 136 to 46 to submit questions about administrative procedures to the Board. The questions, concerning such matters as the profits earned by the GHA pharmacy and how GHA's administrative costs compared with other organizations in the field, indicated a high level of suspicion. President Warne responded that GHA staff salaries were below the Washington standard that had been set by the federal government. Only then did the members approve the increases.[46]

Group Health's attempts to recruit new members occurred in this intensely democratic atmosphere, with its accompanying suspicion of radical changes in the organization that might disrupt its cooperative character. GHA aggressively targeted private employers in the Washington area, including local newspapers, labor unions, and nonprofit and community organizations.[47]

In the summer of 1946, promotional materials included a brochure that, although upbeat in tone, illustrated the organization's serious purpose and its desire to educate the community. "GHA Invites You: To remove the fear and burden of unexpected medical and hospital bills; to benefit from comprehensive medical service of high quality; to budget through monthly payments the costs of your family's medical care, hospitalization, health protection," read the brochure's title. Another piece of promotional material noted that GHA "hires good doctors and the price is right."[48]

Slow in starting, the effort gathered steam in the humidity of the Washington summer; GHA added five hundred new participants during August 1946 alone. Among the early groups to join were employees of labor unions and cooperatives: the CIO National Office and the Research Unit of the National AFL, the salesmen of the cooperatively owned Ohio Farm Bureau Insurance Companies, the six Rochdale Cooperative Stores in D.C., Maryland, and Virginia, and the Potomac Cooperative Federation.[49]

By the end of 1947, GHA had gained enough new members to compensate for its wartime losses. Enrollment reached 4,600 subscribers, or a total of more than 12,000 participants when family members were included. This represented an increase of nearly 4,000 participants since March 1946. Nineteen forty-eight brought further expansion, to more than 6,000 subscribers and 16,000 participants, but the organization was still far short of the 25,000 anticipated earlier.[50]

The nature of GHA's membership was in the process of changing just enough for the organization to avert financial disaster. New members, many from outside the government, augmented the pioneering group. By late 1947, 57 percent of GHA's participants had been in the organization for less than two years. By 1950, 20 percent of GHA's subscribers had joined as part of a group. In a move that foreshadowed later changes in the health care field, some employers paid all or part of the costs of GHA membership for their employees. GHA's law firm, for example, agreed to pay all GHA costs for its firm members and employees.[51]

Despite these changes, GHA failed to enter a period of sustained growth. A 1951 study by McKinsey and Company found that the effort to recruit groups had not provided the enormous spurt of growth that had been anticipated five years earlier. In December 1951, for example, there were fifty-four groups in GHA, only six of which contained more than twenty-five subscribers.[52]

Perhaps these disappointing results stemmed from the organization's own ambivalence about drumming up business, as its treatment of its salesmen showed. GHA's salesmen received a bonus of five dollars per member for every group of ten to thirty employees they recruited and three dollars per member for those of more than thirty. In order to encourage greater activity, GHA also placed a number of them on a commission basis. That lasted until one young supersalesman amassed enough commission to rival the executive director's salary. GHA promptly made this salesman a full-time staff member (at a salary lower than he had been making in commissions) and then terminated the commission system. For the most part, only word of mouth and the occasional streetcar placard advertised GHA.[53]

As a result, GHA remained a small cooperative that relied on a curious combination of individual attention and bureaucratic medicine. When members believed that any aspect of the medical service was less than adequate, for example, they did not hesitate to complain, and they submitted claims for payment whenever they felt that GHA's neglect had forced them to go to a private doctor. Both the medical director and a claims committee, composed entirely of members, reviewed each claim. Until 1980, the full Board of Trustees reviewed each recommendation that the claims committee made.

Some of the complaints from the 1940s and early 1950s included the following:

> A man who had fever, nausea, and abdominal pain became angry when the physician refused to make a house call to see whether he had appendicitis.
>
> A woman who suffered from pain in the chest, which a doctor diagnosed over the phone as a shoulder injury, repeatedly asked to be examined in person, and when the GHA doctors insisted there was no need to see her, her husband took her to an outside physician who discovered she had tuberculosis.
>
> A family waited for seven hours for a pediatrician to see a child with a high fever, despite making repeated calls and being told several times that "the doctor is on the way."[54]

As these complaints illustrate, GHA did not work the same way as did a general practitioner who took pride in having a personal touch. Instead, a group of doctors saw a relatively large number of patients, with an inevitable tendency for some patients to become ensnared in the bureaucratic machinery. A 1950 letter from a member summed up the frustrations of many in dealing with GHA. She called the GHA system an "assembly line" and feared that a planned drive for new members would only exacerbate the problems. "I don't want cheaper doctors," she declared, "I want better doctors, doctors who have the time to treat the patient as an integrated human being, not as an isolated neck or ailing behind." The member wrote that she was attracted to GHA by the idea of medical care divorced from commercial considerations but concluded that "It is a wonderful thought in theory. In practice it has worked out like a madhouse."[55]

GHA conducted membership surveys in 1947, 1953, and 1956.

The responses portrayed care at GHA, in one member's later words, as "high-friction medicine," which was "adequate but irritating." Asked to list the three things they liked best about GHA, members in 1947 cited insurance against heavy medical bills, the competence of the medical staff, their confidence in the medical service, the idea of group practice, and the availability of medical care around the clock. The suggestions for improvement raised most often included adding psychiatric services, shortening telephone waits, reducing clinic waiting time, and ensuring a more courteous, patient attitude by nonclinical staff.[56]

To be sure, members also praised the group aspects of GHA's practice. One woman wrote with approval, for example, of GHA's having a second doctor available to take over while the first had time off. "That is a wonderful thing about GHA, the advantage to everyone of the doctors being able to retain a proper perspective, not being on call at all hours, week in and week out."[57]

The members most satisfied with GHA tended to be those who had the patience to work through the bureaucracy and the tenacity to insist on the services they needed. Those who believed they could make the system work for them stayed; those who found it too difficult left. Many of those who stayed treated GHA like the cooperative it was and took personal responsibility for trying to improve its functioning.

One channel for member participation during the early years was the Advisory Council. The expansion of membership beyond federal employees, however, further complicated the already cumbersome system of agency representation on the Council, and its role became increasingly unclear. In 1953, the Council was quietly abolished because it had virtually ceased to function. Instead, members with time and energy to devote to GHA were encouraged to serve on action committees, nominating candidates for the Board, evaluating the organization's financial report, and reviewing members' claims to be reimbursed for outside medical services.[58]

GHA members could also affect policy merely by voting in the annual Board of Trustees election. Selected for three-year terms, the trustees picked one of their number to serve as president for a one-year term. Each Board election involved an elaborate ritual. A nominating committee of GHA members selected the candidates to appear on the ballot. Candidates could also be placed on the ballot by obtaining twenty-five signatures on a nominating petition. Members then received an election package that contained a ballot, biographical sketches and statements by the candidates, and two envelopes. In order to maintain the anonymity of the ballot while still allowing a check for validity, members were asked to seal their ballot inside two envelopes, the outer one to be signed by the subscriber in the family. When ballots were received at GHA, an election committee of GHA members first verified the signature against the signature on file, then separated the inside envelope from the identification envelope before the ballots were opened and counted by volunteers.[59]

In 1951, McKinsey and Company issued a report that recommended changes in the emphasis that GHA placed on a lay board of trustees. Hired by Group Health to review its administrative operations, the firm observed that members had two conflicting roles: as owners of the organization, they wanted to keep it solvent; as consumers, they wanted to keep prices down and the quality of services up. The consultants also discovered—as the trustees already knew—that only a small proportion of members were active in GHA. Most took no part in GHA activities. The consulting firm recommended that it was time for GHA, which had nearly 20,000 participants, to move from the small cooperative whose trustees and committee members carried much of the burden of day-to-day operations to an efficient corporation administered by a professional staff. According to the consultants, the executive director should run the organization, the volunteer board should be responsible only for setting policy, and the committees should serve an advisory function and not undertake operational responsibilities.[60]

In spite of these strong recommendations, the report produced no major changes, because the members were not ready to hear its message. Some committees were abolished, but the Board remained as active as ever. A small minority of the members continued to be interested in influencing policy; the majority were concerned only with the quality and costs of medical services. GHA resumed its existence as a small, intimate organization, "almost like a family." Until 1948, for example, the *GHA News* listed the names of all the babies born to GHA members in the preceding month. Even when the baby boom forced the abandonment of this practice, the births of twins continued to be reported through 1950; babies born to staff members were mentioned well into the 1950s.[61]

As the McKinsey report suggested, the role of employees in this family-like operation was not clearly defined. During the 1940s and 1950s, GHA grew from a tiny health cooperative into an organization with a budget of almost $2 million. The size of the staff expanded from 40 people in 1942 to 275 in 1960.[62]

The division of responsibility between the staff and the trustees never became very clear in the postwar era. After Melvin Dollar resigned as executive director in the spring of 1953, the terms of the job search for his successor indicated a great deal about the self-image of the organization; the Board sought someone with administrative and public relations skills, sympathy for cooperative organizations and group medical practice, and an understanding of the need for good relationships with the Board, the members, and the medical and administrative staffs. In response to advertisements placed in the *New York Times* and *Washington Post* and notices posted at schools of public health, the organization received two hundred applications. Characteristically, the Board ignored all the resumes and instead selected Dillon S. Myer. A member of GHA, he had spent almost forty years in government, most recently as commissioner of Indian Affairs. Earlier, he had acquired notoriety for his role as director of the War Relocation Authority during the World War II evacuation of Japanese-Americans on the west coast.[63]

Whether Melvin Dollar or Dillon S. Myer directed GHA's activities made little difference. Through the forties and much of the fifties, GHA's small cooperative remained intact. Changes were visible only at the organization's periphery, such as the growing black population in the D.C. area. As Washington's black and white populations essentially reversed their numbers between 1950 and 1970, race remained an abstract matter at GHA, on which members could point to their record with pride.[64] Although few blacks became GHA members, those who met the medical requirements were free to join. Although it was no longer possible for the members to know one another, the organization retained a family quality, particularly among those who played an active role in GHA's governance. No powerful third parties intervened in the relationship between health providers and health consumers; only a few of the GHA members had their dues paid by their employers.

GHA paid a price for maintaining such a small, comfortable cooperative. The intimate scale subjected the organization to periodic financial crises and made it difficult to engage in long-term planning. (In 1958, GHA still had not achieved its goal of 25,000 participants.)[65] Having relatively few members made it hard to initiate new projects, such as expanding the range of medical services or opening up new clinics closer to the members' homes. Adverse selection continued to be a problem, limiting the scope of the prepaid health plan.

In the war and postwar years, GHA remained close to the margin and failed to grow into the large organization that many had predicted in the euphoric period after the war. World War II marked a watershed for the D.C. community and the nation as a

whole. At GHA, despite all the pressures to change, the war ushered in an interlude of calm between the crisis of its founding and
the crisis of its expansion.

CHAPTER FOUR

The Great Change

B etween 1959 and 1964, the nature of GHA changed decisively. In the spring of 1959, the employees of D.C. Transit joined the organization as a special group, and later that year Congress passed a health insurance program for federal employees that proved to be a source of further GHA membership gains. Although the changes raised the number of GHA participants from about 20,000 to 50,000 in a little over two years, they also produced a clash of cultures that pitted the defenders of the small cooperative against the proponents of a corporate health care plan.

As if to symbolize the rebirth of the organization, GHA laid the cornerstone for a new central clinic in the spring of 1962. With the influx of new members, the aging Arlington Building had become inadequate to GHA's needs, and early in 1961, the Association announced plans for a $3.5 million, 87,000-square-foot building at 2121 Pennsylvania Avenue, NW. Executive director Frank C. Watters, who had succeeded Dillon Myer in 1958, stressed that the new center would be designed specifically as a medical center. No longer would GHA have to cope with makeshift quarters.[1]

In December 1962, shortly after its twenty-fifth anniversary, GHA moved its staff and equipment from the Arlington Building to the new location.[2] The staff described the new medical center, located near George Washington University Hospital, as functional, efficient, and, with a gleaming facade of marble and limestone along 125 feet of Pennsylvania Avenue, beautiful as well. Although a government agency occupied a portion of the ground floor and GHA hoped to rent the eighth floor, most of the building housed GHA medical and administrative activities. Special features of the facility included a customized audiograph room for ear examinations, a new cystological x-ray room for urogenitary treatments, and a spacious conference room and compact kitchen. GHA had arranged to rent the building for up to twenty years, with an option to buy after nine years.[3]

Despite this appearance of opulence in the service of science, GHA was hardly a rich organization.[4] New members and new facilities coexisted with old equipment and an administrative structure designed for a far smaller organization. When the new building opened, the small cooperative did not fold up shop. Instead, GHA developed into a different organization, but only after a series of bitter conflicts threatened to destroy it.

UNIONS

Shopping for a large group to recruit in 1953, GHA turned to labor unions. After all, GHA needed new members, and the unions, who shared an ideological predisposition toward prepaid group health, had them. Unions were, in fact, responsible for purchasing nearly a quarter of the nation's health insurance in 1954.[5]

Three factors accounted for the emergence of unions as a force in health care politics. One was the rebirth of the union movement after 1935. Nearly given up for dead during the twenties, unions came to life during the New Deal, particularly after the adoption of the Wagner Act in 1935. Passage of this law helped to produce the right conditions for the organization of such mass production industries as automobiles and steel. As the percentage of American labor that was "organized" rose, unions became a political force of importance.

Also important were the peculiar circumstances created by the Second World War. During the war, the government hoped to avoid work stoppages and large wage increases in an effort to increase production and channel savings into the war effort. To accomplish these objectives, the government needed assurances from the trade unions that labor would not take advantage of the wartime situation by striking for higher wages. One way of improving working conditions and strengthening the unions without detracting from the war effort was for management to grant nonwage benefits to workers. In this manner, health care became an important goal of collective bargaining. After the war, health care and other "fringe" benefits remained on the collective bargaining agenda of many industries.

A third and final factor was the growing realization that Congress would not pass a national health insurance program in the postwar era. That meant that workers and their employers would continue to finance the American health care system. With the government out of the picture, unions grew interested in the establishment of union-controlled health plans. Despite the requirements of the Taft-Hartley Act (1947) that management have a role in health and welfare funds, unions persisted in their efforts to initiate and control private health plans.[6]

These developments coincided with the establishment of the Group Health Association. In the formative years of GHA, the exploits of John L. Lewis and other leaders of the Congress of Industrial Organizations shared the front pages with news of Thurman Arnold's antitrust case against the AMA. People who sympathized with Arnold's fight against the AMA tended also to support the CIO; they saw both initiatives as part of a more general fight against monopoly and privilege.[7]

During the war and immediate postwar years, informal ties of sympathy developed into formal alliances between GHA and the labor movement. The career of Henry Daniels, a long-time active member of GHA, illustrates how political and economic forces brought GHA and the labor movement together. A native of Texas, Daniels received an undergraduate degree and a master's degree in economics from the University of Texas. His advisor there put him in touch with the Farm Security Administration (FSA), and in 1939 he took a job running migratory labor camps in East Texas. One of the more innovative late New Deal programs, these FSA-supported camps provided medical care to the workers who lived in them, an early example of government-financed, prepaid health care.[8]

During the war, Daniels, like many other federal employees, came to Washington. He worked in the labor branch of the Department of Agriculture and ultimately became a field supervisor for health. His experience made him an ideal recruit in 1947 for one of the first and most important of the labor health plans: the United Mine Workers Welfare and Retirement Fund. Because this organization was attempting to bring the benefits of modern health care to miners in isolated areas, it posed many of the same administrative challenges with which Daniels was familiar through his work with the Farm Security Administration.

Although Daniels' work took him deep into the valleys of Appalachia, he operated from Washington. In 1947, he took advantage of GHA's recent decision to admit subscribers from outside of the federal government and joined GHA.

Other officials in the growing Washington offices of national trade unions made the same choice. They saw Group Health's cooperative approach to health care as consistent with the goals of the trade union movement. Both groups wanted to bring their members comprehensive health care benefits, rather than the piecemeal and indirect benefits of most health insurance plans. The union administrators regarded themselves as progressive or liberal in political outlook, and GHA embodied the progressive approach to health care. GHA had few ties to the insurance industry or established health care providers, and it was run by the very people who worked on federal social programs, such as social security.

Relationships between GHA and the unions remained close throughout the 1950s; often membership in the two groups overlapped. A 1955 Labor Health Conference, for example, featured speeches by Nelson Cruikshank and Lane Kirkland, the director and assistant director of social insurance activities at the AFL, both of whom were members of Group Health, and by Kenneth Meiklejohn, a lawyer for the Department of Labor who was president of GHA.[9]

It took several years to translate close ties into a formal agreement between GHA and a labor union. Late in 1953, for example, meetings took place between Local 689 of the Amalgamated Association of Street, Electric Railway, and Motor Coach Employees of America and the Group Health Association. The union's health and welfare fund expected to begin its operations in July 1954, and the meetings explored the possibility of having GHA provide health care to the union members. Walter J. Bierwagen, an official of Local 689 and a Group Health member, brought the two groups together. Bierwagen had deep roots in both the labor and cooperative movements. A former bus driver and shop steward, he devoted considerable time to cooperative activities, serving, for example, as president of the Greenbelt Cooperative.[10]

Local 689 consisted mainly of bus drivers, trolley car operators, and other employees of the D.C. Transit Company. Before 1954, these employees used an informal collection system to obtain health, disability, and life insurance. In essence, the Health and Welfare Plan (or Fund) started a regular system of deducting contributions from the drivers' paychecks for health insurance, life insurance, and temporary disability insurance, and of supplementing these deductions with management contributions. Fund officials entered into a group contract with the local Blue Cross/Blue Shield organizations as a means of paying for the members' health care.[11]

From the beginning, however, the union sought more comprehensive health coverage than the "Blues" provided, and it entertained the idea of constructing a labor health center for members of unions throughout the D.C. area. "We were bus drivers and mechanics but we were building a medical center . . . so we needed help," explained Leon Richeson, a former bus driver who became the administrative assistant for the transit workers' fund. The Fund turned to the American Labor Health Association and the United Mine Workers Welfare and Retirement Fund (UMWWRF) for advice. UMWWRF officials, such as Lorin Kerr, Henry Daniels, and Harold Mayers, whose experience in the prepaid health care field stretched back to the Farm Security Administration, helped the transit workers design a center and suggested that GHA be allowed to run it.[12]

The union leaders saw advantages in this approach: It would end the deductibles that were a part of Blue Cross/Blue Shield insurance and increase worker satisfaction with the "union" health plan. The union, in turn, could leave the management of the health center to GHA.[13]

Discussions between Group Health and the transit workers dragged on for five years, marked by hard bargaining that was not unlike contract negotiations between labor and management. At issue was the discount that GHA would offer to the union. As a prepaid group health organization, GHA traditionally charged one price to all its members in a similar class, such as family or single members, but in return for bringing many members to GHA, the union expected a quantity discount. The situation was complicated by the financial pressures on GHA, which limited the discounts it could offer the transit workers, and by political pressures on the union, which had to win concessions from management before it could negotiate with GHA.[14]

The negotiations made GHA executive director Dillon Myer and medical director Dr. Henry H. Lichtenberg uneasy—Myer because of the financial liabilities for GHA and Lichtenberg because of fears that an influx of union members would undermine the quality of GHA's care. Lichtenberg worried that "the union's goal may not be GHA's." "It seems clear," he said, "that the union want their own center and their own Medical Director."[15]

Despite these reservations, the Board of Trustees pressed on with its plans for a special contract with the transit workers. Reviewing the matter some years later, Frank Watters, Dillon Myer's successor as executive director, noted that the Board "looked on the optimistic side." Local 689 would lead the way for other union groups and, although the initial rates might be low, they could be adjusted on the basis of experience. Dillon Myer, according to Watters, saw the matter in darker terms. He felt that "labor would take over and dominate GHA under the leadership of Walter Bierwagen." On September 10, 1958, the Board swallowed any remaining doubts and adopted a contract with the Transit Employees' Health and Welfare Plan. Within a week, Dillon Myer submitted his resignation.[16]

The trustees of the Transit Employees' Health and Welfare Plan sent a flier to the transit workers stressing their new health benefits. A partial list included "complete medical care in GHA Medical Centers or patient's home," as well as eye care, electrocardiograms in the hospital, and complete obstetrical care outside of the hospital with no deductibles. The transit workers also received a glossy member's handbook from the Health and Welfare Fund that spelled out the advantages of a "PREPAID, COMPREHENSIVE medical care program provided through GROUP PRACTICE on a DIRECT SERVICE basis." The pamphlet noted that many transit workers had avoided seeing a doctor until they were seriously ill; the new plan would eliminate this problem by spreading the costs over a group and providing for regular payments, whether the person was sick or well. It was as if a new generation of participants was discovering the advantages of the GHA approach.[17]

On April 6, 1959, GHA and the transit workers together dedicated the Labor-Management Health Center on New Hampshire Avenue in Takoma Park, Maryland. Senator Wayne Morse of Oregon and AFL-CIO president George Meany spoke at the ceremony, as did officials from the D.C. Transit Company, the transit workers' union, and Group Health. A local labor newspaper reported that, as people toured the new facility in the Coop shopping center, they could not contain their "oohs and ahs, which the beauty of the center brought forth." They viewed the technical equipment with "quiet admiration." Walter Bierwagen appealed to his fellow union members: the furniture, fixtures, and decorations were "tasteful, comfortable, and colorful" and, above all, "expensive." "Treat them as though they were yours," he admonished.[18]

Bierwagen's mixture of pride and apprehension attended the first years of the relationship between the transit workers and Group Health Association. The transit employees, new to the etiquette of GHA, needed to learn how to behave. Some of the union members were upset about having to abandon long-established relationships with their personal physicians.[19] GHA staff members wondered whether the transit workers would appreciate the high quality and comprehensive nature of the care they were to receive. Dr. Arthur Rosenbaum, GHA's chief of internal medicine, suggested that the entrance of the transit workers into GHA led to a clash of cultures. The original GHA consisted of highly educated, white-collar civil servants; Rosenbaum was fond of the image of Phi Beta Kappa keys rattling in the waiting room. The new GHA contained many blue-collar workers. The two groups could be expected to approach health care differently. Dr. Lichtenberg noted, for example, that, although the transit workers attended special orientation meetings in good numbers, they failed to respect the GHA system. They showed up late for appointments or failed to appear at all.[20]

In the first months of the agreement, the transit workers used the health care facilities less often than other GHA members. Over an eight-month period, union members averaged 1.4 doctor visits per participant; other GHA members made 2.9 visits on average. The transit workers, who constituted 30 percent of GHA's membership, utilized only 15 percent of the doctors' visits, 14.4 percent of the injections by nurses, and 17.5 percent of the laboratory services.[21]

When the transit employees did visit GHA doctors, they often presented evidence of neglected medical problems, and for that reason, they had a relatively high hospital utilization rate. Bierwagen, speaking before public health audiences, cited the case of a man whose x-ray taken earlier under the Blue Cross/Blue Shield plan showed a shadow but who did not return for additional x-rays on the grounds that they were too expensive. By the time the man visited a GHA doctor, he was diagnosed as having cancer. GHA physicians also found a case where a child's fractured thumb had been left untreated, and another where a ten-year history of diarrhea had been ignored. Such cases required drastic remedial action. It was too late for the preventive approach; such patients were sent directly to the hospital.[22]

Shortly after the transit workers' program began, Dr. Lichtenberg told a congressional committee that GHA was experiencing a "reservoir . . . of un-met medical needs." Many transit workers had never received the common immunizations such as the ones for diphtheria or tetanus. Their children had missed many of the polio immunizations. Nor had many members been tested for tuberculosis or had their eyes checked. "They have not had the medical sophistication for going out and getting care for themselves . . . and we have to ferret out from them . . . the difficulties they experience," Lichtenberg said.[23]

House calls occasioned the strongest clashes between the professional prerogatives of the GHA doctors and the desires of the transit workers for service. In part, this clash reflected a general GHA trend away from house calls and toward service in the clinic. The union members and the union leadership, however, saw house calls as an important test of GHA's willingness to attend to the health problems of the transit workers. The GHA doctors wanted the right to decide when a house call was necessary, but the union leaders, as Bierwagen put it, "felt it most important, at least at the outset, to be able to say to our member that a doctor would come to their homes whenever they thought it necessary." House calls, therefore, presented a good test of GHA's willingness to alter its routines to accommodate the new members.[24]

The doctors, for their part, found themselves in a private battle of wills with the transit workers. Dr. Dorothy Gill, who spent one and one-quarter days a week at the Labor-Management Center in Takoma Park, recalled an incident in which a transit worker phoned GHA on a Sunday morning, suffering from hemorrhoids, and requested a house call. The transit worker put his request in the form of a challenge: if GHA really makes house calls, come out and prove it. Accepting the challenge, Gill went to the man's house and applied Vaseline to the affected area. Impressed with Dr. Gill's medical sophistication, the man became a convert to group health.[25]

Bierwagen characteristically saw such problems as matters for collective bargaining. In a sense, he equated medical prerogatives with management prerogatives: some were legitimate, but some were not. Speaking before the Industrial Medical Association in 1960, he used the example of a union member who was told that he must be x-rayed to determine whether he had an ulcer. That was a medical decision, and the union member would abide by it. But if the member were told of a three-week delay before the x-ray could be taken, he would not "calmly accept" the delay as a "medical decision." Instead, lessening waiting times would be put on the bargaining table.[26]

The battle of wills involved more than the doctors. The union conducted its business with GHA through negotiations in which it would attempt to gain concessions, much as if it were bargaining with management. This approach tended to become adversarial and to pit the union's purchasing power against GHA's ability to deliver medical care. Before the arrival of the transit workers, GHA had never dealt with a group of members who were both a part of the organization yet somehow outside it as well. Adjustments were required. No longer could decisions be reached through open discussions; the situation now required the strategic responses of collective bargaining.[27]

Contract renewal negotiations with the transit workers in 1960 demonstrated the stresses the union contract placed on GHA. Part of the difficulty was that the union had paid $275,000 to build and equip the Labor-Management Health Center, only to find that three-quarters of the services provided there went to nonunion members.[28] Another part of the difficulty was the sheer technical detail of determining an appropriate rate to charge the Fund. Such a calculation taxed GHA's lay Board of Trustees' power to comprehend the jargon of health care financing.[29] A final complexity stemmed from the unusual relationship between Bierwagen and the Board of Trustees. He was himself a "special" GHA trustee, yet he was in charge of negotiating a rate with the GHA Board.

On August 15, 1960, the Board met and narrowly averted the disintegration of the agreement. One crucial decision involved creating an arrangement under which GHA would rent the Labor-Management Center from the Transit Workers Fund. But how much rent should GHA pay? Group Health's president began the meeting with a proposal of $50,000 in annual rent. Bierwagen called this figure too low and proposed the Association pay $66,000, which he termed a "fair rental" for the 12,523 feet of usable space involved. Bierwagen said that $66,000 had been cleared with his trustees, who would be reluctant to accept less. GHA's president responded with a figure of $63,000. The amended agreement contained this $63,000 figure.[30]

Although difficulties arose each year, the early period was the most confrontational, a common labor relations pattern. In the beginning, the union wanted to gain recognition from GHA and that required a tough negotiating stance. With the passage of time, matters became more routine, as relationships were established on the staff level between the executive director of GHA and the administrator of the Transit Workers Health and Welfare Plan. The continuing presence of Walter Bierwagen, who remained on the GHA Board of Trustees until 1975, also helped to bring stability, if not tranquility, to the relationship.

In 1963, when the two sides worked out an arrangement under which the transit workers were allowed to choose between GHA and Blue Cross/Blue Shield, the overwhelming majority chose to remain with GHA. Only 693 members, or 7 percent of the group, opted out.[31]

FEDERAL EMPLOYEES

Congressional passage of the Federal Employees Health Benefits Program in 1959 affected GHA even more than did the transit workers agreement. Simply put, most GHA members worked for the federal government, and if the government chose to subsidize health care for its employees, it was vitally important for GHA to be included in the program. The federal plan allowed employees to choose from among a variety of plans. GHA needed to do all it could to induce federal workers to select GHA.

The federal program illustrated both the opportunities and the pitfalls that large membership groups posed for a health care provider. The opportunities were straightforward. GHA stood to gain new members who would use their employer's subsidy to elect GHA's comprehensive care. The pitfalls were more subtle. In return for the subsidy, the federal government could insist on a number of expensive services. The government, like any employer, wanted to use its clout to make sure that all employees, regardless of their age or physical condition, were covered. That meant plans like GHA would have to admit older federal employees and pregnant women, to cite two examples.[32]

When Congress passed the Federal Employees Health Benefits Act in September 1959, GHA not only won the right to be included but also was invited to comment on the draft regulations governing the program's implementation. As GHA's administrators and informed members had anticipated, these regulations contained some costly features, most notably the requirement eliminating exclusions based on age. The regulations also established an open enrollment period once a year, in which federal employees could select a health plan or transfer to a new one.[33]

Although it could comment, GHA was in no position to change the draft regulations. It simply filled out the application forms and asked officially to qualify for participation in the Federal Employees Health Benefits Program. The regulations required compliance with strict accounting and reporting procedures and from GHA's perspective permanently set aside the informality of the small cooperative. Complying with the new procedures required the continuing attention of a professional administrative staff.[34]

The federal health program significantly changed the nature of GHA's coverage. It forced the creation of a rate structure that limited GHA's coverage to four basic plans: a standard and a premium plan for both individuals and families.[35]

Since the federal program would not permit restrictions for preexisting conditions, GHA abolished such restrictions for federal employees and others who had been members for two years. This change represented a considerable expansion in GHA benefits, for about 75 percent of general members (those who were neither transit workers nor federal employees) and their dependents had some form of restriction. The members responded enthusiastically to the change. Even though future new subscribers who did not join as part of a group would still be subject to physical examinations and possible restrictions, the new policy exposed GHA to increased adverse selection problems. Federal employees with serious physical ailments might choose Group Health over the other health plans offered because of its comprehensive care, and GHA would be powerless to exclude them. Nor would the federal program allow differential rates to reflect the size of individual families. Now GHA would have to make do with an arrangement that could be characterized as two sizes fit all. Those choosing the family option paid the same amount whether they had one child or eight. And since the civil service did not allow the charging of initial membership fees, GHA eliminated these as well.[36]

Having set the stage, GHA waited for the new members to arrive. When the federal program took effect in July 1960, many federal employees selected GHA as their health plan. As a result, the total number of GHA participants jumped by more than 12,000 to reach 46,300 by the end of the year. The number of federal employees and their dependents in GHA totalled 26,533, meaning that a majority of GHA's enrollees belonged to this special group.[37]

Retired federal employees received far less cordial treatment from GHA. In a letter to the Civil Service Commission, GHA noted some blunt facts about older beneficiaries. The average retiree used many medical services and fell into a high medical cost bracket. For that reason, GHA did not seek new members over the age of sixty. Instead, it based its efforts on "interesting young families in its comprehensive care program . . . ; geriatrics is not emphasized." If a retiree wanted to join, his or her application would be examined for preexisting conditions and the treatment for such conditions would be on a strict "service-at-cost" basis. In other words, retired federal employees could not receive the advantages that accrued to special groups, unless they were already members of GHA before retirement.[38]

Large special groups like the transit workers and federal employees brought in young individuals and families and lowered the per capita costs of providing services. Indeed, the members of the federal employees group proved to be younger than the general membership.[39] As GHA had already seen with the transit workers, groups also brought inconveniences. In the case of the transit workers, these involved the negotiating sessions with Walter Bierwagen and his associates. With the federal employees, the disadvantages stemmed from the way the Civil Service Commission regulated GHA.

A democratic method of setting rates yielded to a regulatory process. The Civil Service Commission required that the rates GHA charged should "reasonably reflect" the benefits provided and reserved the right to review any proposed rate increases. The Commission also decided important matters, such as the sort of advertising that would be permitted. To provide the Commission with the data necessary to make these decisions, GHA was required to submit an annual utilization report that ran over one hundred pages, as well as annual accounting reports and quarterly reports on enrollment. Frank Watters complained of living in a "glass house." "We are subject to as close scrutiny as though we were in fact a government agency being regulated by the Commission," he said.[40]

Although Watters complained, GHA continued to follow instructions with favorable results. Because of its Washington location and its historical association with federal employees, GHA became a major "carrier" in the federal program. Most employees joined a Blue Cross/Blue Shield plan. In 1963, for example, only 90,000 people out of over 2 million chose a group practice, but of the group practice plans, GHA was the overwhelming choice. According to statistics released early in 1964, GHA benefited from the concentration of federal employees in Washington, enrolling more than twice as many federal workers as the Kaiser Foundation Health Plan and considerably more than the Health Insurance Plan of Greater New York, neither of which served the Washington area.[41]

Federal employees who joined GHA received the benefits of comprehensive care, for which they paid a considerable amount out of their own pockets. A pamphlet prepared by the Civil Service Commission in 1963 summarized the benefits under each of the Group Health plans. The description of the high option GHA plan highlighted the fact that the federal employee paid no extra fees for hospital care, office visits, tests, and treatments and received a substantial subsidy for prescription medicines. The only noticeable charge involved the first fifty dollars of hospital charges for maternity care. To obtain this complete care for themselves and their families, federal employees paid $11.51 every two weeks and the government contributed an additional $3.12. The "government-wide service benefit plan," in contrast, cost only $5.82 every two weeks in out-of-pocket expenses.[42]

THE CONTROVERSY

The organization now entered its third phase. First came the period when GHA was under the control of the Federal Home Loan Bank Board and the Home Owners Loan Corporation. Then, faced with the court fight, GHA opened its membership to all federal employees, and a second phase began, which ended in 1959 when the transit workers arrived and the federal health program started. In its third phase, GHA was no longer an organization made up of individuals, many of whom were federal employees, so much as it was composed of two large groups.

As the third phase began, the internal disputes shifted from matters of economics, such as dues increases, to questions of management. Trustees with contrasting management styles fought a long and bitter battle over GHA's identity as a cooperative. Most felt comfortable with a corporate form of organization, but others believed that GHA was a cooperative first and foremost and that destroying the cooperative would mean destroying GHA itself.

In the fall of 1962, executive director Frank Watters pointed to the difficulties posed by the cooperative structure when nearly 80 percent of the members belonged to special groups. He warned that, if the Civil Service should insist on an increase in benefits, for example, and the members refused to support the necessary dues increase, then GHA could go out of business. To prevent such an impasse, he recommended a system in which the Board could set dues without a vote of the membership.[43]

Watters believed that the issue involved GHA's fundamental identity. Considered in its broadest terms, it concerned "how fast GHA should move in the direction of having a corporate type structure," rather than continuing to be run by a board of trustees overseeing an executive director. The new, larger organization demanded a more efficient approach toward managing its affairs. Just like a major corporation, GHA should have a chief executive officer who reported to a board of outside directors. Watters envisioned himself as the CEO.[44]

President William Colman presented the proposed changes to the Board at the beginning of November 1962. Colman argued that the "great change" from a "small personalized organization" to a "sizeable undertaking" required a "transfer of power" from the membership to the Board of Trustees. The Board would become a "highly responsible policy making body," the members would lose the right to approve changes in dues and charges, and the executive director would become "the Chief Executive Officer of the Corporation, selected by and responsible to the Board." (The Board dropped this last proposal before submitting the plan to the members.)[45]

Colman found the metaphor of the great change particularly congenial. It applied to his life inside and outside of GHA. Colman, who headed the staff of the Advisory Commission on Intergovernmental Relations, was an experienced federal manager, and the federal government, like GHA, was evolving from the small and personal undertaking it had been in the late thirties to a massive operation. Colman saw no reason to intervene in GHA's daily operations. Instead, he felt comfortable leaving GHA in the hands of Frank Watters, a fellow manager who specialized in health care.[46]

Colman defined the great change at GHA as moving from "pure democracy" to what he called "representative democracy." Colman said that it would have been "ludicrous to run GHA as a direct democracy." Instead, the Association needed better administration, so that it could gain more control over its affairs and a better ability to plan for the future. "When there is no certainty," Colman said, "you can't budget." The GHA budget, like the budgets of federal agencies, was no longer small, having doubled between 1958 and 1962 from $1.6 million to $3.3 million, as enrollment jumped from 22,000 to 49,000. Just as the federal agencies were being pushed by secretary of defense and supermanager Robert McNamara to engage in budgetary planning, so GHA needed to modernize its budgetary operations.[47]

The fact that the great change might mean an end to the manner of running GHA "like a New England town meeting" troubled Colman little. He had not been attracted to GHA because it was a cooperative. "The prepayment principle drew me in," he said. Colman favored group health for many of the reasons that Edward A. Filene had: it promoted efficiency in the distribution of health care. He therefore accepted the presidency of the organization out of a simple sense of "civic duty."[48]

Many, but not all, of Colman's fellow trustees who debated the changes in the bylaws shared his outlook and views. Like Colman, they were generally those who occupied important positions in the federal or union bureaucracies and regarded themselves as managers or public administrators. An important exception, however, was Mark Colburn. Throughout the debate, he continually objected to the proposed changes, since his goal was to make the organization more democratic, not less. He believed strongly that members should continue to vote on changes in benefits and dues.[49]

The role of the outsider suited Colburn, whom one trustee described as GHA's "avenging angel" and another as "GHA's conscience." His background was fundamentally different from Colman's. Born in 1915, he was almost the same age as Colman, but he grew up in the Bronx, while Colman came from rural Missouri. Colman was Christian, and Colburn was Jewish. When he was growing up, Colburn spoke Yiddish at home. When Colman was at the University of Missouri, studying public administration, Colburn was studying chemistry at City College.[50]

After Colburn joined GHA in 1943, the organization became increasingly important to him as an extension of his interest in cooperative activities and a replacement for the radical politics he largely abandoned during the war. When Colburn first ran for the Board in 1950, he was determined to prove that GHA trustees did not need to have "fancy pedigrees" or "a vita as long as your arm." He won and, as he put it, defeated "rule by status." On the Board (he was a perennial trustee, serving in 1950–1956, and 1962–1965, and again in the 1980s), Colburn regarded himself as a man who watched out for the interests of those who did not want to have changes foisted on them by a remote group of experts exercising their "civic duty."[51]

In a hortatory letter sent to the members in February 1963, the trustees asked for major changes in GHA's structure. As matters stood, GHA had the "ritual but not the substance of democracy," because the contract negotiations with the transit workers and the Civil Service Commission, which determined the rates and benefits for those groups, left members little real choice on whether to raise dues. It was far better, the trustees believed, to recognize this fact

and allow the Board of Trustees to set dues without member involvement.[52]

In a letter of dissent, Colburn posed the question of whether it
was appropriate for GHA to become a "business-type" corporation. He feared that, under the proposed system, trustees would
simply become tools of the permanent staff, who would present
them with technical material to which they would give only cursory
review. "Braking action by the Board to limit dues increases will be
insignificant once the necessity for obtaining membership approval
is removed," wrote Colburn.[53]

Colburn also disagreed with the other major proposal, which
was to give the transit workers the right to vote in trustee elections,
rather than having their own representatives on the Board. He
did not think the interests of the union and of GHA were iden-
tical. "Unions," Colburn noted, "are organized to further the
economic . . . interests of their membership." Voting as a bloc, the
transit workers could control GHA and tilt the allocation of resources in their favor.[54]

Over 8,000 people, a far greater number than usual, voted in the
referendum to settle the matter, which had received coverage in the
local press. In general, federal employees and individual members
sided with Colburn; the transit workers voted with the other trustees. The results were inconclusive, with neither side winning a
clear victory.[55]

On March 25, 1963, a newly elected Board of Trustees met in an
atmosphere of crisis. Mark Colburn now found an ally in new
trustee Aaron Sabghir, whose background resembled his own.
Seven years younger than Colburn, Sabghir had grown up in
Brooklyn and graduated from City College in 1941. Like Colburn,
Sabghir possessed scientific rather than managerial skills and was a
staff member rather than a frontline bureaucrat.[56]

The Board of Trustees decided that, because the vote was so
close, the president should appoint a special committee to come up

with alternative suggestions by November 1963. In the meantime, the proposals favored by Colman would stand as GHA policy, including the right of the transit workers to vote in GHA elections.[57]

Colburn and Sabghir felt so strongly about the matter that they, along with thirteen other members, decided to go to court in an effort to stop the new rules from taking effect. The United States District Court issued a temporary restraining order until a hearing could be held. As various extensions were granted, the business of GHA came to a near standstill. GHA's public relations firm noted in the early summer of 1963 that "until this cloud is lifted, we are not in a position to approach the press in a positive, constructive fashion."[58]

On May 23, 1963, only five days before the case was scheduled to be heard (a continuance would ultimately be granted), a group of trustees, members, and lawyers met with Colburn and Sabghir in an unsuccessful effort to reach a compromise. They proposed a deal: If the lawsuit were dropped, no major actions would be taken until the members could vote on new rules in the fall. In addition, GHA would pay Colburn's and Sabghir's legal fees, up to $3,000.[59]

The rights of the transit workers became the sticking point. Colburn insisted that GHA not enter into an agreement with the transit workers that gave them the right to vote in the general Board elections. The other trustees regarded Colburn's demands as a way of disenfranchising the transit employees. The union, equally firm, asserted that it would not accept "discriminatory restrictions" in its new contract. If the transit workers had the right to vote, Colburn countered, they would have veto power over GHA.[60]

On June 10, the confrontation took another complicated legal turn. Colburn and Sabghir filed a new motion to prevent GHA from reaching an agreement with the Fund that would give transit workers the same voting privileges as other members. GHA members sympathetic to Colburn gathered signatures on a petition requesting a special membership meeting to question the trustees about the contract with the transit workers.[61]

On July 24, the special membership meeting took place in the Department of Agriculture auditorium. The chairman immediately noted the absence of a quorum (which required the presence of 3,000 people) and ruled that the actions of the meeting would not be binding on GHA. The gathering attracted about 460 people, a remarkably high turnout considering the subject under discussion. The two-hour session featured "heated talk" and "intemperate shouting." Toward the end of the meeting, the crowd shouted for all the trustees to resign. The *Washington Post* reported that the session had produced "more heat than light."[62]

By now the majority trustees were beginning to feel harassed by Colburn's legal and public relations maneuvers. Each of them, after all, was serving on a voluntary basis, and each had a demanding and time-consuming occupation. Trustee Robert J. Myers, the chief actuary of the Social Security Administration, wrote a snappish letter to one of the Board's detractors in which he expressed some of his frustrations. In so doing, he helped to place the conflict in perspective.

Myers stated flatly that he did not regard GHA as a consumer cooperative. He confessed that he had joined GHA (in 1940) *in spite of* the fact that GHA was a cooperative. The advantages of group medical practice, he believed, "outweighed the consumer co-op aspects." Myers said that most members wanted a board that would give general supervision to the managerial and medical staff and then allow that staff to provide quality care at reasonable expense. Transit workers, Myers concluded, should be treated the same way as all other members.[63]

Myers felt this way because he was an expert on health insurance. As America's greatest authority on the technical aspects of social security, he was accustomed to making calculations that involved billions of dollars and affected millions of people. Myers, who ran for GHA office "thinking to offer my professional experience as an actuary to the membership," had difficulty taking Colburn and Sabghir seriously; neither could come close to matching his credentials (although Sabghir was a statistician). To Myers, the very notion that members should set rates was "absurd." "The setting of adequate rates," he believed, "must be a 'good faith' technical matter that skilled, paid management does under the general control of a Board."[64]

As with Myers, so it was with his colleagues on the Board of GHA who believed that a trade-off existed between democracy and efficiency, that good works could sometimes only be accomplished outside of the framework of pure democracy. Expertise was, in and of itself, antithetical to pure democracy, since it implied that one person knew more than another and therefore that one person's views should be accorded greater weight than another's. The GHA trustees who felt comfortable with this formulation of public policy found Colburn and Sabghir to be a threat to the long-run survival of the Association. If the dissidents had their way, these trustees believed, then the organization would not maintain the gains it had made in the years between 1959 and 1963.

In a similar manner, Colburn and Sabghir's position stemmed from their experience. Not only did they instinctively regard themselves as outsiders on the Board, where position in the federal hierarchy determined one's status, they also brought perceptions of contemporary politics to the conflict. For them, that meant the politics of the left, a politics of betrayal. The workers' experiment in Russia had been subverted by the tyranny of Stalin, and the workers' struggle in America had been betrayed by the infiltration of communists into the CIO and by the corruption of the labor leaders themselves. Leaders, seduced by power, they thought, had betrayed the rank and file and subverted democracy. Cooperatives offered a middle way between the grip of capitalism and the grip of the state only if the wishes of the members, as expressed through democratic processes, were respected.[65]

Colburn and Sabghir went to such extraordinary lengths because they did not wish to see GHA go the way of so many other experiments launched from the left. And as the other trustees realized, the dissidents were tapping into deeply held values among GHA members.

RESOLVING THE CRISIS

When the Board met on June 24, 1963, it proved difficult even to reach agreement on the order in which the various agenda items were to be discussed. Colburn raised objections to nearly every proposal put forward by the acting president, saying he wanted to avoid "railroading" by the majority. Trustee John Gunther, the head of the U.S. Conference of Mayors, proposed that the Board accept a new contract with the transit workers in which the transit workers were allowed to vote in the GHA elections. Although Gunther had the votes, his motion led to a complicated parliamentary maneuver by Sabghir that necessitated holding another meeting after midnight. Only then could the Board sign the contract with the transit workers.[66]

At the end of July 1963, the committee that was to produce new suggestions on how to structure GHA attempted to steer a middle course between Colburn's pure democracy and Myers' rule by experts. The draft report took the form of a GHA civics lesson as taught by such distinguished health economists and committee members as Rashi Fein (later a Harvard professor) and Louis S. Reed, chief of Medical Economics Studies at the Social Security Administration.[67]

Under this committee's interpretation of GHA governance, the members adopted bylaws, which functioned as GHA's constitution, and chose trustees. The trustees, in turn, became the members' representatives. Pure democracy, the report asserted, was no longer possible. Membership meetings no longer provided a "suitable means" of conducting GHA business. Assembling a quorum of 3,000 people strained the capacity of most of the auditoriums in

Washington. It was now time to delegate the business of GHA to the trustees and to the executive director, who, along with the medical program administrator, should be in charge of the "day to day management of GHA."[68]

Disappointed with this report and with the recommendation that the transit workers should vote in the same way as other members, Colburn and Sabghir initiated a special referendum to prevent the transit workers from gaining full voting rights. Each side took its case to the media. Colburn and Sabghir said that fundamental differences were now "coming to a head." The referendum would resolve the question of whether "Group Health will continue to be a member-controlled health service or whether GHA will be dominated by paid management supported by a special-interest voting bloc." GHA's president noted that Group Health, a $5 million operation serving 50,000 people, could not be managed "like a neighborhood cooperative."[69]

When the ballots were counted, GHA announced on November 4, 1963, that the "dissident forces" had been "clearly defeated." Even without counting the votes of transit workers, the members defeated the proposals by a margin of nearly two to one.[70]

At last, the pieces were falling into place. In a second referendum, the members voted with the majority trustees and formally approved the changes in the organization. The 5,250 people (representing 10 percent of the membership) who bothered to cast their ballots voted three to one in favor on the new rules. Aaron Sabghir termed the result "a defeat for the members of Group Health." Several weeks later, Judge Richmond Keech of the United States District Court dismissed Colburn and Sabghir's suit against GHA, stating that the members' vote rendered the issue moot. He also denied Colburn and Sabghir's request that GHA pay their legal fees. At a Board meeting, Colburn said that he had no intention of appealing the judge's decision. In April 1964, the trustees chose John Gunther of the Conference of Mayors as the new GHA president, and Walter Bierwagen won election as a regular trustee.[71]

That fall, Dr. Thomas Arnett, GHA's medical director, wrote a reflective letter warning a colleague in Los Angeles about the dangers of such internal battles. He believed that the confrontation had damaged GHA in the public's eyes, through the articles that appeared in the press. In addition, the legal fees amounted to over $10,000, and recruitment of physicians became more difficult.[72]

Colburn and Sabghir never intended to inflict this harm on GHA. Colburn has characterized himself as a reluctant leader, goaded into action by the executive director and the other trustees. He saw himself as leading a fight against making GHA "just another HMO," as the matter would soon be put. He wanted to retain the democratic features of the small cooperative.[73]

In the end he was defeated by the bureaucratic imperatives of a large organization. In order to survive, GHA required the members and money that large groups, such as the transit workers, and group subsidies, such as the Federal Employees Health Benefits Program, brought to the organization. The entrance of these groups, however, inevitably made the organization larger and more complex. This complexity did not daunt either the staff, which wanted to increase its autonomy and demonstrate its competence, or a majority of the trustees, who were accustomed to working with large programs. In the name of economy and efficiency, these trustees welcomed the changes. For them, the attraction of GHA lay not in its cooperative nature, but rather in its ability to deliver quality medical care at a reasonable price.

Colburn and Sabghir presented a compelling alternative vision of a small and democratically run health care cooperative, such as had been envisioned in the late thirties. Although the dissidents argued their case with passion and intensity, they lost. In its third phase, as a result of the great change wrought by the transit workers and the passage of the Federal Employees Health Benefits Act, GHA would be a health care provider whose subscribers joined as members of groups and entrusted the management of the organization to the trustees and staff.

After the Great Change

The events of 1963 eased GHA's internal problems and enabled the organization to accommodate large groups. Large groups, although necessary for GHA's survival, could not guarantee GHA's solvency. In the late sixties and the seventies, the organization experienced a series of external shocks that included the implementation of Medicare and Medicaid, severe inflation in the costs of health care, and the arrival of competition in the HMO industry. Because GHA was both a provider and a consumer of medical services, these shocks created pressures that threatened to drive the organization out of business. During most of the 1970s and 1980s, GHA remained on the defensive.

GHA's administrative structure, which failed to change during this period, continued to complicate its efforts to handle these outside pressures. Dropped in the 1963 Board discussions, the proposal to make the executive director chief executive officer did not resurface. In the next two decades, those executive directors who pressed creative ideas to make GHA more competitive found themselves blocked by recalcitrant trustees who remembered the small cooperative and feared any changes that might loosen consumer control.[1] GHA, therefore, faced difficulties in trying to compete effectively in the health care marketplace, provide quality service to its members, and still remain a consumer-run organization.

MEDICARE AND THE CIVIL SERVICE

For most hospitals and many health insurance companies, the 1965 passage of Medicare and Medicaid yielded a bonanza. Hospitals began to receive regular and liberal reimbursement for their elderly patients, from whom it had often been difficult to collect payment in the past. The physicians who worked in the hospitals also increased their income, since Medicaid guaranteed payment of medical care for welfare recipients and Medicare included a voluntary program that covered the doctors' bills of many retirees. Insurance companies benefited because they were able to change their group coverage, allowing the federal government to pick up the expenses of the elderly. They could also exploit the nooks and crannies in the Medicare program by selling what became known as "medigap insurance." The gaps included the ten dollars per day that patients were required to pay after the sixtieth day of hospitalization.

Although Medicare capped a lifetime of effort by many influential health care policymakers who also belonged to Group Health, it offered GHA few of the advantages that accrued to other providers of health care.[2] Because GHA did not own a hospital, it failed to realize any increased revenues for hospitalizing the elderly. In addition, many of GHA's older members had worked for the federal government, whose employees were not included in social security and hence were not eligible for many features of Medicare. Finally, few GHA members were medically indigent and eligible for Medicaid.

As a health care financer in the Medicare program, the federal government worked hard to accommodate health providers; as a health care consumer through the Federal Employees Health Benefits Program, the federal government proved far less willing to accommodate the organizations, like GHA, that served federal workers. Because federal employees constituted approximately two-thirds of GHA's membership in the mid-1960s, the Civil Service Commission (CSC) exerted a substantial influence over GHA's finances and services. The Commission's goal was to protect federal workers by ensuring that GHA remained fiscally accountable and provided the best value for the government's premium dollars, but its actions often created severe problems for the organization.[3]

On September 20, 1967, for example, GHA learned that the Civil Service Commission had refused to approve its request for a 14 percent increase in rates for 1968, recommending instead that the rates remain the same as the previous year. "The United States Civil Service Commission has delivered GHA a solar plexis blow, incredible as it may seem," reported executive director Frank Watters. GHA's only recourse, according to Watters, was to appeal the decision first to the Bureau of Retirement and Insurance and then to the Civil Service Commission itself. Should the appeals fail, he feared, GHA might have to terminate its civil service contract and then, so great was its dependence on its federal employee members, go out of business.[4]

Watters was on a first name basis with Andrew Ruddock, director of the CSC's Bureau of Retirement and Insurance. On September 26, 1967, Frank called Andy and asked to meet about GHA's request for a rate increase. Ruddock wanted Watters to bring any facts "that might turn us in the other direction" with him to the meeting. "Andy, we have given you so many facts already. You have had men in here for six weeks, and we have given them every piece of information we know of," Watters said. "Frank, this is what leads us to our conclusion that there is not justification for a rate increase." Ultimately, GHA and the Commission compromised on an increase of 7.5 percent.[5]

Eight years later, the Civil Service Commission initiated a full-scale review of GHA operations and discovered, not surprisingly, that rising hospital costs had squeezed the organization's income, despite its high premiums. When GHA requested help in recovering its financial health, the Civil Service Commission refused to allow GHA to use money in the contingency fund it had accumulated with the Commission. "The plan is in serious financial condition with little expectation of improvement," wrote Thomas Tinsley of the Bureau of Retirement, Insurance, and Occupational Health. The CSC, therefore, threatened to terminate its contract with GHA.[6]

In a panic, the Board of Trustees reluctantly agreed to a Civil Service Commission demand that would change the nature of GHA's health care. The Commission wanted Group Health to offer only one option to federal members, rather than the existing "dual choice." The Board, therefore, approved a single plan that included many more copayments than either of the existing plans. The trustees' response to the CSC, in other words, was to propose the elimination of GHA's comprehensive, prepaid coverage. They took this action in spite of fears that the plan would backfire by driving members away.[7]

The trustees correctly anticipated the members' reaction, and when more than five hundred people attended a public meeting to protest elimination of the "high option," the Board reversed its position. The executive director and the trustees drafted a letter to the Civil Service Commission announcing GHA's intention to continue offering high and low option plans for federal employees and to withdraw its proposal for a single option. The Commission reluctantly agreed, and the trustees turned to other measures to cut costs.[8]

The Civil Service Commission's influence over GHA was thus pervasive enough to produce conflicts between GHA and its members. By insisting that the federal workers pay only their fair share of GHA expenses, the Civil Service also coaxed changes that affected other GHA groups, such as the transit workers.

Unlike other members of GHA, the transit workers were experience-rated, which meant that the premiums they paid reflected their previous record in utilizing health care. If the costs of serving them dropped, their rate went down. Other GHA members, including federal employees, paid a universal or community rate, which was a single rate that applied to everyone. Community rates tended to be based on projections of future costs. This system of differentiating between the transit workers and other members lasted until 1977, when the CSC asked that the transit workers pay as much as federal employees.[9]

The Civil Service Commission worried in particular that the federal workers often paid more in dues and other fees than GHA spent on benefits for them. GHA did not rebate the surplus to these members but used the extra money to make general improvements that benefited all enrollees, including the transit workers, who paid less under the experience rating arrangement. Consequently, the federal employees were subsidizing the transit workers, who received benefits for which they had not paid.[10] In response to pressure from the Commission, the trustees agreed to "community rate everyone," starting in 1979. Thus, the transit workers were forced to adjust their health insurance premiums to suit the preferences of the Civil Service Commission.[11]

In these two ways and in many others, the Commission and its successor, the Office of Personnel Management (OPM), took advantage of GHA's dependence on the Federal Employees Health Benefits Program to dictate changes in GHA's charges and benefits.

THE ARRIVAL OF THE HMO INDUSTRY

Although the passage of Medicare meant relatively little to GHA, it signalled an important point of transition in the national debate over health care policy. Before the implementation of Medicare, the debate centered on problems of access. Passage of the legislation was interpreted as a way of providing people outside of the labor force, and therefore unable to receive coverage through their employers, with a means of paying for and therefore receiving medical care. After Medicare began, the policy debate focussed on the costs of the medical care system. These rising health costs could be traced to many sources, including the Medicare program itself. Certainly, the passage of Medicare coincided with the beginning of an era in which health care costs rose precipitously. Reciting those statistics can become numbing; it is sufficient to note that, between 1966 and 1980, Medicare and Medicaid costs *doubled* every four years, and in the five years after Medicare began, the cost of medical services grew by 7.9 percent annually, compared to only 3.2 percent a year in the seven years before Medicare.[12]

These sorts of statistics led a new generation to investigate the costs of medical care, just as I. S. Falk and his colleagues had done at the end of the 1920s. The two generations reached similar conclusions, although for different reasons. Like Falk and the members of his committee, reformers in the administration of Richard Nixon recommended the encouragement of prepaid group practice. In the intervening years, however, the concept of a health consumer had changed dramatically. In Falk's time, the consumer was an individual who was encouraged to pool the risk of ill health in a larger group of individuals. In Nixon's time, the consumer was a third-party payer, like an employer or, through Medicare, the federal government. Where the Committee on the Costs of Medical Care sought to encourage new ways of budgeting for the costs of sickness, Nixon's advisors, the most famous of whom was Paul Ellwood, wanted to reduce the costs of ill health.

Both saw prepaid group health as useful to their efforts. Prepayment, which the earlier generation viewed as a way of budgeting care, also provided an automatic incentive to a provider to keep costs within limits; group practice, to one generation a way of encouraging more people to see specialists, also ensured efficient utilization of those specialists. Where one group saw a system that would enable hospital care to be more widely distributed, the other saw a way of reducing the number and length of hospital stays. Both generations, furthermore, emphasized the prevention of health problems as a means of minimizing costs and maximizing well-being. In this manner, health experts in the late 1960s and early 1970s placed a new label on prepaid group practice and discovered the health maintenance organization.[13]

As the differences in emphasis between the two generations illustrate, there was an ambiguity in the uses to which prepaid health care could be put. On the one hand, these practices reduced costs and encouraged efficient utilization of resources. That, after all, had been Edward Filene's vision when he supported the formation of organizations like GHA. On the other hand, prepaid group health also made health care accessible to a broader range of people, one reason that GHA became a "liberal" cause and gained support in its fight against the AMA. This ambiguity, in turn, gave the HMO idea an advantage over other proposals in the health policy arena. Conservatives could point to its efficiency and its potential to cut government spending; liberals could emphasize its humanitarian aspects.

Playing upon this ambiguity, Congress passed the Health Maintenance Organization Act of 1973, which mandated that employers of twenty-five persons or more offer a prepaid group practice plan to their employees, provided that such a plan was operating in the local area. To assist in the creation of such plans, the government authorized loans and grants to HMOs that met the federal requirements. These requirements, such as community rating, reinforced liberal desires to ensure access to the health care system. The law defined community rating as a system under which rates could vary only by family composition. A family of four in Scarsdale and a family of four in Bedford Stuyvesant would, in theory, pay the same fees to a regional HMO. Nor would that HMO be allowed to charge the poor family extra for some of its services. By the terms of the law, copayments could not exceed 20 percent of "the total cost of providing health services to any given group of members."[14]

Like the man who found out that he had been speaking prose all his life, GHA suddenly became the living embodiment of a health maintenance organization. GHA's high option plan already contained most of the benefits the federal government required of an HMO.[15] GHA quickly decided to go through the necessary formalities and qualify as an officially recognized HMO.

A site visit from federal officials uncovered a slight problem. The law required that the "medically underserved population" be represented on an HMO's board of trustees, and that was not the case at GHA. GHA's lawyers recommended that, after the trustee election, the members of the Board should be asked if they wanted to represent the medically underserved areas. Members living in those areas could then vote for their special representative. Deciding not even to go that far, the trustees simply chose one of their number, Dr. Dorothy Gill, to be "particularly responsible for the concerns" of the medically underserved population.[16]

The Board's cynical decision meant that, although GHA was willing to participate in the new federal HMO program (and became an official HMO), the trustee elections were too important in GHA's internal affairs to permit the federal government's bureaucratic interference. GHA's 1977 trustee elections served as a referendum on labor relations with the doctors, and none of the candidates wanted to interject the separate and largely irrelevant matter of caring for the medically indigent. Deprivation based on a patient's geographic location was in any event too complicated a matter to solve through consumer representation on GHA's Board of Trustees. In the end, therefore, GHA managed to qualify under the HMO Act without changing either its basic practices or its structure.

THE COST CRUNCH AND THE POLITICS OF SACRIFICE

The Act did, however, increase national interest in health maintenance organizations and, after good years in 1972 and 1973, GHA planned for major growth. It built a new center in Rockville, a growing section of upscale Montgomery County, Maryland, and it renovated its Pennsylvania Avenue "flagship" center. In 1974, GHA decided not to increase rates, a strategic marketing decision designed to meet competition from new HMOs associated with Georgetown and George Washington universities.[17]

The decision proved to be disastrous. When the Nixon administration removed price and wage controls in the medical care industry on May 1, 1974, costs began to climb precipitously; hospital rates rose by 30 percent in the last half of 1974. That year, the GHA medical program lost $1.7 million, forcing GHA to increase its premiums for 1975 by 20 percent. Partly as a result of the increase and partly because of competition from other HMOs, fewer new members joined GHA than had been anticipated. Also in 1975, George Washington University Hospital, with which GHA had the closest relationship, announced a 23 percent rate increase, bringing to 60 percent the total rise in GHA hospital costs between 1972 and 1975. All these factors combined to exert severe pressure on the 1975 budget.[18]

Just as it had during the war years, GHA once again pursued the politics of sacrifice. Because of the financial crisis, the organization could not continue to function without someone giving up something, yet any cuts had to be sensitive to the conflicting needs of different GHA constituencies. Unlike in the war years, considerations of race and class figured into the organization's decisions. At the time, for example, GHA ran a branch clinic on the grounds of the Washington Hospital Center. The staff hoped to close this clinic to save money, because it was underutilized. Since most of the patients who used the center were black, the trustees worried that its closing might cause resentment among inner city residents. Nonetheless, the branch clinic succumbed to the economy drive in 1975.[19]

An isolated branch could be closed without conflict, but changes at the flagship downtown center proved more difficult to make and more enduring in their impact. A case study of one change illustrates the varying effects such actions could have on members of different economic classes.

Originally, most patients entered the GHA system by visiting a doctor during the day. If they were seriously ill at night, they reached the "on call" physician, who either arranged for a house call or met the patient in an emergency room. By 1961, the membership was too large for these patterns derived from smaller private practices, and a new system featuring an after-hours walk-in clinic began. The next year, this system became more general; a patient could visit the walk-in clinic during the day, without an appointment, receiving medicine on demand.[20]

Inevitably, there developed what might be described as a GHA proletariat, a "reservoir of members," to use the words of Dr. Raymond Turner, without permanent attachment to a GHA doctor, who relied on the walk-in clinic for their care. It became their equivalent of the catch-all emergency room in an urban general hospital. As the clinic grew in popularity, so did the number of physicians required. As a result, in 1967, GHA decided to hire part-time physicians specifically to staff the clinic during the day. In 1971, the clinic moved to larger and more attractive quarters in GHA's downtown center and gained the use of such medical amenities as an x-ray unit, an operating room for minor surgery, and a four-bed holding ward. With this change also came a new title, the Urgent Visit Center.

Early in 1975, in the middle of the financial crunch, more people used the Urgent Visit Center daily than the Adult Medicine Department on Pennsylvania Avenue. In the minds of many GHA doctors and administrators, this pattern only contributed to GHA's problems. It became difficult to provide Group Health's much touted continuity of care for patients in the Urgent Visit Center; patients' charts often did not arrive there in time to be read by the consulting physician. The part-time doctors who staffed the Center, many from local university training programs, tended to order too many x-rays and make too many referrals to specialists, perhaps because they were unsure of their abilities or unfamiliar with the GHA system, or perhaps because they lacked the information ordinarily available through a patient's chart.

A disturbing pattern appeared to be forming. Some patients used the appointment system and developed a working relationship with an internist, even to the point of making special arrangements to see this doctor when no appointment was available. In other words, these patients received most of the amenities of private practice as well as the economies and range of services characteristic of an HMO. The GHA proletariat represented a less privileged stratum of the organization's society. They were newer members (such as Metro workers) who used the Urgent Visit Center and received less coordinated, less thorough, and less prevention-oriented care from part-time doctors. Although no universal rules could be used to separate the strata, the upper stratum tended to be white and middle-class and the lower stratum black and working-class. As Dr. Raymond W. Turner noted in a penetrating paper on the situation, a visit to the two waiting areas (Urgent Visit Center and regular adult medicine) "on a busy day revealed a striking contrast."

In an effort to end this unequal system of care, GHA, as one of its budget-cutting moves, altered the nature of the Urgent Visit

Center, renaming it the Minor Injury Unit. The part-time physicians who staffed the Center during the day were replaced by physician assistants, who cared for relatively simple medical matters, such as mild skin conditions and minor trauma. Everyone else was referred to their regular GHA physician; those without a regular physician were assigned one.

The change saved money. Direct expenditures for the Urgent Visit Center/Minor Injury Unit decreased from $780,500 to $427,700 between 1974 and 1976. Faced with more patients, the internal medicine staff increased its average number of daily patient encounters from fifteen to nineteen. At the same time, the change altered established patterns of medical consumption at GHA in ways that affected patients from every stratum of GHA society. Those who previously enjoyed the best of both worlds now experienced care more typical of an HMO. They saw physician assistants more often than before, and they experienced longer waits for shorter appointments. Some of the lower stratum members gained the benefit of more personal, more sustained medical care in place of impersonal, sporadic, emergency-oriented care. All of the members lost the consumer convenience of medicine upon demand.[21]

By making this and other changes, GHA avoided financial disaster in 1975, but the respite was only temporary. In 1979, for example, another crisis developed, a deficit of $1.2 million between January and August. In 1986, still another crisis threatened to put GHA out of business.

PAYING HOSPITAL BILLS

At the crux of GHA's financial problems stood its inability to gain the most favorable terms from hospitals. Since GHA did not own a hospital, it had to accept the prevailing rates. When Group Health tried to use Blue Cross as an intermediary between itself and hospitals, the effort ended in disappointment and bitter recriminations.

When GHA renewed its bid to build a hospital, it ran into a central paradox of modern health care: at the same time that hospital costs were rising, hospital administrators complained of an oversupply of hospital beds. Because of the disincentives built into Medicare and other forms of reimbursement, hospitals failed to obey the laws of supply and demand. Increased supply also brought increased prices.

Modern experts who have studied the HMO have pointed out that HMOs obtain their cost savings less by securing cheaper hospitalization than by achieving lower rates of hospitalization.[22] Over GHA's fifty-year history, it gradually reduced its annual number of days of hospitalization per thousand participants. The level started out around 800 in the early 1940s and dropped to 590 by 1947. For the next two decades, the figure fluctuated in the 500 range, rarely dropping below 500 or exceeding 600. Beginning in 1972, the number declined to 436 and remained below 500 through 1978.[23]

Unfortunately, as Lawrence Brown has pointed out, even lowering the number of days of hospital care does not guarantee an HMO low costs, as long as it has no control over the operations of the hospitals it uses or is tied to a particularly expensive teaching hospital.[24]

Once firmly opposed to prepaid group health plans, Blue Cross by the early 1960s began to show interest in working with GHA. In 1964 and 1965, the Board of Trustees completed an agreement with Blue Cross to handle the paperwork for GHA's hospital bills through its Group Hospitalization, Inc. (GHI) subsidiary. This was a way for Group Health to take advantage of the considerable discounts that Blue Cross could obtain from hospitals. GHA officials also believed that the Blue Cross contract would reduce GHA's administrative costs by making a large claims unit unnecessary. The arrangement would also ease out-of-town hospitalization for GHA members and simplify GHA's administration of Medicare, since Blue Cross was a "fiscal intermediary" under the Act.[25]

Despite apparently good intentions on both sides, the contract with Blue Cross developed into another of GHA's confrontational relationships. As early as July 31, 1967, for example, Blue Cross asked GHA to increase its payment for administering the contract by 35 percent, and by 1972 GHA gave serious consideration to ending the relationship. A trustee committee estimated that year that GHA could save $75,000 annually by administering its own hospital claims. In a thorough review of GHA operations conducted in 1973, the accounting firm of Touche Ross recommended that GHA discontinue its use of Blue Cross as an agent for hospital service.[26]

The next year, the relationship changed from one of wary tolerance to active distrust. Blue Cross had become involved in the HMO business, helping to sponsor HMOs at George Washington and Georgetown universities. People who joined these HMOs received special privileges from Blue Cross that were not available to GHA subscribers, in particular the ability to switch from these plans to other forms of Blue Cross coverage without penalty. A GHA subscriber who tried to switch might find a ten-month waiting period for maternity benefits and exclusions for preexisting conditions. Although Blue Cross contracted with all three HMOs, therefore, it gave the university plans an advantage over GHA. Group Health's marketing director quite naturally spoke of "trouble in marketing. It isn't free choice if you can opt back from Georgetown or George Washington and can't from our plan." In spite of the uneasy relationship and questionable cost savings, GHA did not finally end the tie with Blue Cross until 1980.[27]

Although GHA conducted an almost constant search for a solution to its hospital problem, it never managed to penetrate the regulatory tangle, overcome the complex politics of health care finance, and build its own.

Traditionally, GHA had pursued relationships with the local teaching hospitals, such as Children's Hospital and George Washington University Hospital, that were convenient to GHA headquarters and provided a showcase for the clinical skills of GHA physicians. But they were also expensive. Consequently, the year after the passage of Medicare, the Board of Trustees reopened the matter of constructing a GHA hospital. At that time, the organization contemplated a 250-to 300-bed hospital costing no more than $8 million.[28]

By 1975, with the financial situation deteriorating, the hospital matter required immediate action, and in March 1976 GHA entered into an arrangement with Doctors Hospital, which was located on I Street, NW. Most patients from the Pennsylvania Avenue Center who needed hospitalization would go to Doctors rather than George Washington. Much cheaper than George Washington, Doctors cost an average of $185 per patient day, compared to $252 at George Washington. GHA stood to save more than a million dollars a year.[29]

Here, the situation grew complicated. Since the contract with Doctors Hospital would terminate in 1980, it represented only a temporary solution to Group Health's hospital problems. GHA still needed to consider whether to enter into an agreement with another hospital or attempt to build its own. To construct a new hospital involved obtaining a "certificate of need" from the Department of Human Resources of the District of Columbia.

This requirement, which formed part of a national effort to control the supply of hospital beds and reduce costs, produced a conflict between two strategies for cutting health care costs. Decreasing the number of beds, government officials and hospital administrators argued, would reduce the number of people admitted into the hospital and also lower the overhead that hospitals built into their rates. As that line of argument indicated, the market for health care worked in a perverse manner; supply seemed to call forth its own demand. GHA countered that health planners should look beyond the numbers of beds and consider the effectiveness of hospital care. In its view, the issue was not the availability of beds so much as their proper management. Without a way to control hospital costs, GHA and other prepaid group health organizations remained at the mercy of operators who could drive them, and their cost-efficient care, to bankruptcy.

Since GHA's strategy would increase the number of hospital beds in Washington, local officials opposed it. The director of Human Resources believed that the District of Columbia already had a surplus of 560 to 1,000 hospital beds. To grant GHA a certificate, he thought, would add to the surplus and defeat the objectives of the legislation that mandated the certification process.[30]

Ignoring this warning, GHA decided to build a new hospital and apply for a certificate of need in April 1976. Constructing a hospital, GHA soon discovered, was one of the most heavily regulated actions in America. Just to complete the application for a certificate of need and enter into a land purchase agreement required the specialized services of health care consultants, accountants, and land contractors. GHA even needed to hire a special staff member to coordinate the hospital project. The goal now was a 200-bed hospital that would cost $20 million. The proposed site was on the corner of Wisconsin Avenue and Upton Street, NW.[31]

As expected, GHA came in for its share of criticism at a meeting of the Health Facilities Subcommittee of the Health Planning Advisory Committee in the fall of 1976. The District could have an excess of 2,500 hospital beds by 1980, it was suggested, and that would make health care more expensive for everyone. A spokesman from Blue Cross argued that Group Health should lease or buy space from existing hospitals. Representatives of the Washington Hospital Center and of Doctors Hospital testified that they were "ready, willing, and able" to provide beds for GHA patients. Indeed, the board of Doctors Hospital already had offered to sell that hospital to GHA for $5.6 million and to build a new physical plant at 19th and L Streets, NW.[32]

At a meeting on November 19, 1976, the city's Health Planning Advisory Committee concluded that it could not legally approve additional beds in D.C. or recommend that beds be taken away from present holders of certificates of need. The Committee noted that GHA had "not validated a need for a hospital . . . on the site it has selected" nor had it "satisfactorily explored all alternatives."[33]

One alternative was a deal with Doctors Hospital. Officials from that hospital met with GHA officials in November and reiterated their offer. GHA should buy Doctors Hospital, which was scheduled for demolition, and build a new hospital at 19th and L Streets.[34]

Then a scandal broke. The *Washington Post* reported that Dominic Antonelli Jr., a land developer and a major stockholder in the parent corporation of Doctors Hospital, owned the property at 19th and L and stood to gain financially if a hospital were built there. Antonelli was also a major stockholder in the Madison National Bank, from which Joseph Yeldell, the city's director of Human Resources, had received a substantial loan. By blocking GHA's certificate of need and renewing the Doctors Hospital certificate, Yeldell guarded Antonelli's interests.[35]

Although Yeldell was soon replaced as the director of the District's Department of Human Resources, the negotiations between Doctors and GHA continued. Interest now shifted to transforming the Metropolitan Hotel on New Hampshire Avenue near M Street, NW, into a facility that would replace Doctors Hospital. Metropolitan Hotel and Doctors Hospital had the same owners. District authorities liked the idea because it would keep a major hospital in the downtown area, but GHA made a feasibility study and decided against it. Shortly afterward, GHA received formal word that the Department of Human Resources had denied its request for a certificate of need.[36]

GHA then turned to the Washington Hospital Center and filed an application to build a hospital on its grounds. The plan called for GHA to build a 150-bed secondary care and ambulatory care center and for GHA to purchase obstetrical, gynecological, and "tertiary care" from the Washington Hospital Center. The Hospital

Center would in turn reclassify eighty of its acute care beds for other purposes such as rehabilitation and nursing care. The vice president of the local Blue Cross/Blue Shield plan noted, however, that the number of acute care beds in the District would still increase. He need not have worried. Citing overcapacity of hospital beds in the District, the Washington Hospital Center voluntarily withdrew from the proposed arrangement in August 1978, announcing it could no longer support a GHA hospital on its grounds.[37]

A year later, in mid-afternoon on Tuesday, September 18, 1979, without any warning, Doctors Hospital declared bankruptcy. The hospital employees were told that their pay would be guaranteed only through the end of the week. Hearing that, GHA decided to transfer its patients immediately to other area hospitals. By 6:00 P.M. on Friday, September 21, all GHA patients were gone from Doctors Hospital, and all elective surgery was cancelled.[38]

Problems mounted. Many of the GHA physicians lacked admitting privileges in hospitals other than Doctors, and GHA needed a place to treat its patients. For once, the District's overcapacity of hospital beds worked to GHA's advantage. Group Health's managers met with officials at Columbia Hospital for Women and, within a day, obtained admitting and clinical privileges there for GHA's obstetrician-gynecologists. Before the end of the week, George Washington University Hospital had granted clinical privileges to GHA's internists and surgeons.[39]

George Washington Hospital became GHA's next serious suitor. Early in 1980, talk surfaced that together GW and GHA would build a small hospital across the street from GW's hospital. Both Blue Cross and the District authorities issued their usual warnings about overbedding in the Washington area, but again they did not need to exert pressure. GHA investigated the $24 million proposition and decided against it. By now, Group Health had begun seriously to entertain the idea of regionalizing its operations, and a central hospital no longer looked so attractive. GHA administrators were less certain that they could hospitalize patients more cheaply than could community hospitals, and they recognized that any hospital affiliated with a teaching hospital would be an expensive proposition. In the meantime, however, George Washington University Hospital continued to be a convenient place to treat GHA patients.[40]

Group Health came back to the Washington Hospital Center, or rather Washington HealthCare Corporation, a holding corporation that ran the Washington Hospital Center and Capitol Hill Hospital, among others. In 1985, GHA and the Washington HealthCare Corporation entered into a three-year hospital contract.[41]

That ended GHA's hospital quest, at least for a time. In a sense, GHA's experience reflected an unsettled and unsettling relationship with area hospitals that characterized its history from the beginning. The experience also demonstrated Group Health's adaptation to the Washington health care market. GHA laid aside its desire to emulate other HMOs and used its market power to take advantage of the oversupply of hospital beds in Washington and secure the best deal available. As with all such decisions, this one involved trade-offs. Better hospital rates meant greater distance from the prestige of a teaching hospital; a relationship with another health provider inevitably lessened GHA's control over events.

GHA'S EFFORTS TO EXPAND

In 1970, GHA grew concerned that Kaiser-Permanente and Group Health Cooperative of Puget Sound were capitalizing on the popularity of HMOs and growing at much faster rates than the sedate pace set by GHA. In 1960, GHA had 46,000 participants, and a decade later it had about 75,000, a record of growth that a staffer properly termed "not dramatic." Growth, always easy to defend in a prepaid group practice, would enable GHA to offer a "better range of services," allow it to penetrate the suburban markets, and lessen its dependence on the Civil Service Commission. In the absence of growth, GHA's costs would rise, its premiums would cease to be competitive, and GHA would in time be just "a noble experiment." By 1970, then, GHA members were being urged to think ambitiously about a market area that included nine counties in Maryland and Virginia in addition to the District and Baltimore.[42]

In the modern era, Group Health did not lack for possible partners in its bids for expansion. In 1965, for example, GHA, seeking to expand beyond its suburban Washington clinics, had explored the possibility of a joint venture with the Johns Hopkins University Hospital and developer James Rouse to start a prepaid group health plan in Columbia, Rouse's planned community in Howard County, Maryland, between Washington and Baltimore. Johns Hopkins, one of the nation's most prestigious medical schools, saw Columbia as a "community laboratory" in which it could conduct research in the delivery of health care and in the epidemiology of diseases. Although a Columbia health plan was ultimately formed, GHA dropped out and others became involved.[43]

In 1971, Frank Watters mentioned rather casually that both the Connecticut General and Aetna insurance companies had been in touch with him, hoping to do business. The trustees, although wary of such ventures, gave Watters permission to conduct "exploratory discussions" and to continue the drive toward creating suburban GHA health centers. At the time, GHA staff thought in optimistic terms that were not borne out by subsequent events. In one presentation, a staff member projected a 1980 membership of 300,000 participants; when that year arrived, GHA had less than half of that number.[44]

While efforts to form partnerships with other organizations generally petered out, GHA succeeded in expanding its own suburban presence. Suburban clinics, nearly everyone assumed, represented the wave of the future, and despite early difficulties in gaining a foothold in suburban markets, GHA persisted.[45] By 1982, GHA had adopted the suburban strategy to the point where it began seriously to consider a policy known as regionalization. GHA would be divided into four regions: Northern Virginia, Montgomery County, Prince George's County, and the District of Columbia. Each of these regions would contain primary care centers serving between 10,000 and 20,000 members and at least one specialty referral center. Each of the primary care centers would provide internal medicine, pediatrics, obstetrics-gynecology, mental health, eye care, radiology, and laboratory services. Each GHA region would be self-sufficient, using local community hospitals and providing regional emergency service, and each region would tailor its services to regional needs, so that clinical staff models might differ. This change in the delivery of care would be matched by a change in management: there would be a regional line management system and a "corporate headquarters" with planning, policy, and coordination responsibilities.[46]

GHA's annual report for 1983 reinforced the regionalization theme. "GHA—growing with our region" read the headline on the glossy white, red, and gold cover. The report emphasized GHA's "start on new directions," in order to "aggressively manage the costs of delivering care." According to the report, regionalization would improve GHA's flexibility to handle a growing membership and provide "better services at a more competitive cost in a timely fashion." Underscoring its commitment to suburban expansion, GHA had opened two new centers in Virginia that year, at Fair Oaks and at Tysons Corner.[47]

The annual report's rhetorical tone, which might be described as corporate, was unusual. For the first time, the clutter of conflicting motives appeared to have been removed in favor of a dominant theme: change through growth. Internal staff memoranda solidified that impression. Where before they had a philosophical, even whimsical quality, and the boilerplate most often consisted of idealistic statements about social uplift, the memos now had a sleeker, streamlined look and they bristled with what Washingtonians (and typesetters) call "bullets," intended to highlight messages about strategic planning. One such memo noted that "we *must* grow," "*must* become more cost effective," "*must* improve access," and "*must* look to other models of delivery." In this optimistic atmosphere, building projects flourished.[48]

Staff leaders, particularly executive director Dr. Robert G. Rosenberg, encouraged the trustees to adopt a corporate mentality and to think strategically. When the George Washington University Health Plan was for sale in 1984, for example, Rosenburg urged the trustees to seize the moment and buy it. He made little mention of social uplift, arguing instead that acquiring the GW plan would "prevent a competitor—and likely a wealthy one—from gaining a toehold in the heart of traditional GHA territory." If GHA bought GW, it would gain access to five hundred employer accounts, and those accounts and GW's name would enable GHA to expand further into "the greater Washington market." If someone else bought GW, GHA would lose "some market share."[49]

The trustees' discussion of the proposal to buy the George Washington University Health Plan revealed the fact that not all of GHA's leaders had abandoned the old religion and converted to the new. They wanted to maintain a fundamental continuity with GHA's traditions, even under changing conditions, and they saw purchase of the GW plan as a point of discontinuity and therefore undesirable. As he had done so many times before, trustee Mark Colburn made the case for those who urged caution in the face of change. He noted that GHA had an overarching objective, one that had nothing directly to do with market shares, and that was to provide quality medical care at reasonable cost to its members. Purchasing the GW plan would not further that objective. Instead, GHA would become a business manager for the GW plan, an unaccustomed and unnecessary role for it to assume and one that would lead to various classes of members within GHA and disturb its cooperative structure. Sensing the mood of the trustees, Rosenberg said that no vote was necessary, but he warned that the Board was relying on outmoded principles in the face of revolutionary competition in the HMO market. When Rosenberg brought the issue back to the next meeting, the trustees turned the proposal down by a vote of 3 to 4.[50]

Dr. Rosenberg's other proposal to expand GHA's market also met with stiff opposition. He wanted to reduce high fixed costs and reliance on capital investment, to gain greater access in the Washington market, and to do so with a minimum of risk. The solution he offered was called "networking," offering care through groups of physicians who would receive a set amount of money per member from GHA each month. These groups would have fiscal responsibility for members' care, including hospitalization, use of the emergency room, and referral to specialists. GHA would aim to provide about 30 percent of a medical group's business. The arrangement amounted to using outside physician groups as "independent practice associations" that would be affiliated with GHA. Networks, it was claimed, constituted the fastest-growing HMO model in the country.[51]

Both the trustees and the doctors reacted cautiously and conservatively to the idea. One trustee identified the concerns of many by noting that, when GHA was started, one fear was that part-time physicians would not treat GHA members as well as their other patients. "But today doctors are hungry," replied the executive director. "Time is running out. By 1986, others will be doing all these things." Failure to accommodate change would render GHA a "vestigial organ."

One GHA doctor expressed the physicians' categorical objection to networking on the grounds that it would reduce the "continuity and quality of care" and raise expenses. "Networking carried to the extreme," he asserted, "would make GHA nothing but an insurance carrier with preferred providers. Even the recent advertising now plays down any semblance of a consumer-owned cooperative, the very principle on which Group Health was founded." The doctor maintained that physicians came to GHA not for "financial rewards" but for the "quality of life an HMO practice permits." Networking, he claimed, would undermine that quality of life.

The nurses' union was more forthright, objecting to networking because they feared it would reduce jobs for nurses, doctors, and therapists. There was also concern that the plan was designed to dilute the power of GHA's unions by decreasing the reliance on staff doctors and nurses, who were unionized. This latter view was early evidence of the lurking distrust of management by GHA's health care providers that would underlie the 1986 doctors' strike.[52]

Nonetheless, in September 1985, after several months of heated discussion, the Board approved a limited test of the networking concept. In practice, the arrangement turned out to be more rather than less costly, and when GHA encountered severe deficits in 1986, the networking experiment was quietly dropped as a cost-cutting measure.[53]

CONCLUSION

Viewed from a national perspective, the HMO industry flourished in the 1970s and 1980s, and competition became the order of the day. When President Carter took office in 1977, the federal government reasserted its encouragement of HMOs. In the first year of the Carter administration, the number of prepaid health plans grew to 203, an increase of 23 percent from the previous year, and the number of people enrolled in the plans reached 7.5 million, an 18 percent increase. The administration pushed HMOs hardest in those areas with the highest health care costs, including Washington, D.C. By 1983, 280 HMOs served 12 million people, and increases in membership averaged 12 percent a year. Furthermore, most of the growth took place in urban areas; 71 percent of the plans operated in areas with populations of more than half a million. Large insurance companies, such as the John Hancock Mutual Life Insurance Company and the Prudential Insurance Company of America, and large corporations, such as American Telephone and Telegraph and Control Data Corporation, became interested in the development of health maintenance organizations. Suddenly, HMOs were hot business properties.[54]

To be sure, there was a certain faddishness to the HMO boom. Insurance companies invested in HMOs not so much for their profitability as health care providers as for the rising value of their stocks. In addition, the boom fed on itself. If Prudential acquired an HMO, then Aetna also felt compelled to do so. Few of the companies made money on these HMOs. They discovered instead that making an HMO profitable required establishing deep roots in the community and slowly building a loyal clientele. In Washington, for example, none of the HMOs could boast of GHA's long record of service.[55]

Despite the obvious advantage of its longevity, GHA needed to face the fact of competition in the prepaid, group health market. As HMOs proliferated, a variety of new forms began to evolve. Independent practice associations (IPAs) and preferred provider organizations (PPOs) joined the more traditional prepaid staff models like Group Health, where members received care from physicians who were employees of the association.[56] The health care "environment" was changing, with Kaiser making aggressive moves to dominate the D.C. market, with IPAs and PPOs springing up, and with the imminent entry of large chains, like PruCare and Aetna, into the D.C. market. The *Washington Post* summed up the situation in a headline: "Army of HMOs Invades Nation's Capital, Stiff Competition Developing in Race to Care for Washington's Affluent Society." The paper estimated that in 1986 between 450,000 and 500,000 people in the Washington area were enrolled in HMOs, about 14 percent of the population, and experts expected the number to grow. GHA remained a "dominant player," but the *Post* reporter expected the "period of quiet" to end. As one example, the *Post* cited the case of HealthPlus, a failing HMO in Prince George's County, Maryland, that was purchased by Sanus Corporation. Sanus could afford to compete, since it was owned by McDonnell Douglas and the General American Life Insurance Company.[57]

GHA's executive director, Dr. Robert Rosenberg, declared that, even though GHA had $12 million in available cash, it might soon need to form an alliance with a larger "deep pocket."[58] Finding this deep pocket inevitably would bring a backlash from those long-time members who distrusted deviations from GHA's self-financing, cooperative patterns. Change always came hard to GHA, even change thrust upon it by external forces.

GHA never found its deep pocket. It turned down offers from larger or richer health care organizations, as its 1986 response to the Prudential Insurance Company revealed. Prudential, like other major health insurance carriers, was broadening its services. One of its new products was comprehensive health insurance, marketed under the name PruCare, which allowed employers to offer a range of health plans, including HMOs, to their employees. Prudential wanted to use GHA as part of its health delivery system in Washington, D.C. The Prudential offer reversed the terms of the earlier networking proposal. Under networking, GHA contracted with external providers to supply care; under the offer, Prudential would contract with GHA to supply services. GHA would, in effect, join Prudential's network and become one of its preferred providers.[59]

Needless to say, the Prudential proposal sparked considerable comment. Would GHA be able to retain its name, or would it become "an afterthought attached to the PruCare name"? Did Prudential do business in South Africa? Would GHA be placed at the mercy of a large company and be squeezed by another unsatisfactory capitation agreement? How much control would GHA have over Prudential's rates, which would probably be determined on an experience rather than a community rating basis? These questions, like the future of GHA itself, remained unresolved as the fiftieth anniversary approached.[60]

Whatever else one could say about GHA, it was no longer possible to speak of the Association in isolation from more general trends in health care finance. After the passage of Medicare in 1965, GHA began to feel the effects of doing business in an inflationary market. This inflation made its relationship with the Civil Service Commission more contentious, intensified the competition it faced in the local market, exacerbated its financial problems, and heightened the dilemmas of obtaining hospital care.

Affected by national trends, GHA nonetheless continued to resist a corporate identity or a corporate takeover. Although much altered by the demands of the modern health care industry, features of the small cooperative continued to characterize GHA, more than twenty years after the great change.

CHAPTER SIX

The Strike

A cooperative like GHA, it had become clear, had difficulty taking advantage of new developments in the health care market in the 1970s and 1980s. Instead of thinking strategically about market share, many of its trustees persisted in relating the provision of health care to a larger social mission. Hence, Prudential's offer to take over GHA was scrutinized as much for its moral validity as for its financial value. To GHA, it mattered vitally that business be conducted in a way that would benefit its consumers and allow them to retain control.

A desire for control also permeated Group Health's relationship with its physicians and other professionals. GHA maintained a straightforward employer-employee relationship with such allied health professionals as nurses, pharmacists, and physical therapists, who were accustomed to working as employees in institutional settings. Physicians, by way of contrast, were difficult to control. As a consequence, the relationship between members and physicians within GHA's consumer cooperative contained many ambiguities that stemmed from the doctor's power over clinical practice. Since consumer control could never be total, its meaning remained murky. The employer-patients would not have presumed, for instance, to advise the employee-physicians on the treatment for a high fever.

A clear line between management of the organization, which after 1946 was handled by an executive director, and management of the medical staff underscored the separation of the physicians from the rest of the organization. A medical director, always a physician, supervised the doctors and controlled hiring and firing. Not surprisingly, repeated attempts to draw the line between the proper concerns of the members and the professional discretion of the doctors bred many conflicts, with physicians and members arguing over who owed what to whom.

Many of GHA's doctors, although deeply committed to the ideal of prepaid group practice, also had more mundane concerns related to professional advancement and financial security. The cultural norm of modest salaries within a cooperative rankled them, particularly as they watched the income of their colleagues in private practice climb. Accustomed to regarding other doctors as their peers, GHA's physicians often overlooked the benefits of regular working hours and financial freedom from having to equip an office and pay a staff.

The struggle for control between physicians and trustees changed over time. Beginning in the 1960s, for example, many GHA physicians wanted to form a partnership in order to improve their professional standing and their financial situation. Most trustees, perceiving this change as one that diluted consumer control, opposed it. They conceded much to the physicians in the realm of making medical improvements, but they regarded the organization's structure as their special sphere of influence. The resulting impasse paved the way for the formation of a physician's labor union and a history of bruising labor battles.

EARLY PROBLEMS

When GHA was founded in 1937, the problems of labor relations solved themselves. The organization struggled for its survival, and the key battle involved a fight over the rights of GHA doctors to practice in a prepaid, member-controlled, group setting. Members who participated in this battle for recognition of GHA inevitably found themselves defending the professional caliber and the personal integrity of GHA's physicians. The fight drew doctors and patients together and tended to raise the morale of members and doctors alike.

In the spring of 1944, when the war entered its final phase, GHA experienced the first real crisis in its relationship with its medical staff. A group of eight doctors met with the Board of Trustees and demanded, in addition to immediate salary raises, to be recognized as independent contractors. In GHA's democratic spirit, the doctors also offered administrative suggestions, which nicely illustrated the differences in outlook between the physicians and the members. Burdened by attending so many patients, the doctors wanted to reduce the incentives for members to consume medical care and to impose deterrent fees, such as a nominal charge for a clinic consultation.[1] In response, the Board granted the salary increase but upheld the principles of prepaid, group practice along the lines of what would later be called the staff model: GHA doctors were employees who offered GHA their services on an exclusive basis.[2]

On May 11, 1944, Dr. Mario Scandiffio, the medical director, announced that he had had enough, and he implied that his resignation was over a matter of principle. That same day, the assistant medical director also tendered his resignation, saying "there has always been too little opportunity for . . . individual achievement."[3]

Like all workers in the late wartime economy, the doctors resented having to work so hard for what they perceived as inadequate wages, especially since the trustees did not seem properly to appreciate the physicians' sacrifices. At a time when medical income was rising, the doctors chafed at working for fixed salaries. In common with other workers, who would make the postwar year of 1946 the most contentious in American labor history, the physicians carried a sense of grievance into the postwar world.

This dilemma would be repeated throughout GHA's history. The demand for physicians in the nation would increase, and their wages would rise. Because of GHA's need to control costs, the level of its compensation would lag behind, and the physicians would become discontented. The dissatisfaction over salaries would in turn expose other frustrations on the part of the doctors, who would then attempt to negotiate with the Board of Trustees to redress their grievances. This process created basic conflicts between the trustees, who were representing the consumer cooperative and striving to keep the cost of GHA within middle-class means, and the doctors, who were trying to uphold their professional interests.

Following the war, many of the underlying tensions between the Board and the staff reached the surface. The doctors complained, in the summer of 1946, that staff morale had dropped to a new low in an atmosphere of "discouragement, confusion, and insecurity." The Board, they wrote, was an elusive adversary, with a membership that changed from year to year and sometimes even from meeting to meeting. When the physicians requested action, they received only "an undeserved run-around." Too often, the Board referred matters to "slowly functioning committees." Far from consulting the doctors, they charged, the Board drew into itself, excluding the physicians from its deliberations.[4]

According to the physicians, the Board's inadequacies were also reflected in the way it handled complaints from patients. Although the doctors conceded that complaints should be handled sympathetically in a cooperative, a lay board lacked the physicians' understanding of human behavior. In their view, the Board was too prone to listen to the chronic complainers, who would never be entirely satisfied. The trustees needed to keep the members happy and satisfied, but the physicians believed that complaints were an area where democracy and consumer control clashed with professional prerogatives. As the doctors expressed it, "good medicine can be practiced [with GHA's limited resources], but luxury medicine, with coddling of every patient, can not, and it is primarily a medical problem to adjudicate these matters." In short, the doctors did not believe that a group of nonphysicians could successfully administer a program of medical care.[5]

The diagnosis presupposed the cure: doctors thought they should be represented on the Board. After all, they pointed out, they had the greatest stake in GHA, which represented their careers, while trustees were only part-time temporary volunteers. The medical staff, therefore, should have the same number of seats on the Board as trustees elected by the membership, and the chairman of the Board should be a physician. Failure to take action on this proposal, they avowed, would lead to a "dissatisfied and insecure" medical staff marked by rapid turnover and providing poor medical care. Acknowledging that many of them had chosen to be associated with GHA because of its "social significance," they concluded that "we cannot continue to make sacrifices for an ideal alone."[6]

A quiet process of consultation quelled the physician revolt, and the doctors never did receive seats on the Board of Trustees. As time passed, relationships between doctors and the Board settled into a durable if not entirely comfortable routine. Both the executive directors and the medical directors became more active, and they managed to mediate disputes.[7]

TOWARD CAPITATION

The substantial membership growth in the early 1960s forced a comparable expansion in GHA's staff, from just over two hundred in 1959 to more than three hundred in 1961.[8] Physicians became hard to recruit and retain in the 1960s; young doctors finishing their residencies commanded higher starting salaries than GHA could afford to offer. New prepaid group plans, such as the Harvard Community Health Plan, intensified the competition for doctors who believed in HMOs.[9]

136

Even before Congress passed the Medicare legislation and helped to launch a sustained period of rising medical salaries, GHA had lost eleven full-time physicians in two years, due to dissatisfaction with pay. At the time, some doctors made as little as $17,000 per year. By the end of 1967, GHA had fallen further behind similar organizations in its compensation. An informal staff study showed that GHA now paid about $3,000 to $4,000 less than the Kaiser Health Plan and the Cleveland Health Foundation.[10]

GHA tried to improve its position by substituting "ancillary personnel" for doctors. In 1969, for example, GHA hired a maternal and pediatric nurse practitioner who, among other things, offered prenatal classes and instructed new mothers in breast feeding.[11] In the years that followed, GHA added certified nurse-midwives to assist obstetrical procedures, nurse practitioners who were teamed with internists, and physician assistants who worked in the minor injury unit.[12] None of these measures solved the doctor shortage.

GHA's physicians were still at the heart of its health care program. Faced with lagging salaries, the GHA doctors wanted to gain more control over their incomes. One approach they discussed was forming a partnership, in which they would no longer be GHA employees and would instead receive an agreed-upon sum for each GHA member. The physicians believed the proposed arrangement offered the advantage of "greater flexibility" in the division of income and increased the incentives to practice medicine efficiently. Further, the arrangement, according to executive director Frank Watters, would increase GHA's ability to attract and retain young doctors. Too often, these doctors acquired experience at GHA and established contacts with patients and then set up private practices, often taking some GHA patients with them.[13]

By the fall of 1968, a majority of the doctors favored a partnership. Only the older doctors, perhaps satisfied with a pay scale related to seniority or relieved at having no management responsibilities, demurred, yet even they recognized that GHA might lose physicians without it.[14]

The doctors saw a partnership arrangement as a way to be masters "of their own destiny," in which they would lower costs and promote efficiency, but the Board was not ready to accept such an approach. The trustees feared that cost-cutting could diminish the quality of care provided. A halfway step that the Board could accept, however, was called a "capitation agreement." Under this arrangement, the doctors would remain employees of GHA but would establish a medical group, which would receive a lump sum from the Association each year. The term "capitation" meant a payment "per head" or per participant, the monthly amount of which would be subject to annual negotiations between the doctors and GHA management.[15]

In response, the doctors met in closed session and listened to representatives from Kaiser and from the Group Health Cooperative of Puget Sound explain the arrangements used by other prepaid plans. On the day after Christmas in 1969, the doctors approved the creation of the GHA Medical Group, an employees' association. Although it allowed the doctors to bargain collectively with GHA, it was not a separate partnership and did not alter the employer-employee relationship between GHA and its physicians.[16]

In February 1970, Frank Watters presented the Board with a draft agreement between GHA and the doctors. Dr. Arthur Rosenbaum, an internist who had spent twenty-five years at GHA and was an emblem of integrity for many of the Board members, strongly endorsed the proposal. There was simply "no alternative to recognition of this need for participation by the doctors," he declared.[17]

The capitation agreement between Group Health Association and the GHA Medical Group, which was made retroactive to January 1, 1970, became one of the central documents in GHA's history. For the next six years, it, along with the "Medical Quality Control Plan," of June 1, 1970, defined the relationship between GHA and its physicians. These documents reflected GHA's original vision projected on a modern backdrop, a world in which well-paid physicians worked for an organization that was no longer either small or informal.[18]

The capitation agreement, which was similar to that used by Group Health Cooperative of Puget Sound, was nothing if not explicit. It specified that new physicians must be recommended by the department head and approved by both the medical program administrator (formerly the medical director) and the Medical Council. There were detailed provisions concerning the number of months of continuous employment required to become a member of the medical staff (18) and the number of months after which a physician's employment would be terminated if he or she were not approved as a member of the staff (21). The document also included items typical of any collective bargaining agreement, such as the statement that "a member of the Medical Staff shall be discharged only for cause." Much of the document concerned the provision of fringe benefits, which were generous, even by modern standards.[19]

Unlike doctors in more conventional practices, GHA physicians enjoyed the benefits of a forty-hour work week. They also had relatively lengthy vacations (without incurring the loss of income that private practice doctors faced when they took time off). After ten years of employment, a GHA doctor was entitled to five paid weeks of vacation annually, in addition to five days of study leave, fourteen days of sick leave, and nine legal holidays. A senior physician who used all of his or her sick leave could be gone for ten weeks of every year.[20]

The documents made it clear that Group Health, rather than the doctors, was taking the economic risks. GHA agreed to supply everything necessary to the physicians, such as offices, facilities, and laboratory services. The agreement also explicitly stated that the doctors were to receive their salary checks every two weeks. At the end of the year, physicians could also receive bonuses out of funds remaining in the capitation account (GHA's payment to the doctors for taking care of its members).[21]

With the capitation agreement in place, the politics of GHA grew considerably more complicated, as the controversy over natural childbirth revealed. This issue, which arose in 1971, became one of the first to test the new rules. Instead of being a consumer issue that members could settle with the Board, it became one on which the Board needed to negotiate with the staff. It pitted a powerful medical specialty, one in very short supply, against a strong consumer interest. Natural childbirth became a rallying cry of feminists who regarded obstetrics as a male-dominated specialty that was insensitive to women's needs.

In 1971, a GHA member who wanted to deliver her baby through natural childbirth checked GHA's policy and found that the obstetricians did not allow men in the delivery room. Fathers could go only as far as the labor room. Her husband, who very much wanted to be in the delivery room for the birth of his child, complained. A Board member with a special interest in the subject told the couple that GHA, a consumer-sponsored organization, should be sensitive to their needs. The medical director disagreed. He felt that GHA had too few obstetricians to implement natural childbirth, and he did not want to start a controversy with the obstetrical staff, which, he noted, "believes that the members should respect the judgment of the staff." Insistence that the staff yield on the matter bordered on "interference with the practice of medicine." After all, GHA provided good obstetrical care; there had been no maternal deaths for fifteen years.[22]

The Board consulted the department chief, who explained that fathers were not allowed in the delivery room because "there are too many patients and not enough time." He admitted that the staff was "unsympathetic" to the procedure.[23]

The issue eventually reached a committee of the Member Advisory Council, which had been formed in the late 1960s to provide a channel for member participation. The Council concluded that natural childbirth was a "legitimate, recognized, and increasingly practiced procedure." Although some GHA members strongly wanted to deliver their babies through natural childbirth, the Council agreed that staff members had a right not to practice this procedure. The recommended solution was for the women to go elsewhere and for the economic burden to be shared by the member and the organization.[24]

Eventually, GHA embraced natural childbirth. On May 26, 1972, the Board adopted the policy of allowing women to go outside for natural childbirth deliveries, with the member and GHA splitting the costs. Less than two years later, the organization began to offer natural childbirth deliveries through GHA's own doctors. The deliberations on this issue revealed the ways in which consumer preferences could push against medical prerogatives, and they exposed the unclear lines of authority between the Board and the doctors.[25]

THE MEDICAL GROUP AND THE MEDICAL COUNCIL

Differences among doctors became apparent in the politics of the Medical Council, which administered the affairs of the GHA Medical Group. The Council's formal composition was carefully divided by medical specialty. Adult medicine and pediatrics, the largest departments, each received two seats. Doctors in the obstetrics-gynecology department had the right to select one representative on the eleven-person council, as did the doctors in the artificially combined departments of dermatology and ophthalmology. Then there came two at-large members, one from the Pennsylvania Avenue Clinic. Finally, the department heads in medicine, pediatrics, and obstetrics-gynecology automatically received Council seats.[26]

The officers were chosen by the Council itself. Dr. Arthur Rosenbaum served as the Medical Council's first president. One staff member described him as a "charismatic leader," who was "altruistic" but also "extremely competent." Having started with GHA in 1941, Rosenbaum represented an important link to GHA's past, but the faction he led among the doctors was relatively young and very committed to prepaid group practice. Dr. Donald Mitchell, who served as the vice chairman of the Medical Council, was a dermatologist, a specialist, who, much more than Rosenbaum, concerned himself with issues of wages, hours, and grievances. His following, composed of doctors for whom secure working conditions and good wages were priorities, might be described as conservative.[27]

The Medical Council met weekly to discuss such matters as quality of care and working conditions, as well as to communicate with the Board of Trustees. Each year, the Council bargained with the Board in what became known as the "capitation" negotiations. Although the doctors made traditional wage demands, the negotiations concerned control of the workplace as much as the usual bread-and-butter issues. To the debate on workers' control, as to so many others, the two sides brought different expectations, based on differing professional backgrounds.

The doctors never became accustomed to their status as employees and feared any agreement that undermined their "identity and autonomy." At one Medical Council meeting, for example, the doctors criticized having the nurses keep time cards to record their hours. The nurses, the doctors said, had no ability to judge the quality and hence the proper length of time for a particular encounter. The doctors said that "punching-a-time clock surveillance by Administration" inevitably undermined professional morale."[28]

The trustees viewed the negotiations from the standpoint of the consumers they represented. Although they relied on the executive director as their negotiator, he was not a physician, and the Board tied his hands on many issues, trying to make sure, for example, that patients would have to wait no more than two weeks for an appointment.[29] In the end, a talented but diverse board of amateurs faced an undisciplined and conflicted group of professionals; together they pushed labor relations into new realms.

REORGANIZING THE MEDICAL GROUP

During 1972, a new leadership team came to GHA. Louis J. Segadelli, recruited from the Group Health Association of America, served as the new executive director, and Dr. Peter Birk became the new medical program administrator.

Both Birk and Segadelli criticized GHA's administrative structure. Segadelli noted that the lines of responsibility were unclear. Birk discovered that the medical program administrator's role was vague, as a result of the agreement with the Medical Group, which did not specify the relationship between the administrator and the Medical Council.[30]

All agreed that the existing arrangement was inadequate. GHA's lawyers advised Segadelli that the Medical Group was "neither a partnership nor a corporation" and created a situation that was "complex, potentially legally dangerous and politically volatile." The Medical Council charged GHA with having an inefficient administrative structure with the "two-headed monster" of Birk and Segadelli.[31]

The physicians, therefore, joined the trustees and the administration in looking for an alternative arrangement for the organization. "How can we protect ourselves from inappropriate inroads from the Board?" asked a special committee of the Medical Council, concerned about what it saw as the Board's voracious appetite for power to set salaries, select department heads, and even guide educational policies. "We physicians," concluded the doctors, "want a physician making decisions about medical care—not a lay administrator." The alternative was to "abdicate to the Board of Trustees."[32]

The more senior physicians, who had formerly opposed an independent doctors' partnership, now changed their minds. Dr. Mitchell, who represented the interests of the senior physicians on the Medical Council, argued that an independent Medical Group "would enhance the self-respect of GHA physicians."[33] At a meeting of the Medical Council in late November 1973, Mitchell moved that the Medical Council endorse the recommendation that the Medical Group "form a separate legal entity distinct from GHA Incorporated." His motion carried by a vote of 7 to 2.[34]

A fact-finding committee distributed a memo to the medical staff that confronted the doctors' hopes and fears. "I would never go in business with you softheads!" was one of the anticipated objections, to which the committee replied, "Although our control is limited we're already in business together." "But, I don't want all that administrative work, that's why I came to GHA," read another of the concerns, to which the committee answered that, if the doctors did not want to do administrative work, the Board and Louis Segadelli were more than willing to "take up the slack."[35]

On December 2, 1973, the doctors met and adopted Mitchell's recommendation "that we proceed to structure a separate legal entity." Some doctors, however, still worried about concerns like those discussed in the committee memo. As a result, the vote was a decisive but far from unanimous 24 to 10.[36]

With that decision made, the physicians attended to the details, with predictable reactions from the members and the trustees. By August of 1974, a special doctors' reorganization committee had received a progress report, prepared by outside consultants, that showed little respect for GHA's traditions. "Fundamental to the entire concept," the report noted, "is the assumption [of] . . . a 'profit motive.' "[37] The statement failed to comprehend GHA's special environment, in which the members instinctively reacted against the notion of a profit motive. The trustees, who faithfully reflected the members' concerns, feared that "efficiency," one of the promised benefits of a partnership, was a code word that meant less service.[38]

In 1974, a dispute over the capitation agreement heightened the fears of both the Board and the doctors about the future of GHA. The Board discovered that, with a capitation agreement, fewer doctors meant more money for those who remained. In fact, during the summer of 1974, GHA temporarily closed its enrollment for want of physicians, even as the capitation account generated a surplus of $300,000. The Board found this situation intolerable and tried to encourage department heads to hire more doctors. The Board also sought to restrict the rationing of the physicians' services by encouraging the doctors to see patients more promptly. The reduction of "appointment delays" became a priority for the Board, which proposed explicit standards, such as obtaining an emergency urology visit within forty-eight hours. The doctors objected to the way in which these suggestions allowed control over professional matters to rest "totally with the Board."[39]

Cases that called the doctors' administrative competence into question also troubled the Board. One such case came to Dr. Birk's attention in the summer of 1974. A patient with a chronic cough went to the Urgent Visit Center, which referred him to an internist for a more complete work-up. On the day of the patient's appointment, the internist cancelled all his appointments, and the patient was told that "he would have to go to the end of the line." In frustration, the patient went outside GHA, to Johns Hopkins, where he was diagnosed as having cancer.[40]

Because of the doctors' desires to form a separate partnership, the 1975 capitation negotiations were marked by a higher degree of conflict than those of previous years. The question of waiting time for appointments figured prominently in the discussions. Another thorny issue concerned the doctors' wish for a "no loss provision" to make sure that the physicians' salaries did not fall below existing levels.[41] As the discussions proceeded, the Medical Council's finance committee concluded "the Board of Trustees and the Medical Group are on a potentially destructive collision course."[42]

GHA's looming financial crisis of 1975 also made the physicians uneasy, and they began to talk again about the need for doctors to be represented on the Board and to become involved in the decision-making process. "Reorganization," said one physician, "must again raise its ugly head."[43] Worried about GHA's solvency, the chief of psychiatry even proposed that his department should separate from GHA and provide care on a fee-for-service basis. The head of obstetrics told the members of the Medical Council in June 1975 that, if GHA continued on its present course, it would fold within a year.[44]

In August 1975, the doctors' reorganization committee met again with outside experts, who explained how to organize a doctors' partnership. One physician discussed the East Nassau Medical Plan, which was part of HIP in New York City. These physicians were totally independent of their contractor and simply entered into yearly contract negotiations. The members received prepaid care, and the doctors were allowed to distribute the profits, if any, among themselves. A doctor from the Rochester Health Plan told the GHA doctors that a separate entity would promote better staff morale, administrative efficiency, and improved relations with the Board of Trustees.[45]

In September, a joint committee of doctors and trustees, who were to devise a "new working relationship," met with representatives of the Kaiser Foundation Health Plan, the Permanente Medical Group of Northern California, and the Group Health Cooperative of Puget Sound. The discussion reflected the trustees' concerns over such matters as appointments and productivity. Dr. John Smillie of the Kaiser group reported that, under their contract with a doctors' partnership, half of his patients were seen on the day they requested. Dr. Harold F. Newman of Puget

Sound explained that questions of productivity were handled through a joint conference committee of three medical staff officers and three board members. Newman mentioned that, although Puget Sound—which had a capitation arrangement similar to GHA's—had some problems, "esprit de corps" and the "concern of the medical and administrative staff" helped to overcome them.[46]

Both the Board and the doctors heard what they wanted to hear in these discussions. In September 1975, the doctors' reorganization committee prepared a report that featured what had become the traditional physicians' analysis of GHA's problems. In the old days, when the organization was small, costs were low, and competition was sparse, GHA performed well with its cooperative structure, volunteer board, and "less than skillful management." In the new era, the physicians could no longer entrust their futures to a voluntary board and a management team that had made "demonstrably poor decisions" and brought the organization "close to the edge of financial collapse." Instead, the doctors needed to form their own independent group and enter into a partnership to plan GHA's future.[47]

On November 24, 1975, the doctors' reorganization committee circulated a formal proposal for a corporation and set December 14, 1975, as the date for the full Medical Group to consider it. Under the plan's terms, the physicians would become shareholders in the Capitol Medical Group, and elect a board of directors. They would work for the Capitol Medical Group, not GHA.[48]

Soon, mention of the doctors' intentions appeared in the press, and, for the first time, the doctors' corporation became a significant issue in the GHA trustee elections. In the spring of 1976, three of the six candidates for the three available seats openly opposed the doctors' corporation. Harold Wool, one of the candidates who believed deeply in retaining the cooperative aspects of GHA, told the *Washington Post*'s Victor Cohn that the corporation would "seriously reduce member influence on medical service." Brent Oldham, an influential member of Washington's black community who had served as GHA president in the early 1970s, also ran in opposition to the doctor's corporation. He told Cohn that the corporation would be GHA's "death rattle."[49]

Louis Segadelli and trustee Jan Lodal disagreed. They worked to prepare the Board for the transition to what Segadelli referred to as the "Kaiser system."[50]

When Wool, Oldham, and Gertrude Ruttenberg, three of the candidates opposed to the corporation, won election to the Board, a serious clash of wills lay ahead. The discussions began at a special meeting of the newly elected Board of Trustees, almost a retreat, held at a hotel near Dulles Airport in April 1976. After electing Oldham president, the trustees were informed by Segadelli that Dr. Birk intended to resign as medical director. "I am not effective as a leader of the physician staff," he stated. Birk suggested that the Medical Group should pick the next medical director, and Segadelli wholeheartedly agreed.[51]

The newly elected trustees heard a litany of reasons why GHA should adopt a doctors' corporation. Segadelli declared, "It can't work on the basis of a strictly employer-employee relationship." A consultant from Arthur D. Little asserted, "In order for the physicians to do an effective job, they must do it themselves." Board members responded with a variety of consumer concerns, including the need for better doctor-patient communication, access to service, and physician competence.[52]

The dialogue illustrated the deadlock that would prevail over the course of a year. Segadelli continued to advocate the Kaiser solution, and the trustees, who were badly divided among themselves, continued to press their consumer concerns. In direct response, the level of contentiousness between the doctors and the trustees rose, as the appointment of a new medical director demonstrated.

The Board invited the Medical Council to nominate a physician for the position of medical program director, but they attached stringent conditions. No longer would the position carry the title "director." Instead, it would be called medical executive, and it would be filled on a six-month experimental basis. The Medical Council objected both to the title and the temporary basis of the job. It took more than two and a half months for the matter to be resolved, but in July 1976 the Board finally agreed to the Medical Council's stipulations, and Dr. Donald Mitchell accepted the position of medical director.[53]

Another event that highlighted the patterns of conflict within the Board and throughout GHA was the resignation of Dr. Daniel Patterson, the chief of psychiatry. On July 14, 1976, Dr. Patterson, long discontented, announced his decision to leave, with a blistering indictment of GHA's policies. Patterson denigrated GHA's cooperative structure, arguing that no one faction respected another. Patterson doubted that patients were well served by the volunteer Board, which could "afford the luxury of making decisions on the basis of principle, secure in the knowledge that if that decision leads to GHA's demise, the decision that they made was 'after all a matter of principle.' " Executives were chosen not for their managerial abilities so much as for their "pledged allegiance to the principles of consumer cooperation." The doctors, Patterson contended, had responded to the crisis only by becoming more concerned with security and maintaining the status quo.[54]

Having made such a strong statement, Patterson then had to retract it, when he saw renewed movement toward a doctors' corporation.[55]

THE END OF THE MEDICAL GROUP

With the system stalemated, it required an outside prod to produce major change. The unexpected spur came in the form of an apparently innocuous request for study leave by Dr. Nancy Falk, who was planning to resign from GHA. The Medical Council turned down her request under a rule that said "no approval for study leave can be granted 90 days prior to a termination of employment." Dr. Falk, whose husband was a labor lawyer, responded by filing a complaint with the National Labor Relations Board, which had recently been given jurisdiction over the health care industry. She charged that the Medical Group was a company union and hence an improper bargaining agent on behalf of GHA employees.[56]

Both GHA's legal counsel and NLRB attorneys agreed. As Dr. Mitchell later said, "We were indeed a company dominated union. We got everything, including paper, from the company."[57] In September 1976, GHA reached a settlement agreement under NLRB auspices. GHA agreed to withdraw recognition from the Medical Group as a collective bargaining agent and the Medical Group agreed to cease within sixty days to function as a collective bargaining agent. Dr. Mitchell, however, went beyond the requirements of this agreement, moving immediately to disband the Medical Group entirely, as a step toward forming a corporation.[58]

The latest crisis produced a new blizzard of paper examining how GHA should be organized. Trustee Edwin A. Deagle Jr. prepared a thoughtful analysis on behalf of the joint physician-trustee committee that contrasted consumer and physician expectations. The consumer expected that GHA would be member-controlled, that it would remain nonprofit, and that it would institute procedures to measure consumer satisfaction. The physicians wanted to be actively involved in policymaking, and to enhance their professional and financial status. Deagle noted that these objectives could be achieved either with the physicians as GHA employees or through a separate legal entity.[59]

Unable to reach a decision, the trustees requested more study of the matter. In mid-November, the Board decided to hire a health care consultant to do a study and determined that, in the meantime, experts should come to talk about other HMOs. (By now, of course, the paths to GHA from Puget Sound and Kaiser were well worn). This action irritated the physicians, who were concerned at the prospect of further delay.[60]

Tempers grew short under the stress of the crisis. One Board member took Segadelli to task for supporting the doctors' corporation. The trustees received a letter from an *ad hoc* Committee for Concerned Members, which expressed shock over the fact that the Medical Council was setting up a private corporation.[61]

The December 1976 Board meeting began with Oldham announcing that the physicians had formed what he called a "precorporation Medical Group Organization." Dr. Patterson, a strong supporter of the corporation idea, headed the new organization, although Dr. Mitchell was to continue as medical director for the time being. The doctors made it clear that they wanted the matter settled before a new Board of Trustees took office; the consumer advocates on the Board clearly sought delay. They reminded their fellow trustees that the Board had decided to hire an outside consultant, and stressed the need for consultation with the Member Advisory Council and the members themselves.[62]

Listening to the trustees' discussion, Dr. Mitchell blew up, declaring that delay would lead only to confrontation. The newspapers would begin to write negative stories about GHA. A trustee replied that the surest way to get bad publicity was to cut corners in the deliberation process. President Oldham, by now converted to the doctors' position, counseled immediate discussion of the doctors' corporation. The proponents of delay, however, were successful, and the Board simply adopted a resolution, promising a "final resolution of the organizational structure by April 1977."[63]

The debate now moved to more public forums, culminating in the trustee election. A pivotal event in GHA's history, the election of 1977 joined the early antitrust cases and the referenda of 1963 as incidents that defined GHA's identity in their respective eras.

In 1977, even more than in 1976, the question of a doctors' corporation became the focal issue for GHA voters. The January and

February issues of the *GHA News* carried a series of essays providing different viewpoints on the doctors' corporation, making it clear that the forthcoming election would serve as a referendum on that issue. Dr. Patterson, the spokesman for the GHA physicians' group, argued that the doctors' corporation would bring doctors and members together in a restoration of GHA's original partnership between physician and consumer. Trustee Robert Greenberg contended that a corporation was not in GHA's best interest and would weaken the members' ability to influence the quality of medical care. He continued to believe that a collegial arrangement between the doctors and the organization could be worked out.[64]

In this atmosphere, the political lines at GHA hardened. In March 1977, the members chose between two slates of three candidates each. One slate, in favor of the doctors' corporation, announced itself "For Common Sense in GHA," and the other, which opposed the corporation, was endorsed by the Committee of Concerned Members. Balanced by race and age, the Common Sense slate included two trade unionists and the chairman of the Member Advisory Council. Although the "concerned members" slate lacked this demographic balance, it included people with distinguished GHA service records, such as Al Raizen, a financial advisor at the World Bank, who had been a member since 1948 and had served on the finance committee since 1970.[65]

The balloting ended on March 24, and all three members of the slate that opposed the doctors' corporation won decisively. Dr. Smillie of the Permanente Medical Group wrote to his friend Lou Segadelli, lamenting GHA's failure to adopt the Kaiser model. "Some members of the GHA Board apparently retain the self delusion that they can control the doctors. They do not nor will they under any arrangement," wrote Smillie, who believed that under the right conditions GHA could have a membership of a million or more. Almost as if in response, Harold Wool told the *Washington Post*, "Some of us are not totally impressed with the way corporate medicine has operated in other parts of the country. We don't necessarily think this is the way of the future."[66]

Harold Wool was placed in a position to help shape the future on March 28, 1977, when the new Board met and elected him president. One of his first tasks was to respond to a letter from Dr. Patterson asking that the "GHA Medical Group, Chartered" (the doctors had already gone ahead and formed their corporation) be recognized as the physicians' negotiating agent. Wool replied that he had a mandate from the voters to develop proposals *within the framework of a single overall GHA organization.*" This phrase was the key to the difference of opinion—whether the doctors would form a separate organization or remain an integral part of GHA. Recognizing that Patterson and his colleagues must have found the election results "a severe disappointment," Wool stated that he counted on the doctors' cooperation.[67]

Wool and the new Board of Trustees soon faced their first crisis. On April 1, nine doctors responded to Wool's letter to Patterson by resigning their administrative positions. Dr. Nicholas S. Gimbel, the chief of general surgery, asked Louis Segadelli to convey an apparent paradox to the trustees: "More 'control' can be exercised through a negotiated contract with a quality medical group than can be exercised by direction of a salaried staff, whether unionized or not." Dr. Donald Mitchell, after resigning his post as medical director, put the matter in less intellectual, more potent terms. "Group Health hasn't had a medical director for the last week," he said.[68]

GHA limped along without medical administrators. Although all the doctors, including the former administrators, continued to see patients, matters like budgetary planning and physician recruiting suffered. It took more than a month for GHA to recruit an interim medical director and to restore a semblance of normality to its medical operations.[69]

In the summer of 1977, a new effort was undertaken to put together a medical organization, this one along the collegial lines favored by the new trustees. Memoranda flew, as the parties at interest staked out their turf; more meetings ensued.[70]

When Dr. Dorothy Millon, the former chief of internal medicine, appeared before the Board in August 1977, she reported that many physicians in her department were threatening to quit, more because of the general atmosphere than because of the pay. Physicians cited the events of the election campaign as reasons for leaving, and those who remained resented the Board's lack of interest in their complaints. The physicians' response to the Board's indifference, she noted, was to work to rule, showing up at nine, leaving at five, and lingering over lunch. She recalled that, at one point, the physicians were so distraught that they were considering resigning *en masse,* in order to bring GHA to "a dramatic crisis" and get the Board's attention. The trustees assured Millon that they were interested in forging a good relationship with the doctors, "within the context of the organization remaining consumer-controlled."[71]

In September, Louis Segadelli submitted his resignation, to be effective June 30, 1978. "I decided to resign since I cannot carry out the major policy of the Board," he said. Wool, accepting the resignation with regret, explained that the rejection of the corporation did not mean that the Board regarded the doctors as "just employees." On the contrary, the Board sought to increase the involvement of the doctors in GHA management.[72]

A PHYSICIANS' UNION

Aware of Segadelli's resignation and mindful of the Board's firm refusal to permit a separate corporation, the doctors in the fall of 1977 decided their only alternative was to organize as a labor union. In June, Wool and Segadelli had sent the doctors a draft proposal for a collegial-style physicians' organization. The organization would be run by a medical director, reporting to an executive director, who in turn would report to the Board. In addition, there was to be a medical staff association that would consult with a committee and the medical director on wage rates and would appoint a nonvoting member to the Board. Unimpressed, the doctors, on October 20, 1977, informed GHA management that they had instead formed an association to negotiate wages and other conditions of employment. "We demand immediate recognition of our association," the letter stated.[73]

Segadelli replied that the trustees wanted to be sure a majority of doctors desired the union and therefore would not recognize the group until it had been certified as a collective bargaining representative in a secret-ballot NLRB election. In response, the doctors filed a formal petition with the NLRB on November 4, 1977. On January 4, 1978, the physicians voted, 53 to 16, in favor of the union, with ten doctors abstaining.[74]

An important line had been crossed. The physicians would indeed remain employees, as the trustees wanted, but the very presence of the union prevented a collegial relationship. The appearance of a duly certified union inevitably made the relationship more formal and hence more distant. The Board learned this fact of life almost immediately. When one trustee suggested a meeting with the whole staff in order to improve communication between the doctors and the Board, a GHA lawyer cut him short. Under the law, communication with nonsupervisory doctors must now go through the union, he said. GHA soon discovered itself in a situation where the law defined much of the form and even the content of its relationship with the physicians. The union was in some ways similar to a separate legal entity, as the doctors had wanted, but the doctors were unambiguously defined as employees, as they had always feared.[75]

Regarded by many as a companion cause to the CIO when both were created in the 1930s, GHA now had given rise to what was believed to be the first physicians' union in an HMO. Unions, which many long-time GHA members had viewed as an important element of the liberal cause, became a divisive force within the Association. In a strange reversal, people who had few previous links to the union movement became the workers; trustees, some of whom had belonged to unions and had close ties to the organized labor movement, were now the bosses. Union member Donald Mitchell's grandparents and great grandparents had been physicians. Trustee Harold Wool had worked for the International Ladies Garment Workers Union and been active in the CIO's United Federal Workers union.[76]

The negotiations Wool and his Board conducted with the doctors were critically important. First negotiations with a new union can set the pattern for subsequent labor-management relations. In this situation, few precedents existed to serve as guides. Perhaps aware of this fact, Segadelli recommended that the Board enter the negotiations without numerical or other goals; it should simply seek the best contract possible.[77]

On March 7, 1978, the Board met to review the progress of the negotiations. Several bargaining sessions had taken place, one lasting fifteen and a half hours, that covered a wide range of issues. A new era in the relationship with the doctors had begun. There was now a formal physicians' union that, in the event of unsuccessful negotiations, might strike.[78]

Briefed about the stalled negotiations with the doctors, the Board members struggled to develop a strategy that would win a new contract and avert a strike. The wage issue remained unresolved. Workload loomed as an even more difficult issue, for the physicians wanted to reduce the number of patients they saw each day.[79]

In trying to set management's negotiating strategy, the trustees were hampered by limited information and experience. Not doctors, they had to accept the judgment of others on the feasibility of their proposals; not career staff members, many lacked an institutional memory. More directly affected by the matters at hand, the doctors shared a lack of experience in labor-management negotiations. They made periodic threats, unaware of whether they could be carried out legally. Most of these threats lacked substance; they represented the bluster of a new labor organization seeking recognition.[80]

On April 3, 1978, the attorney for the union wrote the Federal Mediation and Conciliation Service, announcing the doctors' intention to engage "in a strike, picketing, and any other concerted activity." In the absence of an agreement, these activities would begin on April 13, 1978. The lawyer took this action in advance because health care unions were required by law to give ten days' notice of intent to strike. The attorney anticipated that other GHA employees, such as nurses and other allied health professionals, would observe the picket line.[81]

When the Board met on Thursday, April 13, Segadelli reported that the union had postponed its strike deadline to 1 A.M. on April 15. Agreement still had not been reached on five critical issues, of which productivity, outside practice, and malpractice insurance were the most important. On the productivity question, the union said it would "strive" to have each doctor schedule eighteen patients and also see three unscheduled patients a day. GHA preferred to "require" the physicians to meet this standard. The doctors wanted two hours a day to see patients in the hospital; GHA offered only one hour. As for outside practice, the Board of Trustees insisted that the GHA doctors work exclusively for GHA and that they not be allowed to moonlight. The issue surrounding malpractice insurance concerned the amount of protection against an expensive jury award that GHA should provide. GHA agreed to present a final offer to the doctors by Friday afternoon, which the doctors could take to their membership at seven that evening.[82]

Rhetoric on both sides hardened. On Friday, April 14, the *Washington Post* reported Dr. Mitchell's warning that, if GHA did not improve its offer, "you'll see physicians on the street Saturday morning. . . . They've had all they can take." Wool stressed the need to get agreement "on a fair day's work" to match agreement already reached on a fair day's pay. Dr. Norman Lieberman, president of the union, contended that the issues did not concern economics so much as civil rights, a "God-given right in the United States of America to go out and make more money as a physician."[83]

When on late Friday night the doctors voted 38 to 2 to reject GHA's last offer, a strike became inevitable. On Saturday morning, physicians began picketing outside GHA's Pennsylvania Avenue headquarters. "Doctors on Strike," read the signs they carried. "We are striking a system and the Group Health board members who would force us to live under these conditions," declared Dr. Lieberman. "I deplore this exercise in brinksmanship," said Harold Wool. Registered nurses and other unionized employees honored the picket line, while some members, distressed by the sight of their doctors on strike, organized their own counter picket line.[84]

Dr. Philip Brunschwyler, a pediatrician and one of the fifty-five doctors on strike, tried to describe his feelings. "You get angry at the board because you don't see things the way they do," he said. "No matter how lofty you can be, there comes a time when you have to take care of yourself and your family."[85]

Anxious to explain the situation to members, GHA's management mailed out a brief "GHA Situation Report" at the beginning of the strike. Apologizing for the inconvenience, the circular explained the issues from management's point of view and notified members that emergency services were available, provided by more than twenty supervisory and other physicians, with the assistance of some nurses, physician assistants, and support staff who continued working.[86]

As the strike continued, some issues were moved off the bargaining table.[87] Outside practice was the last issue to be settled. The Board Members who expressed an opinion on this issue said that, although they wanted to retain the flexibility for the doctors to engage in research, training, and pro bono work, they disapproved of "outside paid private practice." The trustees agreed to hold the line on this issue. On Tuesday, April 25, the negotiators broke through the obstacles, and the union voted to return to work, eleven days after the strike had begun. The *Washington Post* reported that the physicians "appear to have won a sizable concession" on the outside practice issue. The final wording contained the proviso against outside practice and then added:

> Where the medical director determines that no possibility of interference with GHA patient care exists, the Medical Director may allow physicians to engage in pro bono medical service, research or teaching. Any fees or payments associated with such pro bono service, teaching, or research may be retained by the physician.[88]

"I am thrilled to be a physician again," Dr. Lieberman told the *Washington Post*. Wool said that he expected easy ratification of the agreement by the Board.[89]

When the *Post* asked Tom Gagliardo, the union's lawyer, to define "pro bono," he replied, "that's one of those loose terms that got us through the contract. It remains to be seen. There's 'pro bono,' and there's 'pro bono.' "[90] On Wednesday evening, April 26, when the Board convened to ratify the contract, the trustees expressed some uneasiness over the meaning of "pro bono." They voted to ratify the contract, but subject to a clarification of the term. To the Board "pro bono" meant only uncompensated work; the union thought it could include some paid activities as well.[91]

At 12:05 A.M. on Thursday morning, Wool and one of the attorneys left the Board meeting and presented the mediator with the trustees' request to clarify the meaning of "pro bono." Forty minutes later, Wool returned to the Board meeting and stated that the union had rejected GHA's clarification of the phrase. The mediator was working with the union negotiators to produce alternative language.[92]

At 1:50 A.M., the union negotiating team and some forty other physicians joined the trustees. "You deceived us! You've lied to us! You must not care very much at GHA," one of the doctors told the Board. Donald Mitchell engaged in an angry shouting match with Harold Wool. "If I have to go out on the streets again, I'll break the organization," Mitchell said. He accused Board member Dr. Dorothy Gill, a former GHA staff member, of betraying the doctors. After observing, "It's with a heavy heart that I'm here to read this," Dr. Lieberman proceeded to read a notice of intention to strike beginning at two A.M. on May 7, 1978, again giving the ten days' notice that the law required.[93]

The trustees sent Brent Oldham to talk to the union negotiators. "They're going to bring down Group Health. Brent, they're destroying the place. They're literally destroying it," Dr. Lieberman told Oldham, apparently referring to the trustees.[94] At 2:20 A.M., Oldham returned to the Board meeting room. He said that he now believed that there had been a complete misunderstanding on the meaning of "pro bono." The two sides appeared to be talking about two entirely different things. At 2:40 A.M., Harold Wool said that nothing more could be accomplished that night. The trustees went home.[95]

Thursday and Friday's papers contained vivid descriptions of the meeting. Wool, who had been greeted each morning by television crews staking out his house, and Lieberman, whose phone had also been ringing with calls from reporters, continued their negotiations in the media. Lieberman accused the Board of "trying to get us to clarify its own language." "We felt that pro bono meant in the community service, maybe for a nominal fee, not designed to be competitive, not a contractual commitment and certainly nothing that commits a substantial bloc of the doctor's time," Wool explained.[96]

Whether the doctors realized it immediately or not, the strike had been broken. It would have required almost superhuman effort of will for the doctors to have worked for the ten-day "notice period," and then to have geared up for another strike. For all of the rhetoric, the issue in dispute was comparatively small and the differences between the two sides relatively minor.

The mediator decided to give each of the parties a cooling-off period until Monday, May 1. He then approached each side with the suggestion that they meet on Tuesday to consider a specific proposal: the GHA trustees would ratify the contract and both sides would submit to immediate arbitration on the meaning of the words "pro bono." Segadelli recommended to the Board that it accept the mediator's suggestion and ratify the contract. Hours before the Tuesday meeting, the Board agreed to the mediator's suggestion. Later that afternoon, Wool and Lieberman signed a stipulation appointing an arbitrator to resolve the dispute. Both the strike and the threat of a new strike were over. Conciliatory statements followed. "GHA is healthy. I think the contract we signed is one both sides can easily live with," Lieberman said.[97]

When the arbitrator issued his award at the end of August, it came as something of an anticlimax. The arbitrator sided with GHA. He ruled that doctors could engage in "uncompensated services, except to the extent of receiving expenses or a nominal fee for them."[98]

GHA paid a tremendous price for this victory. The strike left a lingering feeling of bitterness. For both the doctors and the organization, the strike was traumatic. The members saw a cooperative organization engaged in one of the most uncooperative of acts. Groping for the right metaphor, one doctor said, "It's like the Civil War. You're forced to take a side. Where do we go from here? I think one lesson to be learned is the Board should realize things are not well with the organization and should look in an objective fashion at why things are not well."[99]

One aftermath of the strike was that the union physicians held a grudge against those "physician extenders"—physician assistants and nurse practitioners—who continued to provide care during the strike. Thereafter, the union sought to limit GHA's use of such physician extenders, claiming that they actually made more work for the doctors and recommending that GHA should instead simply hire additional physicians. The Board responded firmly that it intended to continue to use physician assistants, nurse practitioners, and nurse-midwives. Nonetheless, the 1980 collective bargaining agreement with the physicians' union included requirements that the doctor had to be present when the extender examined a patient and that no doctor would have more than one extender to supervise. The terms of the agreement hampered the goals of conserving the physician's time and saving money.[100]

Far from solving the problem, the 1978 physicians' strike proved to be only the beginning of a continuing adversarial relationship with the doctors' union, and with the nurses as well.

In 1975, GHA's nurses and physical therapists formed a labor union, the Registered Nurses and Physical Therapists Association (RNPTA). This union went on strike against GHA in the spring of 1982. One nurse explained that the nurses were "on the front line at GHA," being expected to give advice, set up appointments, listen to patients' problems, and explain treatment techniques. She felt that other areas of responsibility, such as answering the constantly ringing telephones, should be left to clerical personnel.[101]

The strike of eighty nurses and five physical therapists began on April 1 and lasted for thirty days. Most GHA members expressed support for the nurses, believing their demands were justified. "You have to pay for good medical health care," asserted one mother.[102] Reflecting on the strike, executive director Dr. Edward J. Hinman later noted that the nurses were concerned that GHA nursing salaries had fallen behind those elsewhere in the community. The times also contributed to the nurses' uneasiness, Hinman explained:

"The concept of functioning as the 'handmaid' of the physician is no longer acceptable to nurses."[103]

In the next set of labor negotiations with the doctors, the Board, management, and the union all made a concerted effort to avoid confrontation. Talks began in early 1983, amid conciliatory rhetoric. The three-year contract, negotiated and approved by January 1983, included concessions on both sides. The physicians agreed to a contingency surplus payment program that would reward them if GHA could achieve a budget surplus; GHA receded from its long-standing opposition to outside practice. Physicians were permitted to undertake limited outside work if they received specific approval from the medical director. As GHA president Al Raizen explained, "Both parties committed themselves to make a fresh start to develop constructive and supportive joint working relationships." Dr. Mitchell described the result as a "win-win contract."[104]

By the end of the contract period, however, the era of good feelings had dissipated. As the time approached to renegotiate, it became apparent that GHA management and the union had divergent views of the organization's financial condition. A statement by Dr. Nieves M. Zaldivar, the union president, asserted that GHA was enjoying unprecedented prosperity and, unlike in 1983, the doctors expected to share in GHA's financial success. The executive director, Dr. Robert G. Rosenberg, concerned about increasing competition and the business environment, predicted hard times ahead for GHA, which the union viewed as "crying poor." An adversarial relationship had returned.[105]

As the March 1, 1986, contract termination date approached, management became concerned at what it saw as the union team's strategy of delay, meeting as briefly and as infrequently as possible. Since the union had already filed the necessary ten-day strike notice, management began setting up a strike plan, hoping it would not prove necessary.[106]

On March 1, the Board met and determined that continuation of the 1983 contract would not be acceptable. In order to improve GHA's ability to compete in the crowded HMO market, management wanted to raise the number of hours physicians were available to see patients, while retaining the thirty-five-hour work week. In return, the doctors would be granted a 4–5 percent salary increase. GHA also wanted the right to schedule some patient appointments in the evening hours, for the convenience of members who could not take time off from work during the day. Management also planned to institute an incentive system, under which 5 percent of doctors' salaries would be placed in an escrow account, to be paid to specialty groups of doctors at each center if they were able to treat target numbers of patients. The union found none of these proposals to be acceptable. When no agreement was reached, the union voted 90 to 20 to begin striking on March 3.[107]

As the 160 union doctors took turns walking picket lines, GHA's contingency plans swung into action. Both sides did their best to obtain the sympathy and support of the members. Both doctors and management spoke to newspaper reporters. Management issued radio and television spot announcements, insisting that GHA's goal was "quality medical care" and that all medical centers remained open.[108]

Meanwhile, negotiations continued at the headquarters of the Federal Mediation and Conciliation Service. Although many doctors began quietly drifting back to work as early as March 10, the strike dragged on. GHA financial analysts predicted that, even if the walkout ended quickly, the adverse publicity would still cause the organization to lose as many as 4,000 potential members and as much as $2.5 million.[109]

On March 26, the parties reached agreement, and the union voted 80 to 19 to submit most of the controversial issues to arbitration. Under the new contract, the doctors received a 3 percent salary increase for 1986. Minimum office hours per week were set for each specialty, with the understanding that physicians required to devote less than thirty-five hours a week to office visits would spend their remaining time in surgery or hospital rounds.[110]

The strike could not have come at a worse time. It divided GHA management and trustees from its physicians in a period when the organization was under severe outside pressure and needed to have all parties pulling together. The $2 million loss caused by the strike, together with the adverse publicity, exacerbated a growing financial deficit and left GHA's leadership seriously concerned about the Association's future.

As a result, GHA faced the competitive HMO environment with a double disadvantage. Its cooperative structure made it difficult for executive directors to make strategic moves that would enhance the organization's competitive standing. Its labor unions enforced norms that limited physicians' productivity and raised costs. As the fiftieth anniversary approached, GHA no longer stood at the cutting edge of medical care, so much as it traded upon loyalties that had developed over the course of its fifty years. Long the dominant player in the Washington, D.C., HMO market, Group Health, like the dominant American manufacturer of steel, could easily go out of business and for similar reasons: an inability to modernize its operations and improve productivity.

CHAPTER SEVEN

GHA in Historical and Comparative Perspective

This history has no last act. We have followed GHA from its early uncertainty, to moderate success, and back to an uncertain future. Unlike the author of a novel, we do not know whether our central character will live or die. With the competition closing in, the organization faces limited choices: it can fold, sell out to a profit-seeking competitor, or survive, after another period of sacrifice. Whatever the outcome, we know that the members and trustees of GHA will not voluntarily abandon the consumer concerns of the organization, since many of them believe GHA has a mission that extends beyond preserving its market share.[1]

The trouble is that GHA does not have the luxury of elevating ethics and dismissing economics. As we have demonstrated, one cannot analyze GHA in isolation from more general trends in the market for health care. Health care organizations, even those that swear off profit, cannot run away and hide from the market. The dilemma of adverse selection and the costs of doing business make that impossible. Doctors and allied health professionals will not work at wages below the market level in the name of a social experiment, nor can hospitals be expected to offer a nonprofit cooperative a rebate on the grounds of social compassion. GHA has never controlled a sufficient share to exert influence over the medical market. In economic terms, it has always had to operate in an environment that has been dominated by the area's major employer, the federal government. The monopoly power in this market has come from the buyer's rather than the sellers' side. As a price "taker," Group Health must raise sufficient revenues to cover its costs, mindful of the fact that these revenues are also sensitive to the premiums it charges. Everywhere the organization turns, it is limited in its freedom by the dictates of the market.

The market has even influenced the range of benefits that GHA has offered to its members. Some, such as psychiatric services, began at the request of the Civil Service. Mental health care, which started in the early 1960s with a single psychiatrist advising other doctors, grew, as a result of Civil Service pressures, to include both hospitalization and outpatient acute psychiatric care.[2] Other benefits resulted from changes in consumer expectation. During the 1970s and 1980s, for example, GHA increased its commitment to providing extended care for members, adding some nursing home care in 1978 and hospice care for terminally ill patients in 1984.[3]

Each benefit liberalization heightened the financial danger of adverse selection. To guard against this problem, GHA required entrance physical examinations, first of everyone, and later of those who wished to join as individual members; the organization then placed restrictions on certain preexisting conditions that were found. Even today, GHA still screens the small number of members who do not join through groups.[4]

As GHA expanded its benefits, it used a number of methods to help control costs, including a change from depending on outside consultants in many medical fields to hiring its own staff specialists. By 1977, all medical departments, except neurosurgery, were staffed by full-time GHA physicians.[5]

Just as GHA has been influenced by market forces, so it has been affected by governmental actions and public policy. Group Health owed its early prominence to the Roosevelt administration's recognition of its symbolic value as a prepaid group health plan struggling to survive in the face of active opposition from the medical profession. Later, the organization faced rising costs that were due at least in part to the passage of Medicare in 1965, and it encountered serious competition that was substantially attributable to the federal government's encouragement of health maintenance organizations. Its financial and manpower dilemmas often resulted from conditions over which the government exerted direct control, such as the supply of doctors during the Second World War or the duration of wage and price controls in the seventies.

Although national trends have affected GHA, it has remained a profoundly local organization. As such, its history is intertwined with the development of Washington, D.C. One key local influence on GHA has to do with race.

The organization started in a rigidly segregated city; even fifty years later, blacks and whites in Washington tend to reside in different areas. Because health care was intimate and touched the body, racial taboos mattered far more than did class barriers in the provision of medical care, and they persisted longer. In Washington, two separate medical practices developed: one for white residents and the other for blacks. Dependent on the goodwill of the community for patients and hospital care, GHA could not move too much ahead of community norms, despite the liberal opinions of its members. Only after World War II did GHA open its membership to all races.

During the 1960s and early 1970s, Group Health took its social commitment a step further and sought to assist physicians in bringing health care to poor black residents of the District. In 1960, GHA helped a group of Howard University physicians create a group practice to provide care to GHA members who lived in one of the city's many black neighborhoods.[6] The 1968 riots after Martin Luther King's assassination sparked new interest at both the White House and the mayor's office in encouraging low-income health programs, and the federal Office of Economic Opportunity funded a clinic in the predominantly black Cardozo Heights area. This clinic, not aimed at GHA members but launched with administrative help from GHA, built a solid enrollment of 14,000.[7]

In the early 1970s, GHA entered into another social experiment to provide health care for 1,000 Medicaid beneficiaries (all of whom were poor and a majority of whom were black). The creation of the Medicaid program in 1965 had reflected congressional desire to assure welfare recipients and the medically indigent of access to medical care. Administered on the local level and financed jointly by federal and state governments, which in D.C. were the same, the program provided a new market for medical care providers. Care that might previously have ended in the ledger books as "bad debt or charity" could now be reimbursed in a timely manner by the government. GHA took advantage of this opportunity and gave a selected group of Medicaid clients the benefits of prepaid group health, ending, it was hoped, the dependence of the poor on acute care provided in the emergency rooms of local hospitals. When, after three years, the D.C. government found that other providers offered cheaper care, the experiment ended.[8] By that time, GHA had become caught up in its own economic problems, and the Board turned its attention to internal concerns.

For most of its history, GHA's politics centered on those internal concerns, indicating a separation between GHA's political discourse and the ideological debates of conventional politics. The labels liberal or conservative meant little in a GHA election. Nearly everyone was a liberal. Instead, the politics tested the members' commitment to the principles of pure cooperation. The two most controversial issues that GHA confronted both concerned the meaning of cooperation in a health care setting. One involved the rights of the transit workers, a third party brought into the cooperative because of the need to attract large groups of new members. The other issue centered on the right of the doctors to form their own profit-making corporation and, in effect, to secede from the organization.

Both were difficult issues for the members to resolve. In the first case, a democratic impulse triumphed over fear of external influences, and members granted full rights to the transit workers; in the second case, the desire to retain direct control over the quality of medical care outweighed the desire of the doctors for greater autonomy, and members refused the doctors permission to form their own organization.

The results of the two battles meant that GHA stopped being a small cooperative after the transit workers were admitted, yet it never imitated the Health Insurance Plan of Greater New York or Kaiser Permanente in its relationship with the doctors.

In a book about health maintenance organizations, Lawrence Brown contrasts GHA with these two other early HMOs, arguing that the structures and ideologies of both GHA and HIP have hampered them from successfully meeting the challenges of the rapidly changing health care market of the 1980s. Kaiser's structure, in contrast, has enabled it to expand from its original west coast base to form or acquire plans across the country, making it by far the largest HMO in the country, with 4 million members.[9]

HIP grew quickly in the beginning, achieving 200,000 members within its first two years and 500,000 at the end of ten years. Since it simply contracted with existing group practices to provide services, HIP required less capital to finance growth than did GHA. In Brown's view, HIP's problems arose chiefly from the diversity of the physician groups with which it contracted. Some HIP members complained, for example, that they were treated like second-class citizens by doctors who favored their fee-for-service patients.[10] HIP's decentralized structure gave the plan little control over individual physicians and groups, who often found it easier to withdraw from the plan than to improve their treatment of HIP patients. In the 1960s, efforts to increase the percentage of physicians who worked entirely for HIP and build "staff model" centers and hospitals met with only limited success; physicians were reluctant to work full time for HIP or to move to HIP-owned centers. Membership stagnated at 750,000 in the 1970s and 1980s, and costs rose.[11]

Kaiser, by contrast, grew rapidly and continued its growth into the 1980s. Brown's thesis is that Kaiser succeeded because of the durability of its basic structure and its willingness to adapt the structure to meet local needs.[12]

Brown concludes that a successful HMO must "design balanced organizational arrangements for physicians," in which they are neither too subordinate nor too autonomous, and must have a board that does not attempt to interfere in decisions that properly belong to management.[13] He recognizes, however, that Kaiser, HIP, and GHA each remains essentially trapped by the origins that determined its basic structure.[14] The Kaiser plan, the product of a paternalistic, wealthy industrial employer, was created from the top down. Although the HOLC officials who started GHA took a similarly paternalistic approach, an agency of the federal government could not run a health plan, as could a private employer. They, therefore, turned GHA over to its members, starting the organization on its road as a member-owned cooperative.

Kaiser differs from HIP and GHA in the use it makes of its board of directors; it makes no pretense of being "democratic." Henry Kaiser, who noted, "You don't ask your corner grocer to share his ownership with people who buy at the store," originally put only Kaiser Industries representatives on the board of his health plan. Although the board now contains some consumer representatives, most of the unions that use Kaiser have no official representation.[15] Nothing could be further from the cooperative approach of GHA's leaders throughout its history.

Kaiser and GHA also differed in the nature of their membership, a factor that helped to determine their respective organizational characters and structures. From the beginning, GHA served a middle-class clientele, made up in its first two decades of well-educated civil servants. These articulate, politically aware people regarded GHA as a community activity in which they expected to join not passively as patients but actively as consumers. However passionately they believed in prepaid group health, they did not regard their organization as one that could easily be transferred to other communities. The ideology could be exported, but not the cooperative itself, which was tailored to federal employees and to Washington, D.C.

Until the late 1950s, most GHA members paid their own premiums out of pocket, strengthening their sense of commitment. Since the members owned GHA, they felt both the right and the obligation to participate directly in GHA's management.

Formed by an industrial corporation to serve its own employees, Kaiser expanded by enrolling union members. The workers' share of their premiums, for which they received comprehensive care, generally amounted to less than 4 percent of their income. Kaiser's blue-collar enrollees, therefore, tended to be grateful for, rather than critical of, what they received from their health plan, and they had neither the inclination nor the incentive to demand a voice in its management. Management, interested in making money, felt free to expand the plan from coast to coast, hampered only by the availability of local facilities and by the need to find suitable markets. Unlike GHA's cooperative, Kaiser's model was for export.

For both organizations, 1959 marked a time of change. The transit workers' union brought GHA its first large influx of blue-collar members, and the Federal Employees Health Benefits Program introduced white-collar federal workers to the Kaiser plan. By that time, however, each plan had developed its characteristic structure and culture, which continued to determine its development into the 1980s.[16] When HMOs became popular, Kaiser was in a better position than GHA to take advantage of the situation and increase membership. The more that people joined HMOs for pragmatic rather than for ideological reasons, the better things turned out for Kaiser, even within the Washington, D.C., market itself (where, in the Baltimore-Washington area, Kaiser acquired the largest market share by 1987).

GHA, thus, remained a consumer cooperative that tested the ability of a group of educated, sophisticated lay people to exercise authority over professional prerogatives and practices. The doctors, not surprisingly, took steps to protect themselves by following the logic of their employee status and forming a trade union. This union behaved like any other in seeking better working conditions and greater control over the workplace. Some scholars of health care have expressed concern that physicians who work as salaried employees of corporations may become "proletarianized," losing control over both their salaries and their working conditions.[17] Although the situation might be different at a large for-profit corporation, the doctors remain a powerful force within GHA.

The physicians may have protected their interests, but the politics of sacrifice always lay close to the surface at GHA. In general, HMOs have been praised more for their efficiency than for their basic comforts. During GHA's early years, patients put up with the irritations of long waits and other inconveniences because they wanted to establish a new way of providing and financing care. A homogeneous group of consumers, they were also pioneers, prepared to temper their demands in times of emergency, such as the Second World War. Even when the membership became more heterogeneous, the members still knew how to cooperate when the occasion demanded it—for example, during the financial crises of the seventies. In that period, the members accepted less contact with their doctors, and the doctors sacrificed income. Although the fervor of the early pioneers may have been diluted by expanded enrollment, the members still believed they were preserving an important form of medical care and a valuable institution in the Washington area.

Should another crisis require sustained sacrifice, the responses of the members and the staff may be different. Members will no longer accept precipitous premium increases, for competing HMOs offer alternative sources of prepaid, group practice care. Doctors, too, cannot be expected to sacrifice if other providers are willing to pay them more for the same services. A repetition of events in the early forties and middle seventies appears unlikely.

Without demeaning either product, one might make the illustrative analogy that the demand for GHA's care resembles the market for kosher meat. The truly religious will pay a substantial premium for it, but others, who simply prefer its taste or happen to live next door to the market, will not tolerate much of a price rise before they change their habits. A consumer core of activist members, such as the 10 percent of the membership that votes in the elections, will stick with GHA for a long time. They are the truly religious. Others, for whom changing health plans is a simple matter of a phone call to a personnel office, may be tempted to leave.

As this analogy suggests, there is something esoteric about GHA. Fifty years after its founding, GHA remains more than a health maintenance organization. Typical of its highly competitive yet highly regulated industry, GHA is also distinctive. For all that it functions in a market that demands conformity to the principles of health insurance, Group Health continues to be a social institution with its own traditions and institutional concerns. GHA maintains a pattern of active member involvement, for example, with committees working on such matters as finances and claims.

Historically, the trustee elections provide the best example of consumer involvement. Each year, an orderly process for electing trustees unfolds, with a nominations committee putting forward a list of candidates (supplemented by any members who qualified for the ballot by petition) and the members selecting the trustees from that list. The nominations committee always takes its work seriously, basing its decisions on such selection criteria as interest in GHA's basic goal, "the continued availability of high quality medical care at the lowest cost to the membership," and "the disposition to work together and to cooperate."[18] (Indeed, the elections still matter a great deal to the future of GHA. No wonder a recent issue of the *GHA News* featured a bold headline on its cover: "Your Voice Counts.")[19]

In 1977, to cite another example of how GHA operates, the members of the Annandale, Virginia, center were dissatisfied with their clinic's condition. Despite its status as a pioneering GHA suburban outpost, members there believed that management was ignoring the need for improvements in favor of aiding the newer centers in Maryland. The Annandale Member Council called a meeting in March 1977 to solicit ideas on how to proceed. Sixty members attended. They expressed a clear preference for building a new center and began to obtain estimates. Discovering that the costs were prohibitive, they then investigated renovating the old center and asked the trustees to authorize the renovations. The trustees agreed. When the chairman of the local building committee was asked whether the GHA staff had tried to influence the members' decisions, he replied, "No. I would have expected some pressure. And I was surprised when there wasn't any."[20]

Not everything works in this textbook manner; resources are limited, no matter who controls them. Yet GHA encourages far more communication with its members than most other health plans. One trustee founded and chairs an active committee that tracks complaints and tries to resolve problems. Like all GHA committees, it is run by members for other members, and it takes its mission very seriously.

In an innovative yet characteristic approach, GHA also maintains a special assistance fund, created in 1982, that provides short-term aid to GHA members for health-related services. Financed partly from a small percentage of dues payments and partly from contributions, the fund gives members in financial need help with medically related items that are not covered by GHA's regular benefits. Prosthetic devices, for example, are a benefit, but not such "durable equipment" as wheelchairs. Since its inception, the fund has provided aid ranging from a heart transplant (at the time, considered an experimental procedure by GHA) to wheelchairs, back braces, and eyeglasses. In 1984, the fund paid for oxygen for a six-month-old baby suffering from a severe respiratory disorder and helped an eighty-four-year-old member arrange transportation to a dialysis center.[21]

In these ways, GHA remains a cooperative in which members help other members, one that combines social objectives with the more mundane goal of providing medical care. Whether the market will continue to make room for such an enterprise, even one as venerable as GHA, remains an open question in 1987, just as it was in 1937. For the fact remains that GHA has been better at maintaining its principles than its market share; the principles themselves were designed for a world in which consumers, rather than third parties, dealt directly with medical care financing. The issues in the health care policy debate no longer center on ideology, gaining acceptance of prepaid group practice, so much as on controlling costs in an increasingly competitive marketplace. Modern pressures have also made the various components of the GHA community less cooperative. Today, medical staff, the member Board of Trustees, and management often have a fractious relationship. Many observers and participants are convinced that the 1986 doctors' strike was unnecessary, the result of poor communications, miscalculations, and misperceptions on both sides. Some physicians thought that Dr. Rosenberg, the executive director, wanted to "break the union." Rosenberg viewed the doctors as eager to punish management. Many physicians, caring for exceptionally high numbers of patients, felt insulted at the implication that they were not doing enough. These disagreements cast a pall over the organization, just as it reached its fiftieth anniversary.

Few, however, doubted GHA's accomplishments. In 1937, a small group of federal employees succeeded in creating an organization that continued to survive more than fifty years later. They withstood a massive campaign on the part of the local medical establishment to put them out of business. When a slowdown in growth threatened to disrupt GHA's progress in the postwar period, the organization forged a strategic alliance with a labor union and helped to establish the Washington area's first labor health center. GHA also weathered major disputes within its own community that might have destroyed the organization. Yet GHA's democratic structure proved capable of resolving each of the disagreements.

Despite economic uncertainty about the future, members could point to GHA's first half-century as one of fatiguing battles that were not without their moments of exhilaration and, even, of triumph. Whether future clashes would yield similar triumphs was, however, far from clear.

APPENDIX

Group Health Association, Number of Participants by Year, 1937–1985

Year	No. of Participants	Year	No. of Participants
1937	900*	1961	48,000
1938	6,100	1962	50,000
1939	5,500	1963	53,000
1940	5,600	1964	54,000
1941	6,600	1965	56,000
1942	7,800	1966	59,000
1943	8,300	1967	68,000
1944	9,200	1968	70,000
1945	8,700	1969	71,000
1946	9,100	1970	75,000
1947	12,000	1971	77,000
1948	15,500	1972	85,000
1949	17,000	1973	87,000
1950	18,000	1974	98,000
1951	19,000	1975	100,000
1952	19,000	1976	100,000
1953	19,000	1977	100,000
1954	20,000	1978	105,000
1955	20,000	1979	110,000
1956	21,000	1980	111,000
1957	22,000	1981	111,000
1958	23,000	1982	112,000
1959	33,000	1983	115,000
1960	46,000	1984	131,000
		1985	144,000

*Subscribers only.

178

Group Health Association, Medical Centers, 1937–1987

Center Name and Location	Dates
1328 I Street, NW, Washington, D.C.	1937–1952
1422 K Street, NW, Washington, D.C.	1939–1946
2529 Pennsylvania Ave., NW, Washington, D.C.	1946–1951
1025 Vermont Avenue, NW, Washington, D.C.	1951–1962
10620 Georgia Avenue, Silver Spring, Md.	1956–1959
6854 New Hampshire Avenue, Takoma Park, Md.	1959–1977
2121 Pennsylvania Avenue, NW, Washington, D.C.	1962–
7601 Little River Turnpike, Annandale, Va.	1965–
North Central Center, Irving Street, NW, Washington, D.C.	1970–1975
6111 Executive Boulevard, Rockville, Md.	1974–
Prince George Medical Center, 6525 Belcrest Road Hyattsville, Md.	1977–
Marlow Heights Medical Center, 5100 Auth Way Suitland, Md.	1979–
Fair Oaks Medical Center, 12011 Lee-Jackson Memorial Highway, Fairfax, Va.	1983–
Tysons Medical Center, 1577 Spring Hill Road, Vienna, Va.	1983–
Skyline Medical Center, 5109 Leesburg Pike, Baileys Crossroads, Va.	1986–
Silver Spring Medical Center, 8401 Colesville Road, Silver Spring, Md.	1987–

Group Health Association, Hospital Days per 1,000 Members, 1940–1978

Year	Days/1,000 Members	Year	Days/1,000 Members
1940	847	1961	667
1941	800	1962	598
1942	745	1963	649
1943–46	N.A.	1964	584
1947	590	1965	599
1948	549	1966	576
1949	556	1967	555
1950	568	1968	534
1951	537	1969	595
1952	488	1970	583
1953	436	1971	554
1954	506	1972	436
1955	503	1973	416
1956	546	1974	470
1957	523	1975	400
1958	499	1976	418
1959	N.A.	1977	418
1960	541	1978	458

Source: Calculated from information provided in GHA annual reports. Information after 1978 is not comparable because it does not include GHA members who are Medicare recipients.

GHA Presidents

Years	Name
1937	W. F. Penniman*
1938–1939	W. C. Kirkpatrick
1939–1942	Cameron G. Garman
1942–1944	Edith Rockwood
1944–1945	Robert H. Shields
1945	Carl C. Farrington
1945–1947	Harry Becker
1947–1951	William E. Warne
1952–1957	Kenneth A. Meiklejohn
1957–1960	Fordyce W. Luikart
1960–1961	Edward J. Overby
1961–1962	Agnes W. Brewster
1962–1963	William G. Colman
1963–1964	Raymond J. Goodman
1964–1966	John J. Gunther
1966–1969	W. Gifford Hoag
1969–1972	L. Lazlo Ecker-Racz
1972–1974	M. Brent Oldham
1974–1975	Ralph B. Bristol Jr.
1975–1976	Jan M. Lodal
1976–1977	M. Brent Oldham
1977–1981	Harold Wool
1981–1983	Abraham A. Raizen
1983–1984	Mark Colburn
1984–1987	Harold Wool

*Temporary chairman.

GHA Executive Directors

Years	Name
1938–1940	Perry R. Taylor*
1940–1942	Morgan Sibbett†
1942–1946	Walter R. Volckhausen†
1946–1953	Melvin Dollar
1953–1958	Dillon S. Myer
1958–1971	Frank C. Watters
1972–1978	Louis J. Segadelli
1978–1983	Edward J. Hinman, M.D.
1983–1986	Robert G. Rosenberg, M.D.
1986–1987	Robert P. Younes, M.D.(acting)

*Administrator.
†Secretary-Treasurer.

GHA Medical Directors

Years	Name
1937	Henry Rolf Brown, M.D.
1938–1939	Raymond E. Selders, M.D.
1939–1944	Mario Scandiffio, M.D.
1944–1961	Henry H. Lichtenberg, M.D.
1961–1971	Thomas M. Arnett, M.D.
1972–1976	Peter Birk, M.D.
1976–1977	Donald E. Mitchell, M.D.
1977–1978	John Newdorp, M.D.
1978–1982	Robert Van Hoek, M.D.
1982–1986	Robert G. Rosenberg, M.D.

NOTES

CHAPTER ONE

1. Paul Starr, *The Social Transformation of American Medicine* (New York: Basic Books, 1982), p. 260.

2. Ibid., pp. 295–298; Odin W. Anderson, *Blue Cross Since 1929; Accountability and the Public Trust* (Cambridge, Mass.: Ballinger Publishing Co., 1975), pp. 18, 31, 36, 39–40; Steven C. Renn, "The Structure and Financing of the Health Care Delivery System of the 1980s," *Health Care and Its Costs,* ed. Carl J. Schramm (New York: W. W. Norton and Co., 1987), p. 27; Group Hospitalization, Inc., *Celebrating Fifty Years of Service to the Nation's Capital* (Washington, D.C.; Group Hospitalization, 1984).

3. Starr, *Transformation,* p. 301.

4. Ibid., pp. 201–202.

5. Ibid., pp. 303–304.

6. Here and throughout the book, "subscriber" refers to the employee who signs up for Group Health; all the other terms—"members," "participants," "enrollees"—refer to those receiving GHA services, both subscribers and their enrolled dependents.

7. Marquis Childs, *Sweden: The Middle Way* (New Haven, Conn.: Yale University Press, 1944), pp. 50, 161.

8. Interviews with Mr. and Mrs. Edward Hollander, November 6, 1986, Mark Colburn, August 6, 1986, Harold Wool, July 8, 1986, Gertrude Ruttenberg, September 11, 1986, Ruth Ruttenberg, October 2, 1986, and Robert Greenberg, August 7, 1986.

9. Starr, *Transformation,* p. 322; Lawrence Brown, *Politics and Health Care Organization: HMOs as Federal Policy* (Washington, D.C.: Brookings Institution, 1983), pp. 103–107, 114–124.

10. Brown, *Politics,* pp. 107, 114; Starr, *Transformation,* pp. 322, 326.

11. Starr, *Transformation*, p. 326. The Group Health Plan of St. Paul, Minnesota, also relied on staff physicians who were employees. See Mary Jo and Walter Uphoff, *Group Health: An American Success Story in Prepaid Health Care* (Minneapolis: Dillon Press, 1980). At the Group Health Cooperative of Puget Sound, physicians were employees of the Cooperative but belonged to a medical group. In return for a "capitation" payment based on the number of members served, this group contracted with the Board of Trustees to provide services to the members. Harold S. Luft, *Health Maintenance Organizations: Dimensions of Performance* (New York: John Wiley and Sons, 1981, p. 13.

12. "Selecting the GHA Medical Staff," *GHA News,* July-August 1985, p. 6.

13. Interviews with Ruth Ruttenberg and Gertrude Ruttenberg.

14. Jack A. Meyer, Sean Sullivan, and Nancy S. Bagby, *Health Care Today: Issues, Trends, and Developments in Cost Management* (Washington, D.C.: National Chamber Foundation, 1986), p. 21; Brown, *Politics,* pp. 33–44; Renn, "Structure," pp. 36–37; see also Jon Gabel and Dan Ermann, "Preferred Provider Organizations: Performance, Problems, and Promise," *Health Affairs* 4, No. 1 (Spring 1985): 24–40.

15. See Harold S. Luft, "Health Maintenance Organizations and the Rationing of Medical Care," *Milbank Memorial Fund Quarterly* 60 (1982): 268–306, and Luft, *Health Maintenance Organizations, p. 386.

CHAPTER TWO

1. For a succinct introduction to Filene and his relationship to progressive reform, see Edward D. Berkowitz and Kim McQuaid, *Creating the Welfare State: The Political Economy of Twentieth-Century Reform* (New York: Praeger, 1980), pp. 11–16.

2. "Memorandum of the Relation of the Twentieth Century Fund and the Committee on the Costs of Medical Care," n.d., Twentieth Century Fund Papers, Twentieth Century Fund, New York (hereafter cited as Fund Papers).

3. Edward A. Filene to Professor H. H. Moore, November 19, 1926 and Edward Filene to Roscoe Pound, June 8, 1927, Fund Papers.

4. Paul Starr, *The Social Transformation of American Medicine* (New York: Basic Books, 1982), pp. 261–262; Daniel S. Hirshfield, *The Lost Reform: The Campaign for Compulsory Health Insurance in the United States from 1932 to 1943* (Cambridge, Mass.: Harvard University Press, 1970).

5. Daniel M. Fox, *Health Policies, Health Politics: The British and American Experience, 1911–1965* (Princeton, N.J.: Princeton University Press, 1986), pp. 70–93. On historical changes in hospital care, see Morris J. Vogel, *The Invention of the Modern Hospital, Boston, 1870–1930* (Chicago: University of Chicago Press, 1980); Rosemary Stevens, " 'A Poor Sort of Memory': Voluntary Hospitals and Government Before the Depression," *Milbank Memorial Fund Quarterly* 60 (1982): 551–584; David Rosner, *A Once Charitable Enterprise: Hospitals and Health Care in Brooklyn and New York, 1885–1915* (New York: Cambridge University Press, 1982): Charles E. Rosenberg, "Inward Vision and Outward Glance: The Shaping of the American Hospital, 1880–1914," *Bulletin of the History of Medicine* 53 (1979): 346–391.

6. Quoted in Odin W. Anderson, *The Uneasy Equilibrium: Private and Public Financing of Health Services in the United States, 1878–1965* (New Haven, Conn.: Yale College and University Press, 1968), p. 94.

7. Starr, *Transformation*, p. 265.

8. Hirshfield, *Lost Reform*, pp. 32–33.

9. For more on Falk and Sydenstricker see Edward Berkowitz, *Rehabilitation: America's Response to Disability* (New York: Arno Press, 1980).

10. W. Andrew Achenbaum, *Social Security: Visions and Revisions* (New York: Cambridge University Press, 1986), p. 164.

11. Twentieth Century Fund, *Director's Report, 1936–37* (New York: The Fund, 1937), p. 16.

12. Ibid., pp. 18–19.

13. Twentieth Century Fund, Minutes of the Executive Committee, April 10, 1936, p. 8, Fund Papers; Irving J. Levy and Samuel Mermin, "Cooperative Medicine and the Law," *National Lawyers Guild Quarterly* 1, No. 3 (June 1938): 197.

14. Twentieth Century Fund, *Annual Report, 1936* (New York: The Fund, 1937), pp. 10–11.

15. Twentieth Century Fund, *Annual Report, 1937* (New York: The Fund, 1938), p. 34.

16. Born in Manchester, New Hampshire, in 1873, Fahey became the publisher of such papers as the *Worcester Post* and the *New York Evening Post*. Fahey's prominence in progressive causes and his ties to Supreme Court Justice Louis Brandeis and Filene made him Franklin D. Roosevelt's choice to head the FHLBB. "John H. Fahey Dies; Ex-Head of HOLC; Chairman of Federal Group from 1933 to 1948, Former New England Publisher," *New York Times,* November 20, 1950, p. 25; James S. Olson, "John H. Fahey," *Historical Dictionary of the New Deal: From Inauguration to Preparation for War* (Westport, Conn., and London: Greenwood Press, 1985).

17. Raymond R. Zimmerman, "More on GHA's Early Days," *GHA News,* October 1972, p. 2.

18. Quoted in Joseph G. Knapp, *The Advance of American Cooperative Enterprise* (Danville, Ill.: Interstate Printers and Publishers, 1973), p. 459.

19. John W. Ballard to All Washington Employees, October 31, 1936, Record Group 195, Records of the Federal Home Loan Bank Board, Washington National Records Center, Suitland, Md. (hereafter RG 195), Box 77; Ballard to All Employees, January 16, 1937, RG 195, Box 21.

20. Federal Home Loan Bank Board, "Minutes of a Meeting, October 1, 1936," Defendants' Exhibit No. 48, Record Group 60, Records of the Antitrust Division, Department of Justice, Washington National Records Center, Suitland Md. (hereafter RG 60) Box 81; Group Health Association, background paper, December 18, 1937, "GHA Part I," RG 60, Box 92.

21. Horace Russell to Members of the Board, R. R. Zimmerman, Charles A. Jones, Preston Delano, and Nugent Fallon, December 28, 1936, RG 195, Box 3.

22. The following paragraphs, including all quotations, are taken from "A Plan for a Cooperative Medical Service on a Periodic Payment Basis for Federal Employees and Their Families in Washington," Government Exhibit No. 104, RG 60, Box 85.

23. Draft by R. R. Zimmerman of memorandum from Nugent Fallon to All Employees of Federal Savings and Loan Insurance Corp., January

27, 1937, RG 195, Box 21; Group Health Association, certificate, February 24, 1937, Office of Recorder of Deeds, Washington, D.C. Although the certificate did not limit GHA's membership to federal workers in the Washington, D.C., area, the fact that clinic services were located only there made nonresidents unlikely to join.

24. Memorandum from R. R. Zimmerman to Mr. Stevenson, Mr. Catlett, Dr. Hoagland, and Mr. Russell, March 1, 1937, Defendants' Exhibit No. 50, pp. 5350–5352, 5356–5364, RG 60, Box 81.

25. Draft brochure describing Group Health Association, Defendants' Exhibit No. 50, RG 60, Box 81.

26. Evans Clark to Edward A. Filene, March 10, 1937, Fund Papers.

27. Group Health Association and Home Owners' Loan Corporation, contract, March 22, 1937, Defendants' Exhibit No. 10, "GHA, Part I, Formation and Background of GHA", RG 60, Box 92; H. R. Townsend to W. F. Penniman, March 22, 1937, Defendants' Exhibit No. 53, RG 60, Box 81.

28. Group Health Association, Membership Meeting Minutes, March 22, 1937, April 27, 1937, and Board of Trustee Minutes, April 27, 1937, Group Health Association headquarters, Washington, D.C.

29. Group Health Association, Board of Trustee Minutes, May 5, 1937, May 25, 1937; Evans Clark to Edward A. Filene, June 18, 1937, Fund Papers; Henry Rolf Brown, "Why I Quit the GHA," *Medical Economics*, September 1939, p. 39.

30. M. W. Ireland to Dr. Leland, March 27, 1937, Government Exhibit No. 295a, RG 60, Box 81; Group Health Association, Board of Trustee Minutes, June 7, 1937.

31. Medical Society of the District of Columbia, Minutes of a Special Meeting of the Executive Committee, June 24, 1937, Government Exhibit No. 106, RG 60, Box 85; much of the material in the following paragraphs, including quotations, is taken from a verbatim transcript of a meeting between the GHA Board of Trustees and representatives of the Medical Society of the District of Columbia, July 26, 1937, Government Exhibit No. 10, RG 60, Box 85.

32. C. B. Conklin to W. C. Woodward, September 13, 1937, Government Exhibit No. 84, RG 60, Box 85; John F. Hayes to William C. Woodward, July 31, 1937, Government Exhibit No. 186, RG 60, Box 85.

33. Group Health Association, Board of Trustee Minutes, July 13, 1937, August 2, 1937, September 7, 1937; John F. Hayes to William C. Woodward, August 24, 1937, Government Exhibit No. 182, RG 60, Box 85.

34. Henry Rolf Brown to William F. Penniman, October 1, 1937, and attachment, Government Exhibit No. 611, RG 60, Box 85.

35. Hayes to Woodward, August 24, 1937.

36. Bureau of Legal Medicine and Legislation, "Group Health Association, Incorporated: Health Insurance and Corporate Practice of Medicine Under Federal Auspices," *Journal of the American Medical Association* 109, No. 14 (October 2, 1937): 41B–45B.

37. Bureau of Medical Economics, "County Medical Societies and Group Hospitalization," *Journal of the American Medical Association* 109, No. 18 (October 30, 1937): 65B.

38. Group Health Association, Board of Trustee Minutes, October 4, 1937.

39. "Harvard Doctor Hails Inaugural of Group Health," *Washington Post,* October 31, 1937, p. 17; "Group Health Clinic to Open," *Washington Evening Star,* October 28, 1938, p. B1.

40. "Clinic Equipped for Health Group," *Washington Evening Star,* October 29, 1937, p. A3; "Co-operation for Health" (editorial), *Washington Post,* November 1, 1937, p. 6.

41. "Clinic Is Opened by Group Health," *Washington Evening Star,* November 1, 1937, p. B1; "Forty Are Treated as HOLC Staff Starts Clinic," *Washington Post,* November 2, 1937, p. 3. By this time, more than eight hundred HOLC employees had joined GHA. The bylaws required that anyone wishing to become a member submit an application and undergo a medical examination. GHA reserved the right to reject potential members, or to impose limits on the services to be provided, in cases of poor physical condition.

42. "Co-operation for Health," *Washington Post*, November 1, 1937; "HOLC Staff Gets Group Health Aid; Possible Extension of Medical Service to Other Agencies Worries Capital Doctors," *New York Times,* November 7, 1937, p. 6; Mary G. Lynch (secretary to Thomas E. Neill) to William F. Penniman, October 25, 1937, Government Exhibit No. 13, RG 60, Box 85; C. B. Conklin to Holman Taylor, October 30, 1937, Government Exhibit No. 72, RG 60, Box 85.

43. The following information, including all quotations, is taken from notes of a meeting between representatives of the D.C. Medical Society and the AMA in "Conference re Group Health Association, Inc., November 6, 1937," Government Exhibit No. 117, RG 60, Box 85.

44. Olin West to Walter B. Wise, November 10, 1937, Government Exhibit No. 120, RG 60, Box 85.

45. "Report of the Hospital Committee, December 1, 1937," Government Exhibit No. 323, RG 60, Box 81; "Report of Hospital Committee Submitted to the Executive Committee of the Medical Society of the District of Columbia on March 28, 1938," Government Exhibit No. 324, RG 60, Box 81.

46. "Unions Attack Medical Society for Stand on HOLC Health Plan," *Washington Daily News,* November 12, 1937, pp. 1, 26.

47. Louise Sissman, "Group Health Association, Inc. (a Consumer Experiment in the Distribution of Medical Care)," unpublished paper, 1940, pp. 50–53, GHA Headquarters.

48. "Seal Ruling on HOLC Is Awaited; Plan Open to All in U.S. Employ," *Washington Daily News,* December 30, 1937, p. 12.

49. Allan E. Lee to C. B. Conklin, October 30, 1937, Government Exhibit No. 41; Allan E. Lee to Thomas E. Neill, November 11, 1937, Government Exhibit No. 43; R. Arthur Hooe to Executive Committee, Medical Society of the District of Columbia, December 10, 1937, Government Exhibit No. 47; all in RG 60, Box 85.

50. Henry P. Blair to William F. Penniman, November 11, 1937, Government Exhibit No. 366 and Gist Blair to William F. Penniman, November 15, 1937, Government Exhibit No. 370, both in RG 60, Box 81.

51. Sibley Memorial Hospital to J. S. Mann, November 27, 1937, Government Exhibit No. 583, RG 60, Box 85.

52. Walter A. Coole to P. M. Ashburn, December 2, 1937, Government Exhibit No. 539 and Walter A. Coole to Olin West, May 1, 1938, Government Exhibit No. 127, both in RG 60, Box 85.

53. Washington Academy of Surgery, Minutes of Regular Meeting at the Cosmos Club, Friday, December 10, 1937, Government Exhibit No. 444A, RG 60, Box 85; J. C. Alexander to E. M. Rogers, April 28, 1938, Government Exhibit No. 668, RG 60, Box 81.

54. Gist Blair to William F. Penniman, December 30, 1937, Defendants'

Exhibit No. 373, RG 60, Box 81; P. M. Ashburn to Secretary, Houston Medical Society, November 25, 1937, Government Exhibit No. 538, RG 60, Box 85.

55. R. Arthur Hooe to Mario Scandiffio, November 10, 1937, Government Exhibit No. 66, RG 60, Box 85; Mario Scandiffio to R. Arthur Hooe, November 19, 1937, Government Exhibit No. 67, RG 60, Box 85; Mario Scandiffio to R. Arthur Hooe, December 3, 1937, Government Exhibit No. 70, RG 60, Box 85; "Legal Fight Seen If Medical Group Ousts GHA Man," *Washington Evening Star*, March 16, 1938, pp. A1, A5.

56. "Medical Society Expels Group Health Doctor," *Washington Post*, March 17, 1938, p. 1.

57. " 'Gift' of HOLC for Group Health Is Ruled Illegal," *Washington Evening Star*, December 17, 1937, p. A1.

58. U.S. Congress, House of Representatives, *Hearings Before the Subcommittee of the Committee on Appropriations of the House of Representatives, 75th Congress, 2d Session, on the Independent Offices Appropriation Bill for 1939* (Washington, D.C.: U.S. Government Printing Office, 1937), pp. 1351, 1357, 1363.

59. Group Health Association, background paper, December 18, 1937, December 21, 1937, "GHA Part 1," RG 60, Box 92.

60. Group Health Association, background paper, December 18, 1937.

61. Ibid.

62. "House Group Hits 'Gift' by HOLC for Group Health; General Counsel Quizzed, Declares Plan Saves Money: Perfect Farce, Says Chairman Woodrum," *Washington Evening Star*, January 6, 1938. p. A1; Henry E. Moore to Horace Russell, January 7, 1938, RG 195, Box 31.

63. Mr. [Byron] Scott of California, *Congressional Record*, 75th Congress, 3rd Session, Vol. 83, March 22, 1938, p. 3882.

64. J. Ogle Warfield Jr. to W. Warren Sager, February 3, 1938, Government Exhibit No. 313; "Questionnaire," 1938, Government Exhibit No. 295B; Gist Blair to President and Board of Directors, Garfield Memorial Hospital, January 27, 1938, Government Exhibit No. 475; C. A. Aspinwall to Gist Blair, January 29, 1938, Government Exhibit No. 476; Lewis H. Taylor to W. C. Kirkpatrick, June 20, 1938, Government Exhibit No. 421; W. C. Kirkpatrick to Lewis H. Taylor, February 18, 1938, Government Exhibit No. 418; Lewis H. Taylor to W. C. Kirkpatrick, February 5, 1938, Government Exhibit No. 417; Lewis H. Taylor to W. C. Kirkpatrick, Feb-

ruary 21, 1938, Government Exhibit No. 419; R. T. Berry to Lewis H. Taylor, March 30, 1938, Government Exhibit No. 420; all in RG 60, Box 81.

65. Scott of California, March 22, 1938, pp. 3883–3884; Thomas E. Neill to W. C. Kirkpatrick, March 22, 1938, Government Exhibit No. 459, RG 60, Box 81.

66. Extension of Remarks of Hon. H. Jerry Voorhis, March 17, 1938, *Congressional Record,* 75th Congress, 3rd Session, Vol. 83, March 13, 1938, p. 4840; Scott of California, March 22, 1938, p. 3884.

67. "Capper Criticizes Medical Society; Calls on Hospitals for Data: Physicians Offer GHA Their Co-Operation," *Washington Evening Star,* March 27, 1938, p. A1; Mr. [Paul W.] Shafer of Michigan, *Congressional Record,* 75th Congress, 3rd Session, Vol. 83, April 26, 1938, pp. 7652–7653.

68. Sissman, "Group Health," pp. 62, 65–66.

69. Interview with (anonymous) GHA member, September 1986.

70. Group Health Association, Board of Trustee Minutes, December 6, 1937, December 20, 19937; "Health Clinic Opens Drive for Members; 1,500 in Other Government Departments Invited by HOLC," *Washington Post,* December 22, 1937, p. 17.

71. Group Health Association, Board of Trustee Minutes, January 3, 1938, March 7, 1938.

72. Sissman, "Group Health," pp. 62, 65–66; Group Health Association, Board of Trustee Minutes, June 20, 1938, October 17, 1938; "Memberships as of October 15, 1938," attachment to Board of Trustee Minutes, October 17, 1938.

73. Sissman, "Group Health," p. 74.

74. Ibid., pp. 65–66.

75. Group Health Association, Board of Trustee Minutes, February 19, 1938, March 21, 1938, April 18, 1938; Sissman, "Group Health," p. 33; *GHA News Letter,* June 1938.

76. Group Health Association, Board of Trustee Minutes, February 7, 1938; January 17, 1939.

77. "Resolution," attachment to Group Health Association, Board of Trustee Minutes, March 6, 1939.

78. Seeking outside expertise, the Board called in Dr. Hugh Cabot of the Mayo Clinic (Dr. Richard Cabot's cousin) to consider candidates for a new medical director. Group Health Association, Board of Trustee Min-

utes, April 18, 1938; "Brief Summary of Discussion Between Dr. Hugh Cabot of the Mayo Clinic and Members of the Board of Trustees of Group Health Association, Inc. at a Meeting Held on November 30, 1938," attachment to Board of Trustee Minutes, Nobember 30, 1938.

79. Once Dr. Selders resigned, GHA no longer had a staff surgeon and contracted with outside specialists to provide surgical care for GHA members. Not until the mid-1970s did GHA obtain its own staff of full-time surgeons. Group Health Association, Board of Trustee Minutes, December 21, 1938 (special executive session), December 28, 1938, January 11, 1939, January 23, 1939; "Dr. Selders Resigns as Medical Director of Group Health: Decision Actuated by Desire to Practice Surgery, He Says," *Washington Evening Star,* January 24, 1939, p. A1.

80. M. A. McCall, Laurence Ring, W. C. Kirpatrick, R. F. Hendrickson, "Memorandum to the Board of Trustees," March 3, 1939, attachment to Board of Trustee Minutes, March 6, 1939.

81. As its first staff administrator, the Board chose Perry R. Taylor, a trustee who was an Annapolis graduate with considerable managerial experience. Taylor was brought to Washington in 1933 by Morris Cooke of Philadelphia, an expert on public works and a friend of Franklin D. Roosevelt, to serve as his deputy first at the Public Works Administration and then at the REA, until Raymond Zimmerman approached him about working for GHA. Taylor's GHA salary was paid from a donation by the Good Will Fund, an offshoot of Edward Filene's contributions to medical care, during the two-year period from 1938 to 1940. After Taylor's departure in 1940, GHA was run by a paid secretary-treasurer until the Board hired the first executive director in 1946. "Taylor Made GHA Director; Site for Hospital Considered: Dr. Raymond Selders Is Named Association's Medical Chief," *Washington Evening Star,* July 12, 1938, p. A1; "GHA Administrator to Serve Another One-Year Term," *Washington Evening Star,* July 11, 1939, p. B5; interview with Perry R. Taylor, September 24, 1986; Group Health Association, Board of Trustee Minutes, June 20, 1938, July 5, 1938, July 12, 1938; Group Health Association, Minutes of Advisory Council Meeting, July 27, 1938, "Report on GHA Financing Plan," both attachments to Board of Trustee Minutes, August 1, 1938.

82. "Subscription Blank (Draft)," attachment to Group Health Association, Board of Trustee Minutes, August 1, 1938; Group Health Associa-

tion, Board of Trustee Minutes, August 16, 1938, and attached F. O. Billings to O. E. Loomis, August 5, 1938.

83. "Memorandum to Dr. Garman, May 3, 1939," attachment to Group Health Association, Board of Trustee Minutes, May 4, 1939; Board of Trustee Minutes, March 6, 1939, March 16, 1939, April 5, 1939; "Four Doctors Are Added to GHA Staff: Increased Membership Spurs Expansion, New Hospital," *Washington Post,* July 14, 1938, p. 17.

84. "GHA Hospital Permit Is Denied in Montgomery," *Washington Evening Star,* July 26, 1938, p. A1; "Arlington OK's GHA Hospital; Home of Dr. W. N. Sutton Will Be Used by Local Group," *Washington Evening Star,* August 13, 1938, p. A1; Group Health Association, Board of Trustee Minutes, August 15, 1938, November 7, 1938, April 5, 1939; "Civil Workers Urge Chest Aid Group Health; Association Raises Dues as CIO Union Tries to Open Hospitals," *Washington Post,* August 16, 1938, p. 1; "Two More Doctors of GHA Admitted to Garfield Staff: Courtesy Cards Sent; Association Heads Are Gratified," *Washington Evening Star,* January 20, 1939, p. A2.

85. Group Health Association, Board of Trustee Minutes, May 9, 1939, July 17, 1939; *GHA News,* June 14, 1939, p. 1; *GHA News,* July 31, 1939, p. 1; Sissman, "Group Health," p. 22.

86. "A National Health Program and Some Proposals Toward Its Design: A Report from the Technical Committee on Medical Care to the Chairman of the Interdepartmental Committee to Coordinate Health and Welfare Activities," February 1938, Franklin D. Roosevelt Library, Hyde Park, N.Y. This report was later published in slightly altered form as Technical Committee on Medical Care, Interdepartmental Committee to Coordinate Health and Welfare Activities, *The Need for a National Health Program* (Washington, D.C.: U.S. Government Printing Office, 1938).

87. Quoted in Berkowitz, *Rehabilitation,* p. 37.

88. "Medicine on Trial" (editorial), *New York Times,* December 22, 1938, p. 20; interviews with Maurine Mulliner, July 2, 1986, and Ida Merriam, February 26, 1987.

89. Alden Whitman, "Thurman Arnold, Trust Buster, Dead: Respect for the Law," *New York Times,* November 8, 1969, p. 33.

90. "Group Practice versus the American Medical Association," *Yale Law Journal* 47, No. 7 (May 1938); 1199; telephone conversation with

Victor H. Kramer (the student who wrote the article), September 12, 1986.

91. "GHA Winner as Court Rules Activity Legal; Corporation Is Not Engaged in Practice of Medicine, Bailey Declares: D.C. Society Keeps Silent Pending Study of Findings," *Washington Evening Star,* July 27, 1938, p. A1; *Group Health Association v. Moore,* 24 Fed. Supp. 455; Department of Justice press release, August 1, 1938, Government Exhibit No. 21, RG 60, Box 85.

92. Department of Justice press release, August 1, 1938, pp. 2–3.

93. F. O. Billings to Allen Hart, July 8, 1938, July 9, 1938; W. C. Kirkpatrick to Allan E. Hart, October 20, 1938; Morgan Sibbett to John W. Lewin, September 21, 1940, October 17, 1940, October 18, 1940, November 5, 1940; Government Exhibit No. 21, RG 60, Box 85.

94. "Medical Society Denies Liability; Counsel Tells Justice Department It is 'Not Within Range of Antitrust Laws,' " *New York Times,* August 14, 1938, p. 15; "AMA States Its Stand," *New York Times,* September 21, 1938, p. 27.

95. "Jury Is Ordered on 'Medical Trust,' " *New York Times,* October 5, 1938, p. 4; "AMA Is Indicted as Trust Blocking Group Medicine," *New York Times,* December 21, 1938, p. 1 (also contains text of federal grand jury indictment, p. 20, and "Fishbein Sees a Hard Fight," p. 21).

96. Quotations appear in *Journal of the American Medical Association* 112, No. 1 (January 7, 1939): 53–54, 57, and 111, No. 6 (August 6, 1938): 539–540.

97. "AMA Wins Victory on Antitrust Suit: Federal Court Throws Out Indictment of Association in Group Health Row," *New York Times,* July 27, 1939, p. 1; "Murphy to Appeal Ruling for AMA," *New York Times,* July 28, 1939, p. 2; "Government Loses Point in Medical Suit; Supreme Court Denies Short Cut," *New York Times,* October 24, 1939, p. 1; "Medicine a 'Trade,' AMA Must Face Antitrust Charge," *New York Times,* March 5, 1940, p. 1; *U.S. v. AMA,* 28 Fed. Supp. 752; *U.S. v. AMA,* 110 Fed Supp 2703.

98. "Doctors Plead Not Guilty in Monopoly Case; Freed Without Bond at Hearing; Trial in Fall Likely," *Washington Evening Star,* June 14, 1940, p. B1.

99. "Medical Antitrust Trial Jury of Ten Men, Two Women Chosen; One Member Colored; Defense Opens with Attack on Indictment," *Wash-*

ington Evening Star, February 5, 1941, pp. A1, A3; "Plot to Crush Group Health Charged as AMA Trial Opens," *Washington Post,* February 6, 1941, pp. 1, 4; "D.C. Hospitals Put Boycott on GHA, Prosecutor Charges; Patients Turned Away in Some Cases, Expelled in One, He Says," *Washington Evening Star,* February 6, 1941, p. A7; "Group Health Denounced as Scheme to Ruin AMA; Its Medical-Economic Theories Endanger Profession's Ideals, Defense Charges," *Washington Post,* February 7, 1941, pp. 1, 6.

101. "Medical Societies Convicted as Trust" and "Issue Went to Supreme Court," *New York Times,* April 5, 1941, p. 19; "The Doctors of America—for Whom Shall They Toil? Medical Trial to Decide a Vital Question," *Washington Times Herald,* April 27, 1941, p. E3; "The Verdict," *Medical Annals of the District of Columbia,* April 1941, pp. 146–148.

102. "AMA Fined $2,500 in Antitrust Case; Federal Court Also Levies $1,500 on District of Columbia Society," *New York Times,* May 30, 1941, p. 10; "Affirm Conviction of Medical Bodies," *New York Times,* June 16, 1942, p. 24; "Pictures Doctors Engaged in Trade: Arnold Tells Supreme Court They Go Into Market Place to 'Bolster Their Income,' " *New York Times,* December 15, 1942, p. 14; "AMA Loses Fight in Supreme Court on Health Plan; Its Conviction Under Antitrust Law in Cooperative Case Unanimously Upheld," *New York Times,* January 19, 1943, p. 1; *AMA v. U.S.,* 130 Fed Supp. 233, 317 U.S. 519 (1943).

103. Arthur G. Peterson, *The Legal History of Group Health Association of Washington, D.C.* (Washington, D.C.: Group Health Association, 1947), pp. 17–22.

CHAPTER THREE

1. Group Health Association, Board of Trustee Minutes, January 30, 1942, Group Health Association headquarters, Washington, D.C.; "Statement of Operations, First Quarter 1942" attachment to Board of Trustee

Minutes, April 1942; Group Health Association, *Annual Reports for 1942, 1943, 1944,* GHA headquarters.

2. The full-time physicians and part-time specialists were supported by a clinical staff that included an optometrist, two pharmacists, a clinic supervisor, an x-ray technician, a laboratory technician, and seven nurses. C. C. Farrington to Friends and Fellow Members of the Group Health Association, October 23, 1945, attachment to Group Health Association, Board of Trustee Minutes, October 23, 1945; Group Health Association, *Annual Report for 1941.*

3. Group Health Association, Board of Trustee Minutes, December 19, 1941, February 2, 1942, April 13, 1942, September 21, 1942; *GHA News,* April 1, 1942, April, 1943. GHA also changed or bent its rules to meet the wartime needs of its members. As early as 1940, the Board made the clinic's services available without charge to war refugee children who were being cared for by GHA members, although they were not offered hospitalization or house calls. Members serving in the armed forces, including women in the WACs and WAVEs, could suspend their memberships for the duration of their military service, while their family members remaining in Washington continued to receive GHA care. Members who moved away could also suspend their memberships, returning after the war without the need to reapply. By the end of 1943, almost eight hundred GHA subscribers had temporarily suspended their memberships. *GHA News,* January 15, 1942; Group Health Association, Board of Trustee Minutes, February 9, 1942; Group Health Association, *Annual Reports for 1942, 1944;* "Membership Changes as of March 1, 1944," attachment to Board of Trustee Minutes, March 1944.

4. Group Health Association, Board of Trustee Minutes, December 19, 1941, July 7, 1942.

5. Ibid., February 9, 1942, April 13, 1942, September 21, 1942; *GHA News,* April 1943.

6. *GHA News,* January 1944, pp. 5, 7.

7. "Procedure for Admission Without Entrance Physical Examination," attachment to Group Health Association, Board of Trustee Minutes, July 7, 1942; "Trustees State New Policies," *GHA News,* July 1942, p. 1.

8. Data compiled from Group Health Association, *Annual Reports for 1941, 1942, 1943, 1944.*

9. Group Health Association, Board of Trustee Minutes, January 18, 1943; "In Retrospect," *GHA News,* October-November 1949, p. 8.

10. Group Health Association, *Annual Report for 1944.*

11. Group Health Association, Board of Trustee Minutes, March 20, 1944; C. C. Farrington to Friends and Fellow Members, October 23, 1945; Group Health Association, *Annual Report for 1944.*

12. "U.S. Medicine in Transition," *Fortune,* December 1944, p. 162.

13. To accomplish this, Group Health needed to alter its articles of incorporation, which restricted coverage to U.S. government employees, and on April 1, 1946, the organization filed the necessary new incorporation papers. See Group Health Association, certificate, April 1, 1946, Office of Recorder of Deeds, Washington, D.C.; Group Health Association, Board of Trustee Minutes, November 6, 1945; Group Health Association, Annual Membership Meeting Minutes, February 20, 1946, GHA headquarters.

14. Harry J. Becker to John Lindeman, January 31, 1946, attachment to Group Health Association, Board of Trustee Minutes, January 31, 1946.

15. Group Health Association, Annual Membership Meeting Minutes, January 16, 1941; Group Health Association, Board of Trustee Minutes, March 14, 1941.

16. Group Health Association, Board of Trustee Minutes, May 12, 1941, May 3, 1943.

17. Ibid., May 3, 1943, June 14, 1943.

18. Ibid., June 21, 1943, September 20, 1943.

19. "Summary of Letters Received in Response to Board Communication to Members re Admission of Negroes to Membership in GHA," attachment to Group Health Association, Board of Trustee Minutes, November 15, 1943.

20. Group Health Association, Board of Trustee Minutes, December 13, 1943, February 28, 1944; "This Is Our Policy: A Statement by the Board of Trustees," *GHA News*, April 1944, p. 1.

21. Becker to Lindeman, January 31, 1946; Harry J. Becker to Dear Member, February 7, 1946, attachment to Group Health Association, Board of Trustee Minutes, February 21, 1946; Board of Trustee Minutes, January 24, 1946; Group Health Association, Annual Membership Meeting Minutes, February 20, 1946.

22. Becker to Lindeman, January 31, 1946; "Group Health Accepts First Private Unit: Insurance Workers Included in Plan to Extend Service," *Washington Evening Star,* March 31, 1946, p. B1.

23. "Message of the President of Group Health to Membership Annual Meeting, February 1947," attachment to Group Health Association, Board of Trustee Minutes, February 1947.

24. Group Health Association, *Annual Report for 1946*; Harold C. Mufson, "A History of Group Health Association, Inc., 1937–1955," Master's dissertation, School of Nursing Education, Catholic University of America, Washington, D.C., June 1955, p. 63.

25. The assessment, which was approved by vote of the membership, collected from $30.40 to $71.20 from each subscriber, depending upon family size, by the time it ended in 1954. *GHA News,* February 1949, p. 4; Group Health Association, Board of Trustee Minutes, October 20, 1949, September 7, 1949, August 23, 1950, September 6, 1950, September 20, 1950, November 19, 1952, August 28, 1954.

26. Group Health Association, *Annual Reports for 1950, 1952.*

27. Executive Director to Board of Trustees, January 9, 1956, attachment to Group Health Association, Board of Trustee Minutes, January 18, 1956; Eunice S. Grier, *People and Government: Changing Needs in the District of Columbia, 1950–1970* (Washington, D.C.: Washington Center for Metropolitan Studies, 1973), pp. 44–45.

28. Group Health Association, Board of Trustee Minutes, November 22, 1965; John J. Sexton to Robert Denzler, March 5, 1963, attachment to Board of Trustee Minutes, June 22, 1964; "Group Health Association's First Branch Medical Center Open for Service on November 19," *GHA News,* November-December 1956, p. 10.

29. A wholly owned subsidiary of GHA was formed in Virginia to lease space and sublet it to the partnership, which was paid according to a fee schedule for services rendered to GHA members. See Robert T. Barton Jr. to Frank C. Watters, November 27, 1964, attachment to Group Health Association, Board of Trustee Minutes, December 1964; Board of Trustee Minutes, October 26, 1959, November 23, 1959, March 28, 1960, February 24, 1964, January 24, 1965, February 16, 1965, September 26, 1966; Leroy S. Bendheim to Frank C. Watters, February 11, 1964, attachment to Board

of Trustee Minutes, February 1964; John J. Sexton to Robert T. Barton Jr., January 19, 1965, attachment to Board of Trustee Minutes, January 24, 1965; "An Estimate of the Situation on the Proposed Northern Virginia Medical Clinic," attachment to Board of Trustee Minutes, March 16, 1965; John J. Gunther to Dear Member, July 20, 1965, attachment to Board of Trustee Minutes, August 1965.

30. Group Health Association, Annual Membership Meeting Minutes, April 28, 1941; "Tentative Proposed Plan for Dental Service for Group Health Association," attachment to Board of Trustee Minutes, October 13, 1941.

31. Vernon E. West to Commissioners, February 18, 1947, attachment to Group Health Association, Board of Trustee Minutes, February 1947; GHA News, March 1947, p. 6; GHA News, November 1947, p. 1; "Proposal for a Group Health Dental Program," attachment to Board of Trustee Minutes, December 1947; "GHA Members Balk at Rise in Dues, Call for Alternative Plan," Washington Evening Star, February 27, 1948, p. B1.

32. Group Health Association, Board of Trustee Minutes, April 7, 1948; "Report to the Board of Trustees from the Dental Committee," attachment to Board of Trustee Minutes, July 7, 1948; GHA News, June, 1948, p. 2.

33. "Dental Care Plan Set Up in Capital," New York Times, January 1, 1949, p. 11.

34. "GHA's Dental Program," GHA News, October-November 1949, p. 10; Group Health Association, Annual Reports for 1949–1957; "Proposed Prepayment Plan for Dental Maintenance Care, April 15, 1956," attachment to Group Health Association, Board of Trustee Minutes, April 1956; Board of Trustee Minutes, June 20, 1956.

35. Group Health Association, Annual Reports for 1949, 1951, 1957; GHA News, December 1947, March 1948, February 1949; Edward J. Overby to Dear Member, March 11, 1960, attachment to Group Health Association, Board of Trustee Minutes, March 1960.

36. Interviews with Arthur B. Rosenbaum, M.D., August 26, 1986, and Dorothy Gill, M.D., August 27, 1986.

37. Group Health Association, Annual Reports for 1952, 1960, 1968, 1973.

38. "On the Advisability of Purchasing a Building Site at This Time,"

attachment to Group Health Association, Board of Trustee Minutes, April 1, 1946; "Capital Drive Passes 10 Percent Mark," *GHA News,* October 1945, p. 1.

39. Walter R. Volckhausen to Dear Member, attachment to Group Health Association, Board of Trustee Minutes, October 1943.

40. Group Health Association, *Annual Report for 1942.*

41. "Introduction to the 1950 Budget of Group Health Association," attachment to Group Health Association, Board of Trustee Minutes, January 1950.

42. Ibid.

43. Group Health Association, Board of Trustee Minutes, July 13, 1944, March 11, 1947, April 21, 1948, December 21, 1949, April 4, 1951, June 30, 1951, May 15, 1957.

44. Group Health Association, Advisory Council Minutes, April 10, 1941, attachment to Board of Trustee Minutes, April 7, 1941; Group Health Association, *Annual Reports for 1940–1958 GHA News,* April 15, 1941, p. 1.

45. Group Health Association, Board of Trustee Minutes, July 8, 1947, April 21, 1948; *GHA News,* June-July 1947, pp. 1, 4; "Work Papers, 1948 Budget," attachment to Board of Trustee Minutes, January 20, 1948; Group Health Association, *Annual Report for 1947; GHA News,* March 1948, p. 1; Group Health Association, Annual Membership Meeting Minutes, February 26, 1948; "GHA Members Balk at Rise in Dues," p. B1; Group Health Association, Annual Membership Meeting Minutes, March 30, 1948; "A Message to the Membership Regarding the Financial Problems of Group Health Association from the Board of Trustees," attachment to Board of Trustee Minutes, April 21, 1948; "GHA Raises Dues May 1 as Result of Mail Balloting," *Washington Evening Star,* April 22, 1948, p. B1.

46. "Introduction to the 1950 Budget of Group Health Association," attachment to Group Health Association, Board of Trustee Minutes, January 1950; Melvin L. Dollar to Board of Trustees, February 26, 1951, attachment to Board of Trustee Minutes, March 1951; "Health Group's Rate Increase to Be Studied," *Washington Post,* May 3, 1951, p. B2; "Group Health Rate Increase Issue to Be Aired Today," *Washington Post,* May 15, 1951, p. 2B; Group Health Association, Annual Membership Meeting

Minutes, May 2, 1951; "Statement Regarding the Dues Increase by W. E. Warne, President for the Board of Trustees," May 1951, attachment to Board of Trustee Minutes, May 2, 1951; Board of Trustee Minutes, June 20, 1951.

47. Group Health Association, *Annual Report for 1946*; Group Health Association, Board of Trustee Minutes, April 16, 1946; "Report by Albert Hamilton on Membership Drive," July 20, 1946, attachment to Board of Trustee Minutes, July 23, 1946.

48. "GHA Invites You," Group Health Association, July 1946; Frank C. Waldrop, "A Good Buy," *Washington Times-Herald,* February 22, 1946, p. 23, both attachments to Group Health Association, Board of Trustee Minutes, July 23, 1946.

49. "GHA Welcomes Five Hundred in August to Pace Membership Drive," *GHA News,* October 1946, p. 3.

50. "Report on Promotion Program for Last Thirteen Months," attachment to Group Health Association, Board of Trustee Minutes, April, 16, 1947; Group Health Association, *Annual Reports for 1947, 1948*; "Budget Workpapers, 1948," attachment to Board of Trustee Minutes, January 1948.

51. The law firm was Posner, Fox, Arent and Friedburg. Group Health Association, *Annual Reports for 1947, 1948, 1950, 1951*; "GHA Welcomes Five Hundred in August."

52. McKinsey and Co., "Increasing the Effectiveness of Group Health Association, Inc.," consultant's report, January 1952, pp. III-3, I-1.

53. Interview with Daniel J. Sullivan, October 15, 1986; "Promotion Department Program for 1952–53," attachment to Group Health Association, Board of Trustee Minutes, October 1952; "Report on Steps Taken to Reduce Promotional Costs," November 19, 1952, attachment to Board of Trustee Minutes, November 1952.

54. Carroll R. Daugherty to Group Health Association, March 19, 1943, attachment to Group Health Association, Board of Trustee Minutes, March 29, 1943; Henry H. Lichtenberg to Claims Committee, September 13, 1944, attachment to Board of Trustee Minutes, October 1944; James E. Victory to Grievance Committee, October 9, 1952, attachment to Board of Trustee Minutes, October 1952.

55. Mrs. Herman Berman to Frank J. Morris, January 3, 1950, attach-

ment to Group Health Association, Board of Trustee Minutes, October 1952.

56. Interview with Mr. and Mrs. Edward Hollander, November 6, 1986; "Results of GHA Questionnaire," *GHA News,* December 1947, p. 6.

57. *GHA News,* June 1949.

58. Group Health Association, Annual Membership Meeting Minutes, March 18, 1953.

59. "Explanatory Statement to Accompany Ballot on Annual Election of Trustees," attachment to Group Health Association, Board of Trustee Minutes, February 17, 1948; Group Health Association, *Bylaws of GHA,* January 1, 1951, p. 21. The petition requirement was changed to two hundred signatures in 1964.

60. McKinsey and Co., "Increasing the Effectiveness," pp. v, III-1, I-1–I-4.

61. Group Health Association, Board of Trustee Minutes, March 12, 1952; "Checklist of Major Elements in GHA Administrative Review and Reorganization," attachment to Board of Trustee Minutes, June 24, 1952.

62. By 1946, GHA's nonmedical clinical staff included an optometrist, a pharmacist, x-ray and laboratory technicians, nurses, and appointments clerks. The administrative staff, in addition to the executive director, included a business manager, promotional manager, office manager, secretaries, bookkeepers, clerks, telephone operators, maids, and porters. See "Salary Schedule, Personnel Other than Physicians," attachment to Group Health Association, Board of Trustee Minutes, June 26, 1946.

To regulate the treatment of all these employees, as well as the full-time physicians, the Board adopted a personnel policy, setting forth procedures for appointment, probationary periods, dismissal, annual leave, and sick leave. In the years before creation of such a formal policy, the staff members themselves had to draw the trustees' attention to problems. See "Personnel Policy," attachment to Group Health Association, Board of Trustee Minutes, May 14, 1946; Juanita B. Burton to Miss [Edith] Rockwood, January 18, 1943, attachment to Board of Trustee Minutes, February 15, 1943; *GHA News,* January 15, 1942, p. 5; Board of Trustee Minutes, March 29, 1946; Group Health Association, *Annual Report for 1960.*

63. Group Health Association, Board of Trustee Minutes, April 15, 1953, May 20, 1953; *GHA News,* May-June 1953, p. 1; "Report of the

Committee on Selection of an Executive Director for GHA," attachment to Board of Trustee Minutes, June 23, 1953; "Dillon S. Myer," *Current Biography, Who's News and Why,* 1947 (New York: H. W. Wilson Co., 1947), pp. 462–463.

64. In 1950, there were 500,000 white and 280,000 black residents in Washington, D.C. Twenty years later, 500,000 blacks and 200,000 whites lived in the city. Grier, *People and Government,* p. 10.

65. The total that year was 22,879. Group Health Association, *Annual Report for 1958.*

CHAPTER FOUR

1. Gerald J. Miller to Oliver M. Walker, October 21, 1960, attachment to Group Health Association Board of Trustee Minutes, November 1960, Group Health Association headquarters, Washington, D.C.; Frank C. Watters to Palmer Dearing, March 12, 1965, attachment to Board of Trustee Minutes, March 1965; "Program for the Cornerstone Laying Ceremony for the Group Health Association, May 15, 1962," Frank C. Watters papers, privately held.

2. Frank Watters to All Board Members, December 3, 1962, attachment to Board of Trustee Minutes, December 18, 1962.

3. "An Introduction to GHA's New Medical Center," *GHA Bulletin,* November 12, 1962, attachment to Group Health Association, Board of Trustee Minutes, November 1962; Board of Trustee Minutes, November 18, 1960, Gerald T. Miller to Oliver M. Walker, October 21, 1960, attachment to Board of Trustee Minutes, October 1960; Oliver M. Walker to Vernon Graf, November 2, 1960, attachment to Board of Trustee Minutes, November 1960. GHA's lease agreement was with the Lenkin Company, which constructed the building. Financing the project raised old problems, when an insurance company that had planned to provide a $2.25 million construction loan cancelled, in part because of insurance industry opposition to funding a "direct care" plan like GHA. After six months of effort, the money was raised and construction began in the summer of 1961. Frank Watters to Palmer Dearing, March 12, 1965.

4. Frank C. Watters to All Board Members, December 3, 1962, attach-

ment to Group Health Association, Board of Trustee Minutes, December 1962.

5. Paul Starr, *The Social Transformation of American Medicine* (New York: Basic Books, 1982) p. 313.

6. Raymond Munts, *Bargaining for Health: Labor Unions, Health Insurance, and Medical Care* (Madison: University of Wisconsin Press, 1967); Daniel M. Fox, *Health Policies, Health Politics: The Bristish and American Experience, 1911–1965* (Princeton, N.J.: Princeton University Press, 1986), p. 194.

7. Interviews with Mr. and Mrs. Edward Hollander, November 6, 1986, Gertrude Ruttenberg, September 11, 1986, and Mark Colburn, August 6, 1986.

8. Information in this and the next three paragraphs is from an interview with Henry Daniels, October 12, 1986.

9. "Program of Labor Health Conference, April 22, 1955," Leon Richeson papers, privately held; Group Health Association, Board of Trustee Minutes, August 31, 1955.

10. Group Health Association, Board of Trustee Minutes, December 16, 1953; "Walter John Bierwagen," *Who's Who in Labor* (New York: Arno Press, 1976), p. 44. In 1954, looking ahead to possible agreements with large groups like the transit workers, the Board proposed, and the members approved, the necessary amendments to GHA's bylaws. The new Article IX gave the organization the right to enter into contracts with special groups, which would have their own representatives on the Board of Trustees. If such a group had its own Board members, then its members could not vote in the regular trustee election or on changes in the dues that affected general members. "Problems and Questions Arising Out of Group Membership Proposals Which Have Grown Out of Our Discussion with the Transit Operators Group," February 12, 1954, attachment to Board of Trustee Minutes, February 1954.

11. Interview with Leon D. Richeson, July 22, 1986.

12. Ibid.

13. Transit Employees Health and Welfare Plan to All Participating Employees and Their Families, November 26, 1958, Richeson papers.

14. Group Health Association, Board of Trustee Minutes, February 20, 1958, March 26, 1958, April 15, 1958, April 20, 1958, June 17, 1958, August

25, 1958, September 10, 1958; "Notes of a Meeting of Representatives of Local 689, the Transit Company, and GHA, October 28, 1957," attachment to Board of Trustee Minutes, October 1957; Frank C. Watters to Gladys A. Harrison, February 26, 1964, attachment to Board of Trustee Minutes, February 1964.

15. Group Health Association, Board of Trustee Minutes, March 26, 1958.

16. Watters to Harrison, February 26, 1964; Group Health Association, Board of Trustee Minutes, September 10, 1958, September 16, 1958.

17. "Summary Comparison of Services Offered Within Washington Area," November 26, 1958, Richeson papers; Transit Employees' Health and Welfare Fund, "Member's Handbook," April 1, 1959, p. 2, Richeson papers.

18. "Health Center Is Dedicated; Milestone in Cooperation," *Trades Unionist,* April 11, 1959, pp. 1, 4, Richeson papers.

19. Interview with Leon D. Richeson; "Summary Comparison of Services," November 26, 1958.

20. Group Health Association, Board of Trustee Minutes, March 24, 1959; interviews with Arthur B. Rosenbaum, M.D., August 26, 1986, and Theresa Fuller, June 26, 1986.

21. Walter J. Bierwagen, "Medical Care Under the Transit Employees' Health and Welfare Plan," paper delivered at the 1960 Annual Meeting, Industrial Medical Association, Rochester, N.Y., April 26, 1960, p. 7, Richeson papers.

22. Raymond Munts, *Bargaining for Health,* p. 187; Bierwagen, "Medical Care," pp. 8–9.

23. Quoted in "Statement by Fordyce Luikhart, President of Group Health Association, Inc., Washington, D.C. Before Insurance Subcommittee of the Senate Post Office and Civil Service Committee at Hearings of Bill S. 94," attachment to Group Health Association, Board of Trustee Minutes, April 28, 1959.

24. Bierwagen, "Medical Care," p. 6.

25. Interview with Dorothy Gill, M.D., August 27, 1986.

26. Bierwagen, "Medical Care," p. 11.

27. Ibid., p. 10.

28. Experience had shown that most of the transit workers received

their care at GHA's downtown center, perhaps because the location was more convenient for them, while many suburban GHA members took advantage of the Takoma Park center, which had replaced GHA's earlier branch clinic in Silver Spring. Group Health Association, Board of Trustee Minutes, August 12, 1960.

29. One cost analysis, for example, consisted of "taking the annual budgeted direct medical care expense (other than hospital) and applying the percentage usage rate on services for the group to get an amount based on experience; adding to this amount an 'experience rated' hospital charge amount, and adding an amount for indirect and overhead expense computed on the 'GHA community rate' basis." Ibid.

30. Group Health Association, Board of Trustee Minutes, August 15, 1960.

31. Until this time, the transit workers had no choice in their health care plan. J. B. Hanson to Executive Director, October 26, 1964, attachment to Group Health Association, Board of Trustee Minutes, November 1964.

32. GHA's arrangement on pregnancy had always been that a couple needed to belong to the Association for ten months before they could receive maternity benefits. This was designed to prevent women from joining GHA when they were already pregnant, in order to obtain maternity care, and then afterwards dropping out. "Items for Board Review and Recommendations on Policy Matters Which Are Related to the Proposed Government Health Program, February 21, 1955," attachment to Group Health Association, Board of Trustee Minutes, March 2, 1955.

33. Andrew E. Ruddock to Group Health Association, Inc., December 16, 1959, attachment to Group Health Association, Board of Trustee Minutes, January 1960.

34. Ibid.

35. Fordyce W. Luikhart to Dear Member, February 11, 1960, attachment to Group Health Association, Board of Trustee Minutes, February 1960.

36. Ibid.; Edward J. Overby to Dear Member, March 11, 1960, attachment to Group Health Association, Board of Trustee Minutes, March 1960.

37. The remaining participants were about equally divided between the transit worker group (9,403) and general members (9,876). Group Health Association, *Annual Report for 1960*; Group Health Association, Board of Trustee Minutes, July 25, 1960; Agnes W. Brewster, "Enrollment Under the Federal Employees Health Benefits Act," attachment to Board of Trustee Minutes, October 24, 1960.

38. Frank C. Watters to Andrew E. Ruddock, November 30, 1960, attachment to Board of Trustee Minutes, December 19, 1960; Group Health Association, Board of Trustee Minutes, December 1960.

39. Brewster, "Enrollment." Brewster, a medical economist from the U.S. Public Health Service, was also a trustee of GHA and served as its president in 1961–1962. Using her professional skills to assemble a statistical profile of the GHA members enrolled under the new federal health program, she discovered that most lived in the District of Columbia and were relatively young, with only 3.3 percent over sixty. Eight-four percent of the federal employees joining GHA chose the premium, or high option, plan.

40. Andrew E. Ruddock to Frank C. Watters, May 10, 1962, attachment to Group Health Association, Board of Trustee Minutes, May 1962; Frank C. Watters to All Board Members, November 19, 1962, December 20, 1962, attachments to Board of Trustee Minutes, December 1962.

41. "Federal Employees Health Benefits Program, Open Season, October 1–OCTOBER 15, 1963, Summary of Net Changes in Enrollment," attachment to Group Health Association, Board of Trustee Minutes, January 1964.

42. Bureau of Retirement and Insurance, U.S. Civil Service Commission, *Group Health Association,* (Washington, D.C., 1963), as revised November 1963, attachment to Group Health Association, Board of Trustee Minutes, May 1964; "Old and New Health Insurance Rates," *Washington Daily News,* August 21, 1964, p. 22.

43. "Major Items Under Consideration in Bylaw Study," attachment to Group Health Association, Board of Trustee Minutes, October 1962.

44. Ibid.

45. William G. Colman to Board of Trustees, November 6, 1962, attachment to Group Health Association, Board of Trustee Minutes, November 26, 1962.

46. Interview with William G. Colman, October 23, 1986.

47. Ibid.; Group Health Association, *Annual Reports for 1958, 1962.*

48. Interview with William G. Colman.

49. Group Health Association, Board of Trustee Minutes, January 12, 1963, January 28, 1963.

50. Interview with Mark Colburn; "William Gerald Colman," *Who's Who in America,* 41st ed. (Chicago: Marquis Who's Who, 1980–1981), p. 681.

51. Interview with Mark Colburn.

52. Board of Trustees to Dear Member, February 19, 1963, attachment to Group Health Association, Board of Trustee Minutes, February 1963; interview with John J. Gunther, November 5, 1986.

53. Mark Colburn, addendum to Board of Trustees to Dear Member, February 19, 1963, attachment to Group Health Association, Board of Trustee Minutes, February 1963.

54. Ibid.

55. The complex vote-counting method contributed to the ambiguity. On the strength of the total vote, the changes in the bylaws (which were offered as a package rather than as provisions to be voted on separately) were approved, 4,413 to 4,101. The transit workers, who cast 1,493 votes in favor of the changes and only 301 against, supplied the margin of victory. Federal employees and general members voted against the changes. GHA's attorneys, therefore, decided that only certain of the bylaw changes had been adopted, since the transit workers were not eligible to vote on some questions, such as matters relating to dues and benefits for nontransit worker members. "Battle Shaping Up Over Revision of Group Health Association's Rules." *Washington Post,* March 2, 1963, p. D2; "GHA Bylaws Vote Announced," March 22, 1963, GHA news release, attachment to Group Health Association, Board of Trustee Minutes, March 23, 1963; Albert E. Arent to Board of Trustees, March 25, 1963, attachment to Board of Trustee Minutes, March 23, 1963.

56. "Aaron Seymour Sabghir," *American Men and Women of Science: Social and Behavioral Sciences,* 13th. (New York and London: R. R. Bowker Co., 1978), p. 1037.

57. Group Health Association, Board of Trustee Minutes, March 25, 1963, April 22, 1963.

58. Stanley G. House to Frank Watters, May 27, 1963, attachment to Group Health Association, Board of Trustee Minutes, May 27, 1963; "Court Refuses to Enjoin GHA from Signing Contract with Transit Employees' Plan," *GHA News,* July 1963, p. 5.

59. "Memorandum re GHA Offer of Settlement—Colburn v. GHA, May 23, 1963," attachment to Group Health Association, Board of Trustee Minutes, May 27, 1963.

60. Raymond J. Goodman to William F. Schaub, May 28, 1963, attachment to Group Health Association, Board of Trustee Minutes, May 27, 1963.

61. "GHA 'Rebels' Barred from Board Meeting," *Washington Post,* June 11, 1963, p. B2; Jay Cantor to Group Health Association, June 17, 1963, attachment to Group Health Association, Board of Trustee Minutes, June 24, 1963.

62. "Special Meeting Held July 24," attachment to Group Health Association, Board of Trustee Minutes, August 1963; "Petition Hits Group Health Voting Rules," *Washington Post,* July 25, 1963, p. B2.

63. Robert J. Myers to Clark Warburton, June 22, 1963, attachment to Group Health Association, Board of Trustee Minutes, June 24, 1963.

64. Ibid.; Robert J. Myers to Eric Reisfeld, August 31, 1963, attachment to Group Health Association, Board of Trustee Minutes, September 1963.

65. Interview with Mark Colburn.

66. Group Health Association, Board of Trustee Minutes, June 24, 1963; John J. Sexton to Frank Watters, June 28, 1963, attachment to Board of Trustee Minutes, June 25, 1963.

67. "Report of Bylaw Review Committee," attachment to Group Health Association, Board of Trustee Minutes, August 26, 1963.

68. Ibid.

69. Mark Colburn and Aaron Sabghir to Editor, *Washington Evening Star,* October 13, 1963, p. B4; Raymond J. Goodman to Editor, *Washington Post,* October 24, 1963, p. A20.

70. "Group Health Members Vote to Support Board Majority," November 5, 1963, GHA news release, attachment to Group Health Association, Board of Trustee Minutes, November 1963.

71. "New Bylaws Voted by Group Health," *Washington Post,* December 17, 1963, p. C10; "Group Health Trustees Win Bylaws Fight," *Washington*

Evening Star, December 17, 1963, p. B2; "Judge Dismisses Suit by Two GHA Trustees," *Washington Post,* January 26, 1964, p. B6; Board of Trustee Minutes, January 27, 1964, April 27, 1964.

72. T. M. Arnett to Benjamin Lewis, October 14, 1964, attachment to Group Health Association, Board of Trustee Minutes, October 1964.

73. Interview with Mark Colburn.

CHAPTER FIVE

1. Chapter Six discusses these internal tensions in the context of GHA relations with its physicians and other providers.

2. Among these individuals were Nelson Cruikshank of the AFL-CIO, Wilbur Cohen of the Department of Health, Education, and Welfare, and Ida Merriam of the Social Security Administration. For more on Medicare, see Paul Starr, *The Social Transformation of American Medicine* (New York: Basic Books, 1982), and Theodore Marmor, *The Politics of Medicare* (Chicago: Aldine Publishing Co., 1973); Gaston V. Rimlinger, *Welfare Policy and Industrialization in Europe, America, and Russia* (New York: John Wiley and Sons, 1971), pp. 67–68; Martha Derthick, *Policymaking for Social Security* (Washington, D.C.: Brookings Institution, 1979), pp. 319–338; James L. Sundquist, *Politics and Policy: The Eisenhower, Kennedy, and Johnson Years* (Washington, D.C.: Brookings Institution, 1968), pp. 288–319; Eric R. Kingson, *What You Must Know About Social Security and Medicare* (New York: Pharos Books, 1987).

3. Group Health Association, *Annual Report for 1965,* Group Health Association headquarters, Washington, D.C. By the mid-1980s, federal employees represented just under half of GHA's enrollment. Group Health Association, *Annual Report for 1984.*

4. Andrew E. Ruddock to Frank C. Watters, September 20, 1967, and Frank C. Watters to Board Members, September 21, 1967, both attachments to Group Health Association, Board of Trustee Minutes, September 25, 1967, GHA headquarters.

5. "Memorandum on Conversation This Date Between Frank C. Watters and Andrew E. Ruddock," September 26, 1967, attachment to Group Health Association, Board of Trustee Minutes, November 13, 1967; Andrew E. Ruddock to Frank C. Watters, October 23, 1967, attachment to

Board of Trustee Minutes, November 13, 1967.

6. Thomas A. Tinsley to Louis J. Segadelli, June 10, 1975, attachment to Group Health Association, Board of Trustee Minutes, June 16, 1975.

7. Group Health Association, Board of Trustee Minutes, May 12, 1975, June 23, 1975.

8. *GHA News,* September-October 1975, p. 1; Group Health Association, Board of Trustee Minutes, August 5, 1975, September 16, 1975.

9. Louis J. Segadelli to Godfrey Butler, July 29, 1977 and Marie B. Henderson to Louis Segadelli, July 18, 1977, both attachments to Group Health Association, Board of Trustee Minutes, July 25, 1977.

10. Thomas A. Tinsley to Louis J. Segadelli, August 23, 1978, attachment to Group Health Association, Board of Trustee Minutes, August 28, 1978.

11. Group Health Association, Board of Trustee Minutes, March 7, 1978, July 24, 1978, August 28, 1978, January 15, 1979; Louis J. Segadelli to Godfrey Butler, September 26, 1978, attachment to Board of Trustee Minutes, December 18, 1978.

12. Starr, *Transformation,* pp. 384, 406; Susan Feigenbaum, "Risk Bearing in Health Care Finance," *Health Care and Its Costs,* ed. Carl J. Schramm (New York: W. W. Norton Co., 1987), p. 121.

13. For discussions of the two approaches to prepayment, see I. S. Falk, *Security Against Sickness: A Study of Health Insurance* (Garden City, N.Y.: Doubleday, Doran and Co., 1936), pp. 11–35, 50–54, 323, 350–360, and Joseph L. Falkson, *HMOs and the Politics of Health System Reform* (Bowie, Md.: American Hospital Association and Robert J. Brady Co., 1979), pp. 67–87, which describes in detail the development of the Nixon administration's policy on HMOs.

14. Public Law 93–222, Sec. 1301 (B) (1)–(2); Lawrence Brown, *Politics and Health Care Organization: HMOs as Federal Policy* (Washington, D.C.: Brookings Institution, 1983), pp. 296–297. This book is essential for an understanding of the modern HMO movement.

15. J. W. Riggs to Elliot Stern, April 8, 1974, attachment to Group Health Association, Board of Trustee Minutes, April 15, 1974.

16. Louis J. Segadelli to Board Members, May 5, 1978, attachment to Group Health Association, Board of Trustee Minutes, May 5, 1978; Board of Trustee Minutes, June 26, 1978.

17. Group Health Association, *Annual Report for 1974.*

18. Ibid.; untitled document prepared by GHA at request of Civil Service Commission, attachment to Group Health Association, Board of Trustee Minutes, June 23, 1975.

19. Group Health Association, Board of Trustee Minutes, July 15, 1974, July 21, 1975.

20. This discussion is based heavily on Raymond W. Turner, "Urgent Care in the HMO: Evolution of a System in Washington, D.C.," attachment to Group Health Association, Board of Trustee Minutes, November 16, 1977. The clinic was staffed by a nurse, a physician assistant, and one of GHA's internists, who took turns spending half a day there.

21. Group Health Association, Board of Trustee Minutes, October 20, 1975.

22. The work of economist Harold Luft, in particular, has been influential. See Harold S. Luft, *Health Maintenance Organizations: Dimensions of Performance* (New York: John Wiley and Sons, 1981), and Luft, "Assessing the Evidence on HMO Performance," *Milbank Memorial Fund Quarterly* 58 (Winter 1980): 501–536.

23. Information compiled from Group Health Association, *Annual Reports for 1940–1979.* Although the figures for the 1980s are even lower, in the 300 range, they are not comparable, because Medicare participants were no longer included.

24. Lawrence Brown, *Politics*, pp. 72, 174n. Brown even noted that, although he considered it unlikely, some analysts believed that the presence of three HMOs in Washington, D.C., in 1978 might have contributed to the fact that hospital charges in that area were rising 50 percent faster than the national average, on the theory that hospitals raised their rates to compensate for the lower hospital utilization practiced by HMOs. Ibid., p. 468. For comparison purposes, Group Health Cooperative of Puget Sound, which had its own hospital, had a consistently lower number of days of hospitalization per thousand members, ranging from 455 to just over 500 in the period 1965–1969. See Group Health Cooperative of Puget Sound, *View*, March-April 1970, p. 10. In 1972, GHA had 580 days, compared to 496 for Kaiser of Southern California, 420 for Puget Sound (both with their own hospitals), and 549 for HIP, which did not have hospitals. See Ron Jydstrup to Louis Segadelli, February 14, 1972, attachment to

Group Health Association, Board of Trustee Minutes, February 28, 1972. See Appendix for list of GHA hospital days per 1,000 members.

25. Frank C. Watters to Board Members, August 25, 1964, attachment to Group Health Association, Board of Trustee Minutes, August 1964; Chief, Membership Division, to Executive Director, December 29, 1964, attachment to Board of Trustee Minutes, January 1965; Chief, Membership Division, to Executive Director, March 2, 1965, attachment to Board of Trustee Minutes, March 1965; John J. Sexton to Frank Watters, April 23, 1965, attachment to Board of Trustee Minutes, April 1965; "Contract Between GHI and GHA," July 6, 1965, attachment to Board of Trustee Minutes, July 1965; Jerry B. Hanson to Executive Director, August 21, 1967, attachment to Board of Trustee Minutes, August 1967.

26. Group Health Association, Board of Trustee Minutes, July 31, 1967, July 17, 1972, August 25, 1972; Louis J. Segadelli to Board Members, May 1, 1973, attachment to Board of Trustee Minutes, May 12, 1973.

27. Thomas L. Siegel to Louis J. Segadelli, March 28, 1974, attachment to Group Health Association, Board of Trustee Minutes, April 15, 1974; D. S. Farver to Louis J. Segadelli, March 22, 1974, attachment to Board of Trustee Minutes, April 15, 1974; Victor Cohn, "Nader Says Health Unit Plan Biased," *Washington Post*, February 18, 1975, p. A16; Board of Trustee Minutes, October 20, 1980.

28. Frank C. Watters to Board Members, February 28, 1966, attachment to Group Health Association, Board of Trustee Minutes, February 28, 1966; Board of Trustee Minutes, March 26, 1968.

29. Group Health Association, Board of Trustee Minutes, September 22, 1975, February 9, 1976; Louis J. Segadelli to Dear Member, January 23, 1976, attachment to Board of Trustee Minutes, February 1976; Victor Cohn, "Hospital Shift Set by GHA," *Washington Post*, February 1, 1976, pp. A1, A9.

30. Group Health Association, board of Trustee Minutes, March 8, 1976; Victor Cohn, "Group Health May Get Own Hospital by '80," *Washington Post*, April 16, 1976, p. C3.

31. Cohn, "Group Health May Get Own Hospital"; Group Health Association, Board of Trustee Minutes, May 17, 1976; "A GHA Hospital: The Need—the Response," *GHA News*, June 1976 (special GHA hospital issue); Edwin A. Deagle Jr. to Maurine Mulliner, July 30, 1976, Maurine

Mulliner papers, GHA headquarters.

32. Group Health Association, Board of Trustee Minutes, July 19, 1976; Victor Cohn, "Group Health Plan for New NW Hospital Opposed at Hearing," *Washington Post,* October 14, 1976, p. B8; Robert Pear, "D.C. Hospitals Attack Plan by GHA to Build Facility," *Washington Star,* October 14, 1976, p. B5.

33. Betty L. Catoe to Albert P. Russo, December 27, 1976, Mulliner papers.

34. Group Health Association, Board of Trustee Minutes, November 15, 1976.

35. Karlyn Barker, "Yeldell, Antonelli Seen Pressuring Hospital, GHA Link," *Washington Post,* December 16, 1976, pp. A1, A16.

36. Victor Cohn, "Hospital Seeks Facility Shift to Hotel Site," *Washington Post,* April 12, 1977, pp. C1, C7; Albert P. Russo to Louis J. Segadelli, May 17, 1977, Mulliner papers.

37. Group Health Association, Board of Trustee Minutes, June 3, 1977, August 28, 1978, October 16, 1978; Richard Loughery to Louis J. Segadelli, August 25, 1978, attachment to Board of Trustee Minutes, August 28, 1978; Sheilah Kast, "Group Health Seeks to Build Hospital for 103,000 Members," *Washington Star,* September 11, 1977, p. B4; "GHA-WHC to Submit Joint Proposal," *Uptown Citizen,* September 29, 1977, Mulliner papers.

38. Group Health Association, Board of Trustee Minutes, September 24, 1979; "Report: Closing of Doctors' Hospital," *GHA News,* November-December 1979, p. 1.

39. Group Health Association, Board of Trustee Minutes, September 24, 1979; "Report: Closing of Doctors' Hospital."

40. B. D. Colen, "Health Group May Build Hospital," *Washington Post*, February 10, 1980, pp. B1, B4; Robert van Hoek, "Proposal for GHA/GW-Affiliated Hospital, Staff Recommendation," August 25, 1981, attachment to Group Health Association, Board of Trustee Minutes, September 14, 1981.

41. Group Health Association, Board of Trustee Minutes, July 23, 1984; Virginia M. Dollard to Board of Trustees, March 18, 1985, attachment to Board of Trustee Minutes, March 18, 1985.

42. Frank C. Watters to Board Members, November 23, 1970, and Ron Jydstrup to Frank C. Watters, December 9, 1970, both attachments to Group Health Association, Board of Trustee Minutes, December 21, 1970; Group Health Association, *Annual Reports for 1960, 1970.*

43. Frank C. Watters to Board Members, November 22, 1965, attachment to Group Health Association, Board of Trustee Minutes, November 1965; Frank C. Watters to Board Members, undated, attachment to Board of Trustee Minutes, June 1967.

44. Group Health Association, Board of Trustee Minutes, July 19, 1971, September 9, 1971, November 1971; Group Health Association, *Annual Report for 1980.*

45. The Rockville, Maryland, center, which opened in 1974, was followed in 1977 by one at Hyattsville in Prince George's County, Maryland, replacing the aging Takoma Park center. In 1979, GHA inaugurated a clinic at Marlow Heights, Maryland. Paul R. Lenz, "The Future of Suburban Clinics in GHA," March 6, 1975, attachment to Group Health Association, Medical Council Minutes, March 1975, GHA headquarters; Group Health Association, *Annual Report for 1977; GHA News,* January 1978; "Large Turnout at Marlow Heights Dedication—Open House Festivities," *GHA News,* March 1979, p. 1. See Appendix for list of GHA medical centers and dates.

46. Ruth Ruttenberg to Dear Member of GHA, November 16, 1982, attachment to Group Health Association, Board of Trustee Minutes, November 15, 1982; Edward J. Hinman to Board of Trustees, March 22, 1983, attachment to Board of Trustee Minutes, March 30, 1983; Robert G. Rosenberg to Executive Committee, April 13, 1983, attachment to Board of Trustee Minutes, April 18, 1983.

47. Group Health Association, *Annual Report for 1983: GHA—Growing with the Region.*

48. Robert G. Rosenberg to Board of Trustees, February 13, 1984, attachment to Group Health Association, Board of Trustee Minutes, February 13, 1984; "Judiciary Square—Executive Summary," undated, attachment to Board of Trustee Minutes, July 23, 1984.

49. Group Health Association, Board of Trustee Minutes, September 25, 1984; Robert G. Rosenberg to Board of Trustees, September 21, 1984,

attachment to Board of Trustee Minutes, September 25, 1984. Rosenberg, a pediatrician with substantial experience in HMO administration, came to Group Health initially as medical director in 1982. In 1983, he was appointed executive director as well and held the two positions until his resignation in 1986. Rosenberg felt strongly that GHA would have to adapt in order to meet the increasing competition, but he often met resistance from the Board. Interview with Robert G. Rosenberg, M.D., September 3, 1986.

50. Group Health Association, Board of Trustee Minutes, September 25, 1984, October 15, 1984.

51. This discussion of networking is based on Group Health Association, Board of Trustee Minutes, January 25, 1985.

52. Donald E. Mitchell to Harold Wool, May 14, 1985, attachment to Group Health Association, Board of Trustee Minutes, June 17, 1985; Board of Trustee Minutes, February 12, 1985, July 15, 1985; interviews with Alice Hersh, August 7, 1986, and David Krawitz, August 26, 1986.

53. Group Health Association, Board of Trustee Minutes, September 23, 1985, October 1986.

54. It should be noted that HMOs were greatly aided by passage of amendments to the basic act in 1976, which liberalized the requirements and made it easier to qualify as an HMO. Christine Russell, "HMOs Grow like Weeds with Help of U.S. Funds," *Washington Star*, February 4, 1979, p. A3; National Industry Council for HMO Development, "The Health Maintenance Organization Industry Ten Year Report, 1973–1983," 1983; Michael J. Abramowitz, "Army of HMOs Invades Nation's Capital," *Washington Post*, April 14, 1986, "Washington Business," p. 1.

55. These observations are based on conversations with Jon Gabel and other members of the staff of the Health Insurance Association of America, July and August 1987. For a good view of the HMO industry, see Deborah H. Harrison and John R. Kimberly, "Private and Public Initiatives in Health Maintenance Organizations," *Journal of Health Politics Policy and Law* 7 (Spring 1982): 80–95. For some trenchant observations about the viability of HMOs, see Jack A. Meyer *et al., Health Care Today: Issues, Trends, and Developments in Cost Management* (Washington, D.C.: National Chamber Foundation, 1986).

56. IPAs and PPOs have been discussed and defined in Chapter One.

57. Abramowitz, "Army of HMOs."

58. Robert G. Rosenberg to Board of Trustees, January 16, 1984, attachment to Group Health Association, Board of Trustee Minutes, January 16, 1984.

59. Group Health Association, Board of Trustee Minutes, January 27, 1986.

60. Ibid. and February 24, 1986.

CHAPTER SIX

1. Group Health Association, "Meeting of Board and Medical Staff, April 17, 1944," attachment to Group Health Association, Board of Trustee Minutes, April 17, 1944, Group Health Association headquarters, Washington, D.C.

2. Group Health Association, "Minutes of Executive Session, April 24, 1944," attachment to Group Health Association, Board of Trustee Minutes, April 17, 1944.

3. Mario Scandiffio to Robert H. Shields, May 11, 1944, and Russell F. Cahoon to Mario Scandiffio, May 11, 1944, both attachments to Group Health Association, Board of Trustee Minutes, May 1944.

4. Medical Staff to Board of Trustees, June 18, 1946, attachment to Group Health Association, Board of Trustee Minutes, June 1946.

5. Ibid., interview with Ruth Benedict, M.D., November 13, 1986.

6. Ibid.

7. In 1946, the Board created an Executive Council, which served as a forum for discussions among physicians, management, and the trustees. Made up of three Board members, three doctors, the executive director, and the GHA president, the Council could nominate assistant medical directors and department chiefs and possessed veto power over the choice of medical director. In the late 1950s, the Council fell into disuse and ceased to function by the 1960s. Harry J. Becker to Members of the Board of Trustees, July 23, 1946, attachment to Group Health Association, Board of Trustee Minutes, July 1946; H. H. Lichtenberg and F. W. Luikart to Members of the Executive Council, September 8, 1955, attachment to Board of Trustee Minutes, September 1955.

8. By 1965, GHA had the full-time equivalent of 56 physicians, plus 92 paramedical employees and 42 auxiliary staff, 12 dentists, and 124 administrative staff members. See Group Health Association, *Annual Reports for*

1960–1963; "Medical Staff and Consultants Group Health Association, Inc.," January 1, 1963, attachment to Group Health Association, Board of Trustee Minutes, January 1963.

9. Group Health Association, *Annual Report for 1968*.

10. Frank C. Watters to Board Members, March 19, 1965, attachment to Group Health Association, Board of Trustee Minutes, March 1965; Board of Trustee Minutes, December 18, 1967.

11. Group Health Association, *Annual Report for 1969*.

12. Group Health Association, *Annual Reports for 1974, 1976*.

13. Group Health Association, Board of Trustee Minutes, June 24, 1968.

14. Frank C. Watters to Board Members, October 24, 1968, attachment to Group Health Association, Board of Trustee Minutes, April 20, 1970.

15. Group Health Association, Board of Trustee Minutes, January 27, 1969.

16. Frank C. Watters to Board Members, January 29, 1970, and Joseph M. Fries to Frank C. Watters, February 11, 1970, both attachments to Group Health Association, Board of Trustee Minutes, February 16, 1970; Frank C. Watters to Board Members, April 16, 1970, attachment to Board of Trustee Minutes, April 20, 1970.

17. Group Health Association, Board of Trustee Minutes, February 16, 1970.

18. "Medical Quality Control Plan, Exhibit A to Agreement of Group Health Association, Inc., and the GHA Medical Group," June 1, 1970, and "Agreement, Between Group Health Association, Inc., and the GHA Medical Group," approved by Board of Trustees, June 1, 1970, both attachments to Group Health Association, Board of Trustee Minutes, June 1, 1970.

19. The fringe benefits for physicians included membership in GHA (and hence free medical care), free dental care, medical care upon retirement, disability insurance of up to $1,200 a month, and life insurance. There was also malpractice insurance of up to $5 million for a single occurrence and reimbursement for study leave. "Agreement," June 1, 1970.

20. Ibid.

21. Ibid.; Although in a given year there might be no money left to pay a bonus, the doctors would never forfeit their basic salaries. Thus, they

shared in GHA's success without necessarily having to sacrifice in the event of GHA's failure.

22. Group Health Association, Board of Trustee Minutes, September 9, 1971, September 20, 1971, October 18, 1971.

23. Ibid., March 20, 1972.

24. Ibid., February 28, 1972.

25. Ibid., May 26, 1972, January 21, 1974; interview with Joan Goldwasser, September 10, 1986.

26. There was no department of surgery represented on the Medical Council, because until 1976 GHA used outside surgeons on a retainer basis. "Articles of Organization of GHA Medical Group," March 9, 1972, Group Health Association, Medical Council files, GHA headquarters.

27. Daniel Y. Patterson, "HMO Physician Unionization: An Analytic Case Study of Group Health Association of Washington, D.C.," mimeograph, 1980, GHA headquarters.

28. Group Health Association, Medical Council Minutes, November 1, 1973, May 31, 1973, GHA headquarters.

29. Group Health Association, Board of Trustee Minutes, October 29, 1973.

30. Executive Director to Board of Trustees, August 27, 1973, attachment to Group Health Association, Board of Trustee Minutes, August 30, 1973; Dr. Peter Birk to Members of Board of Trustees, February 5, 1973, attachment to Board of Trustee Minutes, February 5, 1973; Medical Program Administrator to Board of Trustees, August 27, 1973, attachment to Board of Trustee Minutes, August 30, 1973.

31. Thomas L. Siegel to Louis J. Segadelli, August 10, 1973, attachment to Group Health Association, Board of Trustee Minutes, September 17, 1973; Group Health Association, Medical Council Minutes, September 27, 1973, October 4, 1973.

32. Chairman, Fact Finding Committee, to All Full Time and Career Physicians, November 14, 1973, Reorganization Committee records, in Group Health Association, Medical Council files, GHA headquarters; Group Health Association, Medical Council Minutes, November 29, 1973.

33. Medical Program Administrator to Full Time and Career Physicians, October 30, 1973, Group Health Association, Reorganization Committee records.

34. Group Health Association, Medical Council Minutes, November 29, 1973.

35. Fact Finding Committee to All Full Time and Career Physicians, undated, Group Health Association, Reorganization Committee records.

36. Group Health Association, Medical Group Minutes, December 2, 1973, GHA headquarters.

37. "Program Report, Medical Group Formation, for Reorganization Committee Group Health Association, Inc.," American Association of Medical Clinics, Alexandria, Va., August 1974, in Group Health Association, Reorganization Committee records; Group Health Association, Reorganization Committee Minutes, September 23, 1974.

38. Group Health Association, Board of Trustee Minutes, September 18, 1974.

39. Ibid., July 15, 1974, July 29, 1974; Group Health Association, Medical Council Minutes, December 12, 1974; Louis J. Segadelli to Board Members, November 6, 1974, attachment to Board of Trustee Minutes, November 4, 1974; Board of Trustee Minutes, September 18, 1974.

40. Group Health Association, Medical Council Minutes, July 11, 1974.

41. Group Health Association, Board of Trustee Minutes, February 24, 1975, March 15, 1975; Louis J. Segadelli, Memorandum for the Record, January 16, 1975, Capitation Negotiation file, in Group Health Association, Medical Council files.

42. Donald E. Mitchell to Ralph B. Bristol, February 26, 1975, attachment to Group Health Association, Board of Trustee Minutes, March 15, 1975.

43. Group Health Association, Medical Group Minutes, March 25, 1975.

44. Group Health Association, Medical Council Minutes, June 12, 1975, June 26, 1975.

45. Group Health Association, Reorganization Committee Minutes, August 26, 1975, August 28, 1975, GHA headquarters.

46. Group Health Association, Medical Council Minutes, July 31, 1975; Board/Physicians Relations Committee Minutes, September 4, 1975, Group Health Association, Reorganization Committee records.

47. Reorganization Committee to GHA Career Physicians, September 16, 1975, Group Health Association, Reorganization Committee records.

48. Medical Group Reorganization Committee to GHA Career and Probationary Physicians, November 24, 1975, Group Health Association, Reorganization Committee records.

49. Victor Cohn, "Doctors in GHA Want Own Firm," *Washington Post,* March 17, 1976, p. C1; *GHA News,* March, 1976, pp. 12–14; interview with Harold Wool, July 8, 1986.

50. Interview with Louis J. Segadelli, September 17, 1986.

51. Group Health Association, Board of Trustee Minutes, April 9, 10, 1976.

52. Ibid.

53. Group Health Association, Medical Group Finance Committee Minutes, July 20, 1976, GHA headquarters; Group Health Association, Board of Trustee Minutes, June 9, 1976, July 19, 1976; Office of Medical Council to Louis J. Segadelli, May 21, 1976, attachment to Medical Council Minutes, May 1976; Medical Council Minutes, May 13, 1976; M. Brent Oldham to Donald Mitchell, May 10, 1976, attachment to Medical Council Minutes, May 1976.

54. Daniel Y. Patterson to Brent Oldham, Louis Segadelli, and Donald Mitchell, July 14, 1976, attachment to Group Health Association, Board of Trustee Minutes, August 16, 1976.

55. Group Health Association, Board of Trustee Minutes, October 18, 1976; Allen G. Siegel to M. Brent Oldham, October 19, 1976, attachment to Board of Trustee Minutes, October 18, 1976.

56. Group Health Association, Medical Group Finance Committee Minutes, June 22, 1976; Medical Council Minutes, September 23, 1976; "Board of Trustees Report on Developments Affecting Relationships with GHA Medical Staff," attachment to Group Health Association, Board of Trustee Minutes, October 18, 1976.

57. Interview with Donald E. Mitchell, M.D., September 4, 1986.

58. National Labor Relations Board, "Notice to Employees," attachment to Group Health Association, Board of Trustee Minutes, September 20, 1976; Donald E. Mitchell to George Joseph and Others, September 27, 1976, attachment to Group Health Association, Medical Council Minutes, September 23, 1976.

59. Edwin A. Deagle Jr. to GHA Board of Trustees and others, October 28, 1976, attachment to Group Health Association, Board of Trustee Minutes, October 18, 1976.

60. Group Health Association, Board of Trustee Minutes, November 15, 1976.

61. Ibid., November 1, 1976; Mollie Kanarek to Trustees, October 30, 1976, attachment to Group Health Association, Board of Trustee Minutes, November 1, 1976.

62. Group Health Association, Board of Trustee Minutes, December 7, 1976.

63. Ibid.

64. Robert N. Greenberg, "A GHA Cooperative: One Board Member's Viewpoint," and Daniel Y. Patterson, "A GHA Cooperative for the Future: The Physician's Viewpoint," both in *GHA News,* January 1977, pp. 6, 7; M. Brent Oldham, "A GHA Co-Operative: One Board Member's Viewpoint," Maurine Mulliner, "A Member's View," and Mollie Kanarek, "A Concerned Member's Viewpoint on the Medical Corporation," all in *GHA News,* February 1977, pp. 1, 2, 4.

65. Mollie Kanarek to Dear GHA Member, March 5, 1977, and "For Common Sense in GHA—Choose These Candidates," undated, both from Maurine Mulliner papers, GHA headquarters; Group Health Association, "GHA Trustee Election—Explanatory Statement," March 1, 1977; interview with Meredith Higgins, October 16, 1986. The struggle over the doctors' corporation convinced one Member Advisory Council participant that better communication was needed with the members about internal organizational matters. As a result, Bertram Strauss started the *MAC Communicator,* which is sent quarterly to about 2,000 interested members, a publication he still continued to edit a decade later. Interview with Bertram Strauss, July 24, 1986.

66. Lawrence Meyer, "GHA Doctors Bid for Change," *Washington Post,* March 24, 1977, p. A8; Group Health Association, Board of Trustee Minutes, March 23, 1977; John G. Smillie to Louis J. Segadelli, December 15, 1976, Medical Group notebook, 1976–1977, Medical Council files.

67. Daniel Y. Patterson to M. Brent Oldham, March 28, 1977, and Harold Wool to Daniel Y. Patterson, March 29, 1977, both in Medical Group notebook, 1976–1977 (emphasis added).

68. Victor Cohn, "GHA Officials Quit in Policy Protest," *Washington Post,* April 2, 1977, p. D5; Nicholas S. Gimbel to Louis J. Segadelli, April 4, 1977, attachment to Group Health Association, Board of Trustee Min-

utes, April 4, 1977.

69. Group Health Association, Board of Trustee Minutes, April 18, 1977, May 16, 1977.

70. M. Brent Oldham to Harold Wool, July 11, 1977, and Louis J. Segadelli to Board Members, July 18, 1977, both attachments to Group Health Association, Board of Trustee Minutes, July 25, 1977.

71. Group Health Association, Board of Trustee Minutes, August 15, 1977.

72. Ibid., September 27, 1977; Louis J. Segadelli to Harold Wool, September 27, 1977, and Harold Wool to Louis J. Segadelli, October 3, 1977, both attachments to Group Health Association, Board of Trustee Minutes, September 27, 1977.

73. Norman Lieberman to Group Health Association, October 20, 1977, and Harold Wool and Louis J. Segadelli to Dear Doctor, June 17, 1977, both attachments to Group Health Association, Board of Trustee Minutes, October 25, 1977.

74. Sheilah Kast, "Group Health Doctors Asking to Be Recognized as a Union," *Washington Star,* November 5, 1977, p. D2; Louis J. Segadelli to Norman Lieberman, October 25, 1977, attachment to Group Health Association, Board of Trustee Minutes, October 25, 1977; Board of Trustee Minutes, November 16, 1977, January 9, 1978.

75. Group Health Association, Board of Trustee Minutes, January 9, 1978.

76. Interviews with Harold Wool and Donald Mitchell and with Gertrude Ruttenberg, September 11, 1986.

77. Group Health Association, Board of Trustee Minutes, January 9, 1978.

78. Ibid., March 7, 1978.

79. Ibid.

80. Ibid.

81. Thomas J. Gagliardo to Robert W. Donnahoo, April 3, 1978, GHA Physicians' Union, 1978 Contract Negotiations file, GHA headquarters.

82. Group Health Association, Board of Trustee Minutes, April 8, 1978, April 13, 1978.

83. Lawrence Meyer, "Strike by Doctors of Group Health Possible Saturday," *Washington Post,* April 14, 1978, pp. C1, C3. Although the idea of

physicians striking and refusing to treat their patients was unusual, it was not totally unprecedented. For three weeks in July 1962, for example, physicians in the Canadian province of Saskatchewan conducted what they called a strike to protest a compulsory new government program that would use tax revenues to pay for medical care for the province's 900,000 citizens. In that case, however, the doctors did not belong to a labor union and were in private practice or employed by hospitals, and the strike was inspired and coordinated by the medical society. Although there was no question of doctors' becoming employees, they were concerned that, because the government paid the bills, it would somehow control their practices and that the prepaid plan would encourage excessive use of their services. The circumstances and issues in the Saskatchewan strike were thus closer to organized medicine's opposition to GHA's creation in the 1930s than to GHA's physicians' strike in 1978. See Robin F. Badgley and Samuel Wolfe, *Doctors' Strike: Medical Care and Conflict in Saskatchewan* (New York: Atherton Press, 1967).

84. Lawrence Meyer, "GHA Doctor Strike Today Is Approved," *Washington Post,* April 15, 1978, pp. B1, B3; Lawrence Meyer, "GHA Physicians Go on Strike as Negotiations Fail," *Washington Post,* April 16, 1978, pp. A1, A13. GHA had agreed to permit a union shop, meaning that all nonsupervisory full-time GHA doctors would be required to join the union. At the time, GHA had a total of ninety-seven physicians, eighteen of whom held supervisory positions. Fifty-five of the doctors were union members; many of the remainder worked only part time for GHA. Meyer, "Strike by Doctors"; Group Health Association Board of Trustee Minutes, March 7, 1978.

85. Lawrence Meyer, "Obligations Weigh on Striking Doctor," *Washington Post,* April 19, 1978, pp. C1, C5.

86. "GHA Situation Report," undated but marked "received April 19, 1978," Mulliner papers. Many of the doctors who reported for work supported the union position, writing to the Board that they were working only "to maintain patient care and not to split the physicians." Meyer, "Obligations Weigh on Striking Doctor"; Lawrence Meyer, "Negotiators Try to Settle Strike by GHA Doctors," *Washington Post,* April 18, 1978, p. C3; interview with John Newdorp, M.D., October 20, 1986.

87. Group Health Association, Board of Trustee Minutes, April 23, 1978, April 25, 1978.

88. "Award and Opinion," August 7, 1978, attachment to Group Health Association, Board of Trustee Minutes, August 18, 1978.

89. B. D. Colen, "Doctors Accept Two-Year GHA Pact, Will Work Today," *Washington Post,* April 26, 1978, pp. C1, C5.

90. Ibid.

91. Group Health Association, Board of Trustee Minutes, April 26, 1978.

92. Ibid.

93. Ibid.; B. D. Colen, "GHA Doctors Again Vote to Strike as Accord Collapses," *Washington Post,* April 28, 1978, pp. C1, C3; interviews with Harold Wool and Donald Mitchell.

94. Colen, "GHA Doctors Again Vote to Strike."

95. Group Health Association, Board of Trustee Minutes, April 26, 1978.

96. Kenneth R. Walker, "GHA Doctors Vote to Resume Striking Early Next Month," *Washington Post,* April 27, 1978, pp. B1, B2; interview with Harold Wool.

97. "Stipulation," May 2, 1978, attachment to Group Health Association, Board of Trustee Minutes, May 15, 1978; Board of Trustee Minutes, May 2, 1978; B. D. Colen, "Nine-Year Buildup of Distrust Led to Doctors' Strike," *Washington Post,* May 4, 1978, p. C1.

98. "Award and Opinion," August 7, 1978.

99. Colen, "Nine-Year Buildup."

100. Daniel Y. Patterson, "HMO Physician Unionization," pp. 40–41.

101. Lewis M. Simons, "Nurses Take to the Streets," *Washington Post,* April 6, 1982, pp. B1, B2.

102. Lewis M. Simons, "Nurses' Strikes Reflect Women's Equality Issue as Well as Pay," *Washington Post,* April 12, 1982, pp. B1, B2; Lewis M. Simons, "Most GHA Patients Back Nurses, Say Strike Causing No Hardship," *Washington Post,* April 22, 1982, pp. B1, B8.

103. "Executive Director's Report on RNPTA Negotiations 1982," September 17, 1982, attachment to Group Health Association, Board of Trustee Minutes, September 23, 1982.

104. Group Health Association, *MAC Communicator* 6, No. 4 (Early Spring 1983).

105. Nieves Zaldivar to Dear GHA Board Member, February 24, 1986, and Robert G. Rosenberg to Dear GHA Physician, February 24, 1986,

both attachments to Group Health Association, Board of Trustee Minutes, February 24, 1986.

106. Group Health Association, Board of Trustee Minutes, February 24, 1986.

107. Ibid., March 1, 1986; Peter Perl, "Group Health Doctors Extend Contract as Strike Deadline Nears," *Washington Post,* March 2, 1986, p. B1; Peter Perl and Martin Weil, "GHA Physicians Vote Strike Starting Today," *Washington Post,* March 3, 1986, pp. D1, D2. Since 1978, GHA's enrollment had grown substantially, from around 100,000 participants to 144,000 in 1985, leading to comparable growth in the number of physicians, to a total of about 180. Group Health Association, *Annual Reports for 1978, 1985.*

108. Perl and Weil, "GHA Physicians Vote Strike"; Robert Rosenberg to Dear GHA Member, undated, attachment to Group Health Association, Board of Trustee Minutes, March 3, 1986; Peter Perl, "GHA Physicians Hit the Picket Line," *Washington Post,* March 4, 1986, pp. C1, C2; Board of Trustee Minutes, March 3, 1986; Peter Perl, "Physicians Authorize Strike at Group Health Association," *Washington Post,* March 1, 1986, p. B5; GHA radio announcement, March 4, 1986, and Robert G. Rosenberg to Dear GHA Member, March 5, 1986, both attachments to Board of Trustee Minutes, March 10, 1986; Board of Trustee Minutes, March 10, 1986.

109. Group Health Association, Board of Trustee Minutes, March 10, 1986.

110. "Strike Settlement Agreement," March 26, 1986, attachment to Group Health Association, Board of Trustee Minutes, March 26, 1986; Peter Perl, "GHA Doctors Accept Pact, End Strike," *Washington Post,* March 27, 1986, p. B4; Group Health Association, *MAC Communicator* 10, No. 1 (Spring, 1986), 10, No. 2 (Summer 1986), and 10, No. 3 (Fall 1986).

CHAPTER SEVEN

1. See "Mission Statement of Goals and Objectives, 1983–1987," Group Health Association, *Annual Report for 1982,* pp. 13–14, Group Health Association headquarters, Washington, D.C.

2. Group Health Association, Board of Trustee Minutes, May 28, 1962,

June 29, 1964, GHA headquarters. GHA pays for up to thirty days of hospitalization and up to twenty outpatient visits per year when recommended by a Group Health psychiatrist. See Group Health Association, *Annual Report for 1976*; Federal Employees Health Benefits Plan brochure on GHA for 1987, GHA headquarters.

3. Group Health Association, *Annual Report for 1978, 1984*; Federal Employees Health Benefits Plan brochure on GHA, 1987.

4. More than 90 percent of participants are members of groups. Even among the 10 percent or less who are so-called "self-pay" members, many originally belonged to a group and exercised their right to convert to individual memberships without a physical examination when they retired or changed jobs. See Group Health Association, *Annual Report for 1985.*

5. Group Health Association, *Annual Report for 1977.*

6. Group Health Association, Board of Trustee Minutes, January 25, 1960, October 24, 1960, November 26, 1962, September 14, 1964, February 28, 1966, May 22, 1967, February 26, 1968; Paul Cornely to Dear Friend, September 26, 1961, attachment to Board of Trustee Minutes, January 29, 1962. By 1966, only four hundred GHA members were using the clinic.

7. Group Health Association, Board of Trustee Minutes, May 27, 1968; interview with Frank Watters by Dr. Tom May, November 1, 1974, Frank Watters papers, privately held; interview with Frank C. Watters, July 23, 1986; telephone interview with Henry Daniels, October 24, 1986; Upper Cardozo Neighborhood Health Center, *The First Seven Years, 1968–1975: A Report on Program Activities of Community Group Health Foundation, Inc.* (Washington, D.C.: The Center, 1975).

8. Group Health Association, Board of Trustee Minutes, May 17, 1971, July 20, 1970, October 19, 1970, July 15, 1974, August 19, 1974; *GHA News*, September 1971, p. 2; Louis J. Segadelli to Joseph P. Yeldell, July 16, 1974, attachment to Board of Trustee Minutes, July 29, 1974; Louis J. Segadelli to Z. Ozella Webb, August 21, 1974, attachment to Board of Trustee Minutes, September 9, 1974; interviews with M. Brent Oldham, July 23, 1986, and Dorothy Jane Youtz, July 11, 1986.

9. Lawrence Brown, *Politics and Health Care Organization: HMOs as Federal Policy* (Washington, D.C.: Brookings Institution, 1983), p. 125.

10. This, of course, was exactly the problem that GHA's trustees had

feared if its doctors were permitted to undertake outside practice.

11. Brown, *Politics,* pp. 114–120.

12. Kaiser, it should be recalled, consisted of three basic entities: the doctors' Permanente partnership, which provided the medical services and staffed the hospitals; the Kaiser Foundation Hospitals, which owned the organization's hospitals; and the Kaiser Health Plan, which managed the program. Brown believes that the cooperation between the three groups resulted neither from "a sophisticated socialization process alone" nor from "mere good fortune" but from conscious choices that developed a strong organizational structure and character that has proven "highly conducive to extensive but stable growth." Ibid., p. 123.

13. Ibid., p. 127.

14. Ibid., p. 125.

15. Ibid., p. 124.

16. The information about Kaiser in the above three paragraphs was provided by Rickey L. Hendricks from her Ph. D. dissertation, "A Necessary Revolution: The First Three Decades of the Kaiser Permanente Medical Care Program," University of Denver, 1987, and in a conversation, April 25, 1987.

17. For discussion of physicians in corporate settings, see Paul Starr, *The Social Transformation of American Medicine* (New York: Basic Books, 1982), pp. 446–449; Robert Ebert, "The Changing Role of the Physician," *Health Care and Its Costs,* ed. Carl J. Schramm (New York: W. W. Norton and Co., 1987), pp. 180–184.

18. Nominations Committee to John J. Gunther, November 25, 1964, attachment to Group Health Association, Board of Trustee Minutes, November 1964.

19. *GHA News,* March–April 1987.

20. As this example implies, the Member Advisory Council, created in the late 1960s as an updated version of the old Advisory Council that was terminated a decade earlier, has become a major GHA institution, with subsidiary councils at the various medical centers. Ray Johnson, "MAC Corner," *GHA News,* March 1978.

GHA's tax status. It had previously been a nonprofit organization under section 501(c)(4) of the Internal Revenue Code, meaning that contributions to it were not tax deductible. After 1982, it fell under section 501(c)(3), allowing those who contributed to the Fund to take a deduction on their income taxes. Group Health Association, Board of Trustee Minutes, October 18, 1982.

INDEX